THE STRANGELOVE LEGACY

Also by the Author

Keeping Going

Growing Up American: Contemporary Children and Their Society
(with Joan Costello)

THE
STRANGELOVE
LEGACY

*Children, Parents, and Teachers
in the Nuclear Age*

———◆———

PHYLLIS LA FARGE

1817

HARPER & ROW, PUBLISHERS, New York
Cambridge, Philadelphia, San Francisco, Washington
London, Mexico City, São Paulo, Singapore, Sydney

Many high-school students in schools across the country responded in short essays to the presentation of the Changing the Silence Tour in their schools. With the kind permission of John Burt, their words are quoted frequently in this book. "Changing the Silence Tour" (produced by John Burt, created and directed by Maya Scott Gillingham, with songs by Jody Simone Lester) was based on—but is distinct from—"Changing the Silence," a theater piece and videotape conceived and directed by Maya Scott Gillingham at the Northfield Mount Hermon School in the spring of 1983.

Grateful acknowledgment is made for permission to reprint:

Excerpt on page v from *The Minimal Self: Psychic Survival in Troubled Times* by Christopher Lasch (W. W. Norton & Company, Inc.). Copyright © 1984 by Christopher Lasch. Reprinted with permission.

Illustrations on pages 49 and 50. Courtesy of Patricia Hoertdoerfer.

Photograph on page 68 of the Children's Campaign for Nuclear Disarmament. Reproduced with the kind permission of Barbara Zahm.

Illustration on page 77. Reproduced with the kind permission of Karen Gersten-Rothenberg.

Illustrations on page 91. Reproduced with the kind permission of Joshua Bloom:

Excerpt on page 127 from "Will She Reach 51?" by Roger Wilkins. Reprinted with the kind permission of the author.

Excerpt on page 239 from "The Role of Film in Nuclear Education" by Robert W. Zuber. Reprinted with the kind permission of the author.

Excerpt on page 240 from "Nuclear Education in the Elementary School" by Katherine Schultz. Reprinted with the kind permission of the author.

FIRST EDITION

Designed by C. Linda Dingler

Library of Congress Cataloging-in-Publication Data

La Farge, Phyllis.
    The Strangelove legacy.

    1. Children and war.   2. Nuclear warfare—Social
aspects.   3. Child psychology.   4. Parent and child.
I. Title.
HQ784.W3L3   1987   355'.0217'088054   86-45667
ISBN 0-06-015699-6

87 88 89 90 91 RRD 10 9 8 7 6 5 4 3 2 1

The first time I ever seriously thought about nuclear war was when the Russians shot down the airliner 007 over Soviet air space and ever since then it sticks with me in the back of my mind wherever I go.
—high-school student

My response is that no matter how hard anybody tries no one will change the plans for nuclear war since it has been around for so long. The government is more powerful than the people.
—high-school student

You people are far too pessimistic. My God it is absolutely ludicrous for you people to think that you, yourself can prevent a nuclear war. Don't dwell upon the fact that you will all die. Stop thinking about the extremes and live your fucking lives.
—high-school student, responding to presentation
by teenage antinuclear activists

Sunrise breaks, the bombs are falling,
You'd better hope your car ain't stalling,
For all you know, Reagan's calling
The missiles from their home.
Pershing, cruise, and MX flying,
Maybe soon we'll all be frying—
Now we know that Reagan's lying
When he says there's nothing to fear.
—from a play by Children for Nuclear Disarmament

The question of whether children suffer from a "new precocity" or from an unnecessarily prolonged period of economic and emotional dependence— equally plausible interpretations of contemporary childhood, advanced by critics of current child-raising practices—is probably misconceived. Neither way of thinking about the condition of children captures the quality of childhood in a society that appears indifferent to the needs not merely of children but of future generations in general. The neglect of children is part of a broader pattern of neglect that includes the reckless exploitation of natural resources, the pollution of air and water, and the willingness to risk "limited" nuclear wars as an instrument of national policy.
—Christopher Lasch, *The Minimal Self*

CONTENTS

ACKNOWLEDGMENTS

First of all, I want to thank the young men and women whose feelings and opinions are the foundation of this book. My special appreciation and respect go to Maya Scott Gillingham, Roxanna Tynan and other members of Kids Outreach in New York City, Vali Rajah, Hannah Rabin, and Josh and Zeke O'Brien. I also wish to thank Karen Gersten-Rothenberg and Joshua Bloom for kindly permitting me to reproduce their drawings.

I am especially grateful to my friend, John Burt, for his generosity in making available to me essays written by students who had seen the *Changing the Silence* tour he produced.

Many others were generous in a variety of ways, in particular Roberta Snow, Tony Wagner, James and Gloria Umenhofer, Anthony Catalano, Elizabeth Crow, Donna Lawson, Tom Roderick, Ernest Drucker, James Tobin, Samuel Brian, Robert Veeck, Barbara Zahm, Robert W. Zuber, Scott Haas, Benina Berger-Gould, Jeffrey Gould, Phyllis Berman, Lenore Duensing, Martha Cleaves, Pat Fellers, Patricia Hoertdoerfer, Diana Morley, Lynn Johnson, Katherine Schultz, Eleanor Mahar Deegan, Roger Wilkins, Herbert Kohl, Betty Bardige, Herbert Mack, and Ann Cook.

My researchers, Mark McColloch, Marjorie Alpren Jelin, and Dahlia Kandiyoti, were unfailingly thoughtful in their help. I want to express my appreciation, too, to my editor, Carol Cohen, who believed in the project from the beginning and was willing to wait.

Two friends, Elaine Sorel and Frances Ferguson, offered me what a writer needs most—a room of her own—and just the right degree of support and discretion to go with it.

THE STRANGELOVE LEGACY

INTRODUCTION

One afternoon in October 1982 I was sitting at my desk at *Parents* magazine reading a manuscript. The author wrote that her teenage daughter was afraid and angry about the threat of nuclear war. Now and then talking with the young woman seemed to help, but there were times when she made it clear she didn't want to hear about the issue at all. Groping, her mother on some days insisted on talking with her forthrightly, on others held back, feeling that her own modest degree of activism against the arms race was somehow a burden for her child.

This manuscript was the third in as many months on the same subject sent unsolicited to the magazine. The other two had taken somewhat different tacks. One man had written about his feelings of appalled anger that his children could not count on a future. Another woman had written about the way in which her teenage children had started her thinking about the issue. Somehow they had been ahead of her in their consciousness of the risk of nuclear war . . . How had that happened? she wondered.

Three essays received by one magazine in three months on the same subject may seem no indication of widespread concern. But for each person who has the knack of setting thoughts down on paper and the need to do so, hundreds, if not thousands, think similar thoughts, feel similar feelings.

What was going on? I picked up the telephone and called the woman whose essay I had just read; no, the magazine couldn't publish her piece, it wasn't the right thing for us (or some such phrase, beloved of cornered editors). But could we meet? She lived in Vermont—but I was going to Vermont over Christmas.

So began an exploration that led to this book, taking me from a Vermont hillside to New Mexico, California, Pennsylvania, upper

1

New York state, Oregon—and to a hillside in France. I talked with scores of young people and read their essays; visited classrooms and interviewed parents, teachers, and mental-health professionals.

In a deeper sense than the geographic ground I covered or the numbers of individuals I interviewed, the book is an exploration as well. Rivalries, policies, politics, weapons and other technologies that are distant and abstract in relation to our individual daily lives, yet at the same time are part of our fate, have made trying to imagine what is impossible to imagine—nuclear annihilation—part of consciousness for a growing number of people in the world. How much do young people share such a vision? Is its impact on them different from its effect on adults? These were the questions I found myself setting out to explore. I found that different people said different things, often very vehemently.

One reason for their disagreements—and one problem in an exploration such as mine—is that it is difficult to conceptualize sound approaches to thinking about the meeting of the "big world," or issues from the "big world," and the "little world" of the individual psyche. Two thoughtful commentators, John E. Mack and William R. Beardslee, both psychiatrists, have noted: "In our experience, the fields of child psychiatry and child psychology lack models for understanding the impact of children's and adolescents' responses to domestic politics and threatening international realities." [1]

They add, however, that "some contemporary political and social events perhaps provide partial analogies." Drawing on recent research that has begun to document the influence of events or institutions in the "big world" on the "little world" of the individual, they name as "partial analogies" the disillusioning influence of parental job loss on a family's sense of well-being; the long-term effects of sudden traumatic events such as the Chowchilla kidnapping; [2] and from yet another perspective, the now well documented influences of television on children's attitudes. But, as Mack and Beardslee note, losing a job is a real, concrete experience, not a threat that one hopes will never be made real. Moreover, although "an aspect of the reaction of adolescents in becoming aware of the nuclear threat" may be like a traumatic event, it is nevertheless very unlike a kidnapping; and television's influence is so broad that it is not directly comparable.

The truth is we are still just beginning to learn how to listen to our children—or to ourselves—in an entirely new era, new not only with respect to our ability to destroy ourselves with our own technology but in our ability—also the result of technology—to convey images and information, making world issues an intimate part of consciousness. With respect to these extraordinary changes we are still early explorers, bringing back from our expeditions what-ever data we can; in my case, the words, written and spoken, of young people. It will never be easy to interpret this data: it is always a slippery business to make sense in an area where the intimate and the vast are brought together. But difficult as it is, it is here that we must learn if we are to find out what we are becoming—and not become the tools and the victims of what we have ourselves made —that is, of our politics as well as our technology.

I intend this book primarily for parents, with the hope that it will help them understand what their children are likely to feel—or not feel—about the nuclear issue and the arms race. However, al-though clearly the nuclear issue is like no other, to a certain degree what I have to say also applies to children's feelings about environ-mental and other "big world" issues, and there were many moments when I wished I had set out to explore young people's responses on a wider range of subjects.

I have devoted many pages to the subject of how to educate about the nuclear issue, and this book is for teachers as well as parents. Very often teachers have an important and delicate role *in loco parentis* in relation to young people with respect to world issues. But I believe parents as well as teachers must make judgments about the way children are educated about these issues, and I hope they will be interested in these pages.

I have included the voices of adults along with those of young people because I believe that the impact of "big world" issues—and the nuclear issue in particular—on children cannot be understood except in the light of a process of socialization that involves parents, teachers, and many adults the child will never know personally but who appear in glossy color on the television screen—or create the images the child sees on the screen.

When people have asked me what this book is about and I have told them that it includes the voices of adults as well as those of children, they have generally not wanted to hear what I said, quickly altering it to suit themselves: it's a book *for* children or a book about children exclusively. It has seemed to me that the idea that children were concerned about the threat of nuclear war made them uncomfortable enough; the idea that adults were in any way implicated was too much.

Although it aims to be helpful, this book is no "how to" of the kind often directed at parents. The issues are far too complex for that. Clearly, the apocalyptic vision nuclear weapons have implanted in our imagination, probably permanently, is the chief reason for the lack of simple answers, but another is the difficulty, already mentioned, of thinking about the impact of an issue that is distant and abstract in relation to individual life.

What one might call a problem of language has been another source of complexity. During the past several years the phrase "nuclear fear" has been increasingly used to describe children's feelings about the threat of nuclear war. New research has appeared on the subject, films have been made, talk-show hosts have discussed the subject with young people and "experts." But what does "nuclear fear" mean? The psychologist Jerome Kagan has noted our tendency to use one word to describe a variety of feelings and states of mind, thus running the risk of obscuring or confusing what we are talking about.[3] For instance, if a researcher asks a group of children to enumerate their principal fears, as many have done recently, a number of children may list fear of a parent's death, fear of doing poorly in school, and fear of nuclear war. For them, three very different situations have a sufficient amount in common to be associated with the same word. But beyond this we know very little. We do not know if children would have used their word for *fear* to describe all three situations if they belonged to another culture. Nor do we know that they would have chosen the word if we did not already tend to lump so many feelings under one term; if we were more precise in our descriptions of feelings; or if we had a better term to describe the cluster of feelings associated with the nuclear issue. What if we had a common term for death anxiety, or one simple word that described a vision of the apocalypse? Or what if we found, as researchers are beginning to, that nuclear fear or nuclear anxiety is not "unidimensional" (to use a bit of social-science jargon)? What if we found that in one individual it may be associated with a sense of despair and a tendency to withdraw from the political process, and in another with a feeling that might as accurately be called concern as fear or anxiety—a feeling that, unlike a sense of despair, is associated with an inclination to active political involvement? I make these points because only when adults begin to recognize the complex feelings the nuclear issue arouses—in themselves as well as in young people—can they begin to explore the possible consequences of such feelings.

But let us return to the word *fear,* for whatever it is worth. To use the word *fear,* however imprecisely, raises a question about the consequences of fear. One consequence of fear is a feeling of vulnerability. This feeling is appropriate if there is a reason for fear (and, if there is not a real reason, psychologists would say we should use *anxiety,* not *fear*). But what if in some way a particular fear (if fear is the right word) and a particular sense of vulnerability are too crippling to feel? Then, it seems, most of us simply do not feel them. But if this is the case, aren't we less safe as a result? These are the questions that I was gradually led to ask by what I was told by adults as well as young people. I believe they are the key questions each adult must ask himself or herself in relation to nuclear weapons and the arms race. But they are also key questions that parents and teachers must ask about children and the "big world" institutions and issues that increasingly shape our lives. They are questions that need answering from many perspectives: military and political, moral and psychological. In fact, all these points of view are necessary if we are to understand our predicament with respect to nuclear weapons and the arms race—or, for that matter, our predicament with respect to the depletion of natural resources and the degradation of our environment.

These questions—about a sense of vulnerability and the risks that may be involved if appropriate fear is not felt—lead immediately to another set of questions: what makes people feel strong and what makes people feel vulnerable? I did not set out to interview children or adults about these questions, but in reflecting on what they said or wrote I found that everyone, including quite young children, had at least an implicit conception of what constitutes strength and vulnerability.

We live in a time of worldwide debate about these conceptions with respect to military and economic, national and international power. The questions raised are hard ones and hotly argued. Again and again a hawk's fear is a dove's anxiety, and vice versa. Technology, by introducing new dangers into the world (at the same time that it has alleviated old ones), by making our world much smaller and all of us more interdependent, has made it essential to continue the debate and pose our questions more searchingly than ever before. We need to raise children who are equipped to participate in this debate.

Despite the difficulty of the debate, everyone will surely agree on one thing: fear and vulnerability are very hard feelings to tolerate. One has to "do something" even if doing something means building ever more weapons or merely blocking the feelings themselves—or both, as is often the case. But, contrary to what hard-core hawks say, more and more people the world over believe that ever more weapons are not the way to a sense of restored strength or relative invulnerability. At the same time, contrary to the perspective of hard-core doves (if that's not a contradiction in terms), people will never accept feeling defenseless. This suggests that we are in need of new conceptions of strength if not invulnerability, ones that take into account the true risks of our contemporary situation. Moreover, it should lead us to ask if we are rearing and educating our children in ways that are appropriate or adequate to the world they are growing into.

The debate about the impact of the possibility of nuclear annihilation on children's consciousness is in many ways a manifestation of the debate about strength and vulnerability. If children are concerned or angry or scared about the possibility of nuclear war—and, as we shall see, a number have been expressing this for more than twenty years (when anybody bothered to listen to them)—then in some measure we have failed in our role as protectors: we have not been as strong as we thought we were. Or, put another way, the policy of deterrence, for all its military and political success, has not been an equal success psychologically. What was conceived of as providing strength—and, in the short term, can be said to have done so—has not provided everyone with a feeling of strength (not surprising, since it was built on terror).

I have no idea what the consequences of such a "psychological failure" will be and I am not sure that anyone else does either. But I am enough of a believer in the links between the individual psyche and the "big world"—ultimately between the psychological and political—to believe there *will* be consequences, however hard to trace. One might be that people will make real efforts to achieve a safer world. Another might be a world made yet more dangerous by the pursuit of pseudoinvulnerability through schemes like the Strategic Defense Initiative.

Meanwhile, we can note that for those who subscribe to the conception of strength on which the arms race and the strategy of deterrence depend, any hint of "psychological failure" is unacceptable. This is one reason many people, particularly the politically conservative, do not want to hear that children are afraid of nuclear war—that they feel vulnerable.

Antinuclear activists, on the other hand, have underscored children's fears and vulnerability. In part, they are motivated by a desire to help children, but in part, too, they want to emphasize the vulnerability of all in the nuclear age. They believe they have found in the image of the child a potent means to this end.

As so often, our feelings about children have much to tell us about ourselves: in this case about our perceptions of our own strength and vulnerability and our conception of what is necessary, precious, or expendable in our lives and in the world.

CHILDREN
AND THE
NUCLEAR VISION

The names and descriptive details of certain individuals whose real identities are not central to the true story told in *The Strangelove Legacy* have been changed.

MAYA

Late in the afternoon of a day in January 1984, the hour between the end of school and the beginning of homework, Maya Scott Gillingham entered a gymnasium at the "Y" on Ninety-second Street and Lexington Avenue in New York City. She was about to conduct a special workshop for a dance class, featuring a videotape of *Changing the Silence,* a theater piece that is a bold outcry against the possibility of nuclear war. Maya had directed the play a year earlier when she was a junior at Northfield Mount Hermon, a prep school in northern Massachusetts.

When Maya entered the gymnasium she mingled with the dance students who were already gathered there. Among the twenty-five or so young women, there were girls as young as eleven, their bodies slim, flat, and childlike in their leotards, and shapely seventeen-year-olds, fully-grown women.

The dance teacher introduced Maya and she in turn introduced her companions: her friend and partner in the workshop, Jody Lester, and John Burt, a drama therapist and producer, no more than ten years Maya's senior, who had arranged a cross-country tour for the workshop.

Maya is tall and long-limbed; her face is broad and her hair blond. That afternoon it hung loose on her shoulders. There was a certain coltishness and gentleness about her as she introduced herself that made her easy to imagine at a much younger age. As she spoke, she was ingratiating, almost diffident, friendly—very much the teenager who does not want to stand out too much from her peers.

Jody Lester is a little shorter, a little more compact. Her nose is pert and her eyes large; she is pretty. But she has a look, not always associated with prettiness, of quiet wisdom and assurance.

And—notable in the almost all-white audience of the gym—she is black.

After her introductions, Maya asked the group to form a large circle and start jumping "like popcorn in a pan." Once they were all jumping, she asked them to jump one at a time into the center of the circle and tell the others their names and something they loved in life. The smallest, youngest, slightest dancer, an elf in a red-and-yellow leotard, was the first to jump into the middle; she loved hot chocolate. The others followed; they loved their families, their friends, walking on the beach, running in the wind in spring, ice cream.

When everyone had said her piece, the group still stood in a circle and Jody sang a song she had written, a part of *Changing the Silence.* "I may be peace, wider than water, deeper than fire," the song begins. In counterpoint to the song Maya recited facts that jarred the air almost obscenely: three babies die of malnutrition in the world every minute; the average family will spend $20,000 on the arms race over the next five years; 140,000 people died in the bombing of Hiroshima, August 6, 1945. Jody concluded her song. Maya concluded her recitation, saying "Even if we die, no one can take away the fact that we're alive today."

Now Jody led the group in an exercise called "embracing the tiger." "Think of something you are really afraid of," she told them. "Then embrace it, draw it in, rest your hands on its shoulders." Around the circle slim arms encircled the emptiness before them, cupped hands on the shoulders of invisible, private monsters.

"Now," said Jody, holding her right arm extended, palm at right angles to it, like the blessing hand of Christ in a Byzantine mosaic, "imagine there is energy and light radiating from the palm of your hand that connects you to the world around you, mountains in front of you, sky above, sea behind." Hands liberated from the creature of fear stretched out to contact an imagined universe.

"Imagine you can hold the world in your hands," Jody went on. At first arms scarcely managed an unwieldy globe. No one tried to lift it above her head; it was too heavy (but if these had been boys would someone have played Atlas?). Jody saw the trouble the group was having. She urged them to make the world really small. For some it became no bigger than a tennis ball, lovingly cradled. When everyone had made the world her own, the exercise was over, and Maya, taking over from Jody, invited the group to sit down. They sat on the floor. Most of them encircled their knees with their arms. *Changing the Silence,* Maya told them, was her way of "embracing the tiger," of finding strength by confronting fear. "And," she continued, "the most important thing was that it was a way of looking my peers right in the face." There was a challenge in her words. She looked boldly at her audience. She was no longer just one of them. Her ingratiating tinge of diffidence was gone.

Now the lights in the gym were turned off and the videotape of *Changing the Silence* turned on.

There was Maya speaking to them again, but now from the screen. She said:

> Day after day I go on
> Pretending I don't know the world could end tomorrow.
> Pretending I don't know that everything I love—
> My mom, my brother, my best friend—
> Could die in an instant.
> I go to school
> Pretending 1 + 1 means anything to me or this dying world
> I go on . . .
> But the world could end
> Just like that.
> And I don't say anything
> Because I *don't want to know*—
> I'm only seventeen,
> I haven't even gotten out of high school yet—
> Why should I have to know that?
> I want to grow up,
> I want to have a family,
> I want to travel . . .

Changing the Silence has a cast of seven. A series of monologues is interspersed with mimed scenes including those of a high-school graduation, Thanksgiving, and New Year's. It is not so much a play—there is no plot or character development—as a cry of fear, a wistful plea for comfort ("So where do I turn for comfort? No one can say it's gonna be all right anymore . . ."), and an outburst of frustrated rage at adults for endangering the future of the world. It rages against adult "silence"—that is, our monumental failure to respond adequately to the dangers of the arms race. It is raw evidence of a need to speak out and a longing to be heard; at the same time it admits infection with the same pathology of silence that infects adults:

I'm so disgusted to be a human being
And yet I'm silent.
Don't we feel?
Don't you feel?
Can't I feel?
What are we doing?
What am I doing?

Most of all, perhaps, it is an outcry against a sense of a jeopardized future—

What's the use of going to college?
What's the use of making money?
What's the use of preparing for a future
When I have none?
What's the use of loving if the people I love are going
    to die
Before I can ever express my love for them?
What's the use of living?
I feel as though I'm dead right now.
My grave was dug
Before I was even born.

—and of an overwhelming sense of powerlessness in the hands of forces beyond any individual's control:

This is my first year of being an adult
. . . Yeah,
I can work, vote, drink, go to prison, be drafted,
    die—
My parents tell me
"Now you're responsible for your own life,
Make it what *you* want it to be."
But I can't.
I'm not in control.
People who I don't even know,
Who don't even know me
Are controlling my future,
Planning my death
And I'm letting them.

For many adults *Changing the Silence* is crude, ungainly, embarrassing, the kind of outcry that makes them uncomfortable. It makes adults want to distance themselves by saying that kids will outgrow feeling this way, it is just a stage. Or they may say that the kids who put together such a thing cannot be typical; they are "too emotional," "hypersensitive," "extra vulnerable." For others, it is simply more honest than they themselves dare to be.

And *Changing the Silence* is the kind of thing that the kids who are "cool" (or whatever word is fashionable) reject as definitely uncool.

How did it come about?

I asked Maya this question two months before her workshop at the Y in New York. One November afternoon, already dark at four, we sat on her bed eating corn nuts from a plastic bag in her dormitory room at the Northfield Mount Hermon School. The room was large and cold; we both wore overcoats. Maya wore silver earrings that dangled and khaki-colored sneakers. I noticed that her eyes were beautiful and distinctive, gray-blue, extra bright, with a look of being neatly chiseled out of her fair-skinned face.

On the wall were a couple of posters from China depicting starry-eyed young workers posturing heroically, and a reproduction of a Winslow Homer painting of a fair young woman in a salmon-colored dress—perhaps the Maya of another era.

In the fall of 1982, Maya told me, her stepbrother had died in a car crash. It was the first time a family member had died and the event broke through the normal defenses we all erect against thinking about death. For the first time Maya found herself confronted with the actuality of death. But it was not just the possibility of personal, "ordinary" death—her own death, her stepbrother's—that overwhelmed her, but the possibility of global death through nuclear war. "I struggled with the issue of my own mortality," she said. "At the same time I realized what the death of the whole world would be. I came to the point where I couldn't just not think about it."

Maya had been concerned about the threat of nuclear war for some time. The previous spring she had worked for the antinuclear student-teacher organization STOP, which at that time had its national headquarters on the Northfield Mount Hermon campus. But she had done so with very mixed emotions: "I worked at STOP," she said, "and I felt strongly, and I did think there were things you could do, in a sense. But I didn't feel I had a future, and my actions at the deep level were motivated by despair."

She had trouble finding words to describe the quality of her fear or precisely the role it had played: on the one hand, she said that her fear of nuclear war was "theoretical" until her stepbrother died; on the other, she was aware that "every time I imagined myself having children, this little voice would say, '*If* I have children . . .' "

But all at once, that autumn after her stepbrother died, what she felt was not expressed in a "little voice," nor was it any longer "theoretical." Despair was no longer "at a deep level" but overwhelming. She felt that what she went through was epitomized by a dream. "I was surrounded by darkness and I wasn't able to scream and there were people dying all around me but not being dead. A horrible dream and I woke up shaking and very, very scared."

She called her mother, Molly Scott, a singer and songwriter with strong ties to the peace movement. "You'd better come," Maya told her mother. "We're not going to be here long." Molly drove to Northfield from the family home in Charlemont, Massachusetts, and took Maya home for a few days. She suggested that Maya attend a workshop run by Joanna Macy, a therapist who has devised a workshop in which participants can confront and work through their feelings about the dangers posed to the world by nuclear weapons and environmental degradation.

Maya attended the workshop in November 1982 and, as she put it, had a "real hard time." But she came out of it with a new sense of the validity of her feelings, and the beginnings of a conviction that her own experience could have meaning for others. She decided that what she had been through "wasn't just me. It was something that in different ways, at different times, a lot of people go through."

Meanwhile, during the winter term, the idea for *Changing the Silence* was "just kind of hatching" in her mind. Originally she thought of it as the "escalation of one symbol," or rather of two symbols—for the symbol of nuclear death that had appeared to her in her first dream had evolved in a subsequent dream into an image of birth. The darkness of death and destruction had become the darkness of the womb. "What I had seen as death and darkness all around me, pressure and darkness, became a birth," she said. "The way I interpret it, the pain I was going through was giving me the birth of a new vision." Her inner movement from fear of death to the birth of a new vision gave her the underlying action of her theater piece.

Maya posted a sign-up sheet advertising for those who were interested in creating a play about the threat of nuclear war. She auditioned those who responded, favoring candidates who she sensed had a "screaming inside them" as opposed to those who simply thought the subject matter was a "good issue." And although she chose people who could act, she did not make her choices from among those who were the experienced actors of the school. "I figured, I think pretty rightly," she said, "that teenagers who are experienced actors have learned to distance themselves from their own emotional selves, but I wanted people to speak right from the heart.

"One of the things that started me was the sense that each person has an individual nuclear story, an individual voice, and individual resources that can be transformed into power. I didn't tell people what to say. I gave them a form that would bring out their own personal stories. Then the group put them together."

After she had chosen her cast Maya led workshops with them and others involved in the production of the play. She began by helping each person work through the feelings he or she had brought to the endeavor. She used some of the improvisational, experiential techniques she had learned from Joanna Macy, added exercises of her own, and assigned reading. "Forget the end product," she told the group initially. "We have to work through our own fears." In retrospect she saw it as "an incredible time," one in which strong bonds were forged very quickly.[1]

Together Maya and her colleagues explored through improvisation the stories of Hiroshima survivors. They read, talked, kept dream journals, and did more improvisations based on their journals. Sometimes someone rebelled—"Do I have to talk about nuclear war when I have two papers due?" Sometimes everyone rebelled. "We would just go out and play and run around in the fields. Playing was important; laughing and playing was a crucial, crucial, crucial part of our work."

Out of their own feelings the players began to fashion the play. In the course of creating it Maya decided they should use masks. "I wanted something physical," she said, "that would represent the blocks we have, and a mask seemed like a really appropriate thing." The actors made their own masks, molding them in plaster over gauze on each other's faces. Then they added "the distortions of our fears" with wads of plaster and paint.

The players do not put on their masks until the last part of the play. In a tableau they read newspapers, bombarding each other with statistics about the arms race until one screams, "I don't want to know this, I don't want to be." Then all the characters put on their masks and drop their newspapers. But the players do not stay masked for long. Painfully, each tears off his mask, which he then attaches to his sleeve, a reminder of how easy it is to hide from knowledge and hide from feeling.

In the course of the spring term the play took shape, although the monologues that are its chief feature were not written down in final form until two days before the first performance in May 1983. "The immediacy that brought was really good," Maya said. "When they came on stage they had nothing to do but be themselves."

In the hall outside Maya's room a bell rang, an intrusive reminder of the institutional life of schools. In a few minutes it would be time for her to eat dinner. It had become even colder in her room. We had finished the corn nuts. We both got up, but there was a question still on my mind—how was she feeling this autumn, compared with last?

"I look around this room," she said, "and for the first time I think these walls will be here in thirty years."

We went out the door and down the stairs.

Did *Changing the Silence* have meaning for young people beside Maya and her friends? Or was it the aberrant outcry of a small group of particularly vulnerable kids? I found one answer at the workshop Maya gave at the Y.

The videotape of *Changing the Silence* ends with these words:

> When I wear my mask I cover my love, I cover my compassion. I cut off my connection to other human beings. And I look around me feeling there's no hope; no peace. What is peace? One day a friend told me, silently . . . wordlessly . . . "Peace is changing the silence." [2]

When the lights were turned on everyone in the gym was still sitting on the floor, arms still clasped around knees or propped behind her. Everyone was silent. From the look on each face I felt as if the silence was laden, emotional.

Picking up on the last words of the play, Maya asked the group what peace meant to them. But it soon became clear that peace was not what most had on their minds.

As a preliminary to answering Maya's question, their teacher now led them in a series of exercises. First they paired up, kept eye contact, and mimed each other's gestures. The gestures they chose seemed to express "sad" and "cold."

Then Jody instructed them to pair up once again and talk with each other about peace. Then each was to dance an improvisation of what the other had said. Pairs formed around the gym and chatted quietly. In the very feminine way they held their bodies, each leaning toward the other, they seemed to coax the other's reply.

A twosome of thirteen-year-olds talked about their fears, not about peace. "I feel scared and angry because the government spends a million dollars a minute on something we'll never use—hopefully," one said. "And we have to pay taxes for it. I'm scared because every time I walk out in the morning I never know if I'll see the next night." Her legs were still chubby in her black leotard. She was wearing a white T-shirt.

Her companion responded, "I think I'm sort of confused and angry and afraid. I think I have mixed feelings. I'm angry because why do you have to spend the money when people are going hungry? But I'm scared because every time I go out I might go *poof.* This thing might come at me out of the sky. I'm confused because it's like juggling with your life. On one hand it's safety—the government is trying to keep you safe—on the other hand it's your life."

Now it was time for each to dance her interpretation of what her partner had said while her partner described it in words. Most danced a sense of confusion and peril with many glances upward toward "this thing that might come at me out of the sky."

But a few danced a vision of peace.

"Peace is when you don't have a schedule," said the elf in red and yellow while her partner danced. "When you don't have obligations and there are no clocks around the house. I'd stay around the house. I'd read. I'm sure I wouldn't be bored."

"My vision of peace is a perfect day," another said. "Sunlight, clouds, and if you're with someone, you have no conflict, you agree, you know the world is okay."

A third said, "Anyone who's very close to you is not going to go away, and there's no sense of pressure."

The gestures of their partners were lyrical and expressive of the joys of the intimate, personal world—not of peace attained in a "big world" rife with conflicting interests. Like most efforts to express happiness, they were a little trite—greeting-card visions.

Then all at once there were no more volunteers. The circle of dancers was silent, but not with the same silence as earlier. Now something—or many things—had been expressed. But what next? What was to be done about these feelings, these hopes, these fears let loose in the room like awkward offspring? At last one of the dancers suggested a way out: everyone would dance. And they did; Maya, Jody, and John joined them. Their dancing was an affirmation, the expression of a bond, and perhaps of hope.

Then the workshop was over. A few dancers lingered, talked to Maya or Jody. Most hurried off. It was time for dinner, phone calls to friends, homework.

MIKE

Mike Seely is a veterinary surgeon in Paradise, California, a town that dozes under Ponderosa pines along a low foothill of the Sierras about three hours north of Sacramento. One day in the spring of 1984 Mike sat in his office at the back of the animal hospital he had designed. He tipped back in his desk chair—a tanned, athletic man of forty-four with a still boyish look. Now and then a dog barked in another part of the building and once or twice the telephone rang, but mostly Mike talked uninterrupted.

"Okay," he began. "I was eight years old and we were living in Visalia, in an old house. There were four of us children and there was an old cottonwood next door that I had a tree fort in, and we would get up at three A.M., four A.M. to watch the A-bombs go off. They were testing at White Sands, that's over in New Mexico, and here we were in southern California and you could see the flash from the atomic blast, and it was a big thrill. You'd read about it in the news, you'd hear it on the radio, and you knew that tomorrow morning at four A.M. one of the A-bombs was going to go off. And here we are, little eight-year-olds—my buddies would be with me—we'd be huddled under a blanket watching the A-bomb go off."

"What did you see?" I asked.

"You see out the window there?" Mike said. We both looked out his office window into the California sunshine. "Imagine it was night, and there was this lightbulb out there around the other side of the building that went on and then died down, and you didn't see the bulb but you saw the light go up and then go down."

Mike was sitting in the cottonwood tree with his buddies in 1948. He is a member of the first generation of children to grow up during the era of nuclear weapons. During the same period he participated in civil-defense drills at school.

"I was in the third grade in the Cary Barnet School in Visalia. My teacher's name was Miss Diamont and I had a crush on her. It was one of those brick buildings with the high windows and the window shades, and the reason I mention this is that we had A-bomb drills. If there was an atomic attack we were to crouch under our desks and cover our heads with our arms, and those people who were lucky enough to be sitting near the window had to jump up and pull down the shades."

I expected Mike to say that even as a child he had been skeptical about the civil-defense drills, but he replied: "I always took things like that seriously. I'm probably a little different from other people. I never realized duck-and-cover wasn't going to do it."

The vision of the flash seen from the cottonwood tree, and the duck-and-cover drills at the Cary Barnet School, were images and memories that did not leave Mike.

"So here I am, carrying them through with me, these vivid memories. I remember them sticking with me through a constant reminder on the radio. Conelrad, they do it today. It's a national tie-in of the radio stations for civil defense, so that if there's a disaster you will hear it on the radio.

"I moved up to Oroville when I was fourteen, and I always used to go to bed with my radio on. I'd listen to *Lucky Lager Dance Time.* I'd keep that radio on until midnight and then I'd wake up and turn it off, but I always had it tuned to a Conelrad station. I was thinking that I wanted to be ready, I wanted to be prepared, I wanted to know what to do in case there was an atomic attack. And the thing that would really click in with that was living with Beale air-force base due south. We'd hear sonic booms, and in the middle of the night, sound asleep, I'd hear a sonic boom and immediately awake and turn on the radio and pray that I wouldn't hear the Conelrad thing. When I heard *Lucky Lager Dance Time,* I'd relax and go back to sleep and know that it was probably a sonic boom. Years I lived with that—thirteen, fourteen, fifteen; I probably stopped doing it by the time I was graduated from high school."

During these high-school years Mike thought of becoming an architect. Courses in architectural drafting provided him with a new medium for expressing his anxieties about nuclear war.

"The other thing I remember," he said, "was, when I got into architectural drafting and I began to draw houses where I'd like to live, I always included a bomb shelter. You know, I am built to survive, and from eight years of age—or even before that—I did what I needed to survive."

His concern with survival has continued into his adult years: "That's one of the reasons I live in Paradise instead of the Bay area. I live in terror of driving into the Bay area, and if there is a nuclear attack, I know I'm finished. If I did live in the Bay area I'd live on a boat, so if there was an attack I could at least go out on the water—because I know the highways would not be functioning."

But he thinks about survival even in Paradise: "Behind my house where I live on the canyon there are old mines and I know where they are, and mentally I'm prepared to take food and water and hide in one of those mines. I have other friends who are like that; so we grew up with that thing."

What else did he grow up with? How had his anxieties about nuclear weapons shaped him?

"Well, I think the general effect on me is my lack of believing that there is some kind of future. And I live my life that way. In town here I'm probably considered the crazy bachelor—I've been through three wives—and I have a sailboat and I used to race cars. I know how to have fun." He paused for a few seconds, thoughtfully. "I probably live on two levels. I'm not really sure I have a future, but what there is of it I'm planning. I invested in this building. I put everything I've got into it. I'm optimistic enough to want to have children in the hopes that, you know, the faith . . ."

He did not finish his sentence but reached forward and turned toward me a framed photo of a pretty woman, his fiancée.

"Susan and I are going to get married in June and we hope to have a couple of kids. A lot of younger people say to me, What are you going to do that for, you're going to raise them up in this world? And I say, Well, I'll make my world the way I want it, and if it's not okay, I'll go somewhere where it can be okay. I'll get on a sailboat—"

He glanced out the window, realized what he was doing, then said, "I used to keep my boat on a trailer just outside."

At one point in our conversation I asked him if he had ever talked to his parents about nuclear weapons as a child.

"I don't have any direct recollections of discussing them with my parents," he replied. "I know my dad and I did talk about things like that. I can remember talking to him about sex and cars, but I don't remember talking to him about anything like that."

Then he paused, as his memory was suddenly sparked.

"Oh, I do remember one thing. The subject was A-bombs, and

he said, Don't worry about it—they outlawed mustard gas, and some day they'll outlaw A-bombs. It was that simple for him."

CHILDREN'S AWARENESS—THE FIRST STUDIES

How many young people feel like Maya, or like Mike? In 1948, no one really wanted to know what Mike Seely or other children felt, despite the dominating presence of the atomic bomb and atomic energy as a public issue.[3] World War II was won; it was time to get on with the business of peace. At the same time the Cold War had begun, and nuclear weapons were deemed a necessary and relatively inexpensive ingredient of supremacy. The Cassandras who foresaw the dangers of a weapon that had just helped win the war and that promised to maintain peace, even at the price of terror, did not succeed in mobilizing opinion.

Psychologists had, however, begun to speculate about the effect of the bomb on individual consciousness. In May 1946, for instance, the Society for the Psychological Study of Social Issues issued a statement that began with these words:

> Atomic energy has become a psychological problem. Our warmest hopes and deepest fears have been caught in it.
> Atomic energy is producing an international fear psychology. But such a fear is not necessarily bad, for human fear releases great psychological energies. When the source of fear is well understood and a constructive solution is seen, these energies serve as powerful supports of well-directed efforts to overcome the danger. But when the source is not well understood, and no clear solution is seen, those energies lead to a general, vague anxiety accompanied by panicky behavior, helplessness or despair.[4]

Prescient though these speculations were, they led to no research, and certainly none on children's feelings. Although there was concern that the duck-and-cover civil-defense drills carried out in schools during the 1950s might be upsetting to children, it was a "minority opinion."[5] In general, authorities on child development took the position that secure children, and those whose parents had not frightened them unduly about world events, would not be upset by the drills, a position for which they could find support in Anna Freud's work with children during World War II.[6] This point of view, whatever its validity, in effect acquiesced to the cold-war climate of the day and gave school administrators, burdened with the task of civil-defense training, the reassurance they wanted.

That was the way things stood until the early Sixties, when Milton Schwebel, a psychologist on the faculty of New York University School of Education, and Sibylle Escalona, a child psychiatrist at Albert Einstein Hospital in the Bronx, conducted the first two investigations of young people's feelings about the threat of nuclear war. When they began their research they did not know each other and were unaware of each other's work, although later they became, in Schwebel's phrase, "a sort of vaudeville team on the subject"—a not very apt metaphor for two people characterized by almost courtly good manners and the slightly weary, restrained style of those whose professions demand that they make a high art of being good listeners.

"In a sense we've complemented each other," Schwebel told me. "Sibylle comes out of child and infant studies and I worked with older children and students.

"What precipitated my first study in the fall of 1961," he continued, "was what was going on in New York state. Nelson Rockefeller was pushing for bomb shelters. Some of us felt this was irrational and destructive; irrational in the sense that it was implying there was protection, and destructive in that it was giving children a model of this kind of adult." Schwebel and likeminded colleagues drafted a petition against the governor's plan, but they had no evidence to support their assertions that atomic weapons and civil defense indeed concerned children.

Although a certain amount was known about adult opinion on these subjects, mostly from public opinion polls, nothing was known about children's feelings, "so that," as Schwebel put it, "when some of the politicians would say, You're making a big fuss—children are hardly aware of the nuclear threat, look at them, they're out playing—there was no effective counterargument."

Schwebel made his decision: "I wanted to know as objectively as I could, recognizing that I was involved, what children felt. What I did first—I was living then in Rockville Centre, Long Island—was to start talking with neighborhood kids and then with the children of some people I knew in New York. I was rather astounded by the intensity of their feelings. It was something that wasn't known to us. Not only was it not discussed in the schools but I surmised it wasn't discussed at home."

What Schwebel found in his first interviews was fear, running deep at times, and anger, "amounting sometimes almost to the level of outrage." He thought at first that he had a biased sample: "Rockville Centre is middle-class, upper-middle-class; the families I associated with in New York were the same."

He decided to extend his study and recruited graduate students, school counselors, and teachers, arming them with the starkest of questionnaires, consisting of the following questions: Do I think there is going to be a war? Do I care? Why? What do I think about fallout shelters? By early 1962 he had obtained three thousand responses from elementary, junior-high, and senior-high students in New York state, Connecticut, New Jersey, and Pennsylvania.

"What I found was that I hadn't had a biased sample in my initial pilot study. The concerns were considerable. The young children, particularly, had distorted notions of what would occur; nevertheless the possibility of war aroused tremendous fear on their part, as much as the reality would justify."

In reply to Schwebel's first question, 45 percent of junior-high students expected a war (older children were only slightly more optimistic), 46 percent disagreed, and 9 percent were non-committal.

To Schwebel's second and third questions (Do I care? Why?), nearly all the children answered yes, "and some were affronted by it."[7] Awareness on the part of young people of the catastrophic nature of nuclear war emerged in replies to the fourth question, about fallout shelters: "Even if I survive, what will there be worth living for, with millions dead?" wrote one student.

Replies to the fourth question showed contrasting opinions between older and younger students. Whereas 48 percent of junior-high students favored them, only 21 percent were in favor among senior high school students, nearly 70 percent being opposed. The great pessimism among older students about shelters may have reflected greater knowledge of the nature of nuclear war.

Sibylle Escalona's work supported Schwebel's findings. Starting in the summer of 1962 and continuing until early 1963, Escalona, working with a group of colleagues, questioned a much smaller sample of young people—the final report was based on the responses of 311 children aged between ten and seventeen. Escalona was motivated in part by scientific interest—"it just seemed like an interesting thing to do," she told me. Moreover, she had encountered some children in her clinical practice who were troubled by air-raid drills. In part, too, she was motivated by the hope of raising political consciousness: "If it was true that children were concerned, it seemed

an entry wedge to interest people in the topic." Her implication—
that the child is the path to adults' awareness of issues they would
otherwise keep at arm's length—has been a recurring motive in the
work of almost all those who have subsequently investigated children's feelings about nuclear weapons.

Where Schwebel had been direct, Escalona was indirect: her
questions made no reference to war or peace, but instead elicited
children's feelings and opinions about the future. "Think about the
world as it may be about ten years from now. What are some of the
ways in which it may be different from today?" "How would you like
it to be different?" "If you had three wishes, what would they be?"
These were some of the questions she asked.

The replies were startling. Seventy percent of the children
mentioned the issue of war and peace. A number spoke of the future
in very gloomy terms, even if they did not envisage war within the
next ten years. For instance, an eleven-year-old wrote, "In ten years
countries will still be quarrelling—larger countries will be preparing
bombs to wipe out the world." [8]

Schwebel and Escalona presented and published their work,
but little followed, even within their professions. "Professional organizations did not want to touch the issue," Schwebel commented.
Both he and Escolona went on to other work. In 1974, Schwebel
threw out his questionnaires. "I sold my home and I was cleaning
out the attic, and you know, if you've accumulated things and you're
moving into an apartment, you look for things to throw out. There
was my box, with three thousand responses. And I threw it out." He
shook his head ruefully, and went on, "What I'm trying to convey to
you is my understanding of the détente. Whoever thought we would
reach the insanity of allowing that to end?"

With few exceptions it was the mid-1970s before anyone
took an interest again in young people's feelings about nuclear weapons. [9] But during this period intellectual interest in the effects of "big
world" events on the "little world" of the individual psyche increased and became more sophisticated. In 1967, the psychiatrist
Jerome D. Frank published *Sanity and Survival: Psychological Aspects of War and Peace.* This comprehensive study has been a basis
for subsequent thinking about the psychology of the arms race in the
nuclear age. Not only did Frank examine the psychological factors
underlying international aggression, but he also analyzed the socialization of children for aggression, including the influence of television. Also in 1967, the psychiatrist Robert Jay Lifton published *Death*

in Life: Survivors of Hiroshima, a book about the effects on consciousness of nuclear war and nuclear weapons—and Lifton conducted the research for the book in 1962, roughly the same period that Schwebel and Escalona conducted their studies. Lifton's book is about Hiroshima survivors rather than those who fear another war, but it is seminal to our understanding that nuclear weapons have brought and are bringing about a change of consciousness. In describing the responses of victims in the face of experience too devastating to be fully admitted to consciousness, Lifton formulated the concept of "psychic numbing"; by extension, he and others have used this term to describe the ways in which people respond—or don't respond—to the threat of annihilation as well as to the actuality of disaster. In a subsequent work, *The Broken Connection,* Lifton explored the effect of the Nazi holocaust—as well as the development of atomic weapons—on our sense of transcendence—and, therefore, on the meaning people are able to find in their lives. A later formulation that Lifton shares with other political and psychological thinkers is the concept of "illusions" in relation to the possibility of nuclear war—among others, the illusion that war can be limited and controlled; the illusion of feasible preparation for nuclear war; the illusion of the possibility of stoic behavior in time of war. We will see that the concept of illusion is useful in understanding adults' perception—or lack thereof—of the presence of an apocalyptic vision in young people's imagination.[10]

In 1975, Jerald G. Bachman, a social psychologist at the Institute for Social Research of the University of Michigan, and his colleague Lloyd Johnston, began an ongoing study of social trends entitled *Monitoring the Future.* Each year a nationally representative sample of high-school seniors—15,792 in the first year, and 17,000 to 18,000 thereafter—have responded to comprehensive questionnaires on a broad range of questions. From the start Bachman and Johnston included questions related to the nuclear-arms threat. One question asked respondents to note how often they worried about the chance of nuclear war. In 1975 more than 7 percent replied that they "often" did, while another 32.6 percent said they "sometimes" did. By 1984, 29.5 percent said they often worried—almost four times as many—and 39.9 percent said they worried "sometimes." Moreover, by 1982 the percentage of respondents who agreed with the statement "Nuclear or biological annihilation will probably be the fate of all mankind within my lifetime" had risen from a little more than a fifth to more than a third.[11] To date, this study contains the most statistically reliable information on young people's opinions about the nuclear threat.

It was not this study, however, that finally had an impact on the public but one that was far less sound methodologically. It came at the right time, however—that is, when awareness of the perils posed by nuclear weapons was intensifying. In 1977, at the suggestion of a Philadelphia psychiatrist, Perry Ottenberg, the American Psychiatric Association voted to form a task force to examine the psychosocial effects of nuclear weapons and nuclear power, including their impact on the feelings of young people.

"Perry came along and recommended this task force, and all of us thought, Why now?" recalled the psychiatrist John E. Mack, co-author, with another psychiatrist, William R. Beardslee, of the task-force report. "We didn't even know about Schwebel and Escalona's work specifically when we started.

"It's a far from perfect study," Mack continued. "In one of our meetings we simply developed a questionnaire that asked these simple-minded questions. We didn't sharply distinguish nuclear power from nuclear weapons, we asked leading questions, we committed every methodological atrocity you can imagine.

"The findings were very obvious: a number of kids are frightened of nuclear war, some say they won't grow up, some say it affects their sense of their own future. There was nothing in there a little common sense wouldn't have led you to believe."

For all its methodological limitations, the task-force study accomplished something that earlier studies had not done (and were not designed to do): it put some descriptive flesh on children's concerns. Most telling were longer responses elicited from a small group within the overall sample. They revealed a keen awareness of the human predicament posed by nuclear technology:

> Nuclear means a source of energy which could provide the world
> with energy needed for future generations. It also means the
> destruction of marine life whose environment is ruined by nuclear
> waste. Also the destruction of human life when used in missiles.

> I was probably ten or eleven, and all I thought of was "blowing up
> places" with bombs. I didn't realize that nuclear power could be
> used for things other than bombs. Now, I think nuclear power
> could be a very important asset, but first we should find a safe way
> to use it and dispose of the waste.

I think nuclear weapons are very necessary for our national security if we intend to remain a major power. We have to keep up.

I think that nuclear weapons are completely unnecessary for protection of the U.S. All they do is cause more death and destruction. If there was a nuclear war right now, the earth probably wouldn't survive it.[12]

These responses were voices the public had not heard, although it could have heard something very like them at the time of the Schwebel and Escalona studies nearly twenty years earlier—or, if it had been able to listen to kids like Mike Seely, not quite thirty-five years earlier. But now it was ready to listen.

"The findings became known," said Mack, "right at the heart of the 1980 presidential election and the hostage crisis. We were interviewed a lot in 1980 and 1981, although the report wasn't published until 1982. Suddenly this bit of committee work was a matter of national sensitivity. Reagan was talking about prevailing in nuclear war, and suddenly we were all on television; suddenly what children had to say about nuclear war became of national interest."

In 1982, the year the task-force report was published, the introduction of cruise and Pershing missiles in Western Europe was in the offing, the MX missile was an important issue, and the administration was obliging the peace movement with its bellicose rhetoric. Nineteen eighty-two was the year of Jonathan Schell's "Fate of the Earth" articles in the New Yorker, important examinations of the risk posed by nuclear weapons and our difficulties in comprehending that risk; the year of the June 12 rally in New York, which brought three-quarters of a million demonstrators out into the city streets in protest against nuclear weapons; the year in which the public imagination was captured by the concept of freezing nuclear weapons at current levels as a first step leading to their negotiated reduction. For a brief moment, at least, a public nerve was sensitized to the arms race and to the threat of nuclear war to a degree it had not been since the movement to halt above-ground testing twenty years earlier. Concern with children's fears and anger was part of this new sensitivity. It was as if the public had at last pushed itself into Mike Seely's bedroom, sat down at his bedside, turned off *Lucky Lager Dance Time,* and asked him what was on his mind—except that it was not Mike they were listening to but people like Maya, who might have been his child and—in the case of those younger than Maya— very nearly his grandchildren.

*   *   *

In the years since the American Psychiatric Association Task Force study was published, new research has reinforced earlier findings. One example is a survey conducted by a psychologist, Benina F. Berger, working with her physician husband Jeffrey Gould and another colleague. In 1983, during the weeks immediately following the downing of the Korean airliner 007, they surveyed 1,778 students, aged between eight and seventeen, in thirty schools throughout the United States, using the same questions Schwebel had used more than twenty years before. To some extent the tensions of this period paralleled those of the period when Schwebel's large study was conducted in 1961, just after the Berlin crisis had passed its peak but while it was still in the news. (Schwebel had also obtained a second, smaller sample at the time of the Cuban missile crisis.)

In reply to the first question ("Do I think there is going to be a war?"), 62 percent of the Berger–Gould respondents—compared with Schwebel's 45 percent—thought there would be a war; 20 percent felt there would not; and 18 percent answered "maybe." These young people were even less confident about the future than those Schwebel had questioned.

To the second and third questions ("Do I Care?") the overwhelming majority (91 percent) responded that they did; but more interesting was what they cared about. When Berger and her associates analyzed statistically the content of the replies (something Schwebel had not done), they found that 63 percent of the students surveyed referred to *loss*. Fear of loss itself had many subcategories —a sense of global loss, that is, the loss of life in the world; loss of family and community; loss associated with self and one's own life; and loss due to radiation. In general, the older the child, the deeper his sense of the threat of loss. At every age level global loss was most feared. One could argue that this fear is evidence of the forging of a new kind of global consciousness.

The fourth question, about fallout shelters, was not as relevant as it had been at the time of Schwebel's study, and 84 percent of fourth and fifth graders, 24 percent of ninth graders, and 16 percent of twelfth graders did not know what they were. (The researchers included the question not only because they wanted to repeat Schwebel's study exactly but because they wanted to elicit students' thoughts and fantasies about the possibility of surviving nuclear war.) Of those students who knew what a fallout shelter was, 39 percent thought they were unequivocally good and another 31 percent gave qualified approval ("I think they're good to a certain degree—except what's going to be left after the war has ended?"). Twenty-nine percent thought that they would not work. Pessimism about their effectiveness did not distinguish older from younger students, as it had in Schwebel's findings.

The analysis of the content of students' replies allowed a deeper understanding of their feelings about the threat of nuclear war. Only 8 percent wrote in terms of fear—although "nuclear fear" has become *the* catch phrase to identify children's responses to the issue—whereas 11 percent wrote of feelings of helplessness and resignation; 24 percent of humanitarian feelings; and 22 percent of anger.[13]

The Berger–Gould repetition of Schwebel's study is a particularly good demonstration of what numerous other recent American studies have indicated—that concern about the possibility of nuclear war continues to be present in the consciousness of great numbers of young people.

International research has corroborated investigations in the United States. One of the soundest of all the studies is a survey conducted early in 1983 of a large national sample of Finnish students aged between twelve and eighteen years old. Respondents were asked to list their three main hopes and three main fears. Fear of war exceeded every other fear, being mentioned first by 79 percent of twelve-year-olds and 48 percent of eighteen-year-olds. There was a broader distribution of answers concerning hopes, with the hopes for employment forming the largest category (32–39 percent)—but among twelve- and fourteen-year-olds hopes for peace formed the second and third largest categories (22 and 16 percent, respectively).[14]

A 1984 Swedish study of adolescents aged between thirteen and fifteen asked respondents to rank their greatest worries, adding nuclear war to a group of worries known to affect teenagers. Forty-two percent indicated that nuclear war was their greatest worry; the second highest worry was concern over the possibility of a parent's death—11 percent.[15]

An informal survey of Soviet children was conducted in 1983 by a team of American psychiatrists who interviewed Soviet youngsters about their concerns about nuclear war. Approximately sixty young people between the ages of ten and fifteen were interviewed on videotape, and 293 ranging in age between nine and seventeen responded to a written questionnaire. The Soviet young people were found to be well informed about the dangers of nuclear weapons and concerned about the possibility of war. More than eleven percent thought nuclear war likely in their lifetime compared with the 11.6 percent in the 1983 Bachman and Johnston survey who agreed with the statement that nuclear annihilation was likely within their lifetime. However, their views differed from American young people in certain ways. They tended to be much more pessimistic about the possibility of personal or national survival in the event of war—2.9 percent, versus 16.4 percent of the Americans in the Bachman sample, thought they would survive. They were also more optimistic about the prevention of war—93.3 percent, versus 65.2 percent.[16]

   The findings of the various studies would seem incontrovertible; they have been sharply criticized, however, for their research methodology. Were the samples on which the studies were based broad enough, or were they drawn from special populations of children? The answer is that some studies—the Finnish study, for instance, and the Bachman *Monitoring the Future* study—were based on large, reliable national samples, whereas many other studies have been based on less representative populations.
   Did the questions "lead" respondents, and therefore risk having more to do with the bias of the investigators than with the states of mind and heart of their subjects? This is a more complicated issue.
   "There are problems with every kind of study," Mack commented. "If you use intensive questionnaires, you're going to get lots of detailed answers having to do with what you want to know, but you're also going to lead the kids. If you bury the nuclear issue in a number of other concerns, you correct for the problem of leading but all you get then are statistical differentiations. If you interview kids intensively, again you have the problem that kids will tell you what you want to hear. But if you don't ask specifically about the nuclear issue it's like any taboo subject; you won't get at it."
   In the conservative journal of opinion *Commentary,* the psychologist Joseph Adelson and the educator Chester E. Finn addressed the "leading question" issue in an essay that is an unsparing criticism of the "nuclear fear" research—and a maddening mixture of the penetrating and the tendentious. Adelson and Finn argue that ". . . it is evident that in dealing with so subjective a matter as a person's emotional state [such as an individual's response to the nuclear-fear issue], responses will be conditioned by his vocabulary of self-report, and even more by his sense of what the questioner is up to, what *kind* of answer the interviewer has in mind."[17] The critical factor,

they maintain, is that the "interviewers ordinarily establish a context which influences and at times governs the answers given. . . ."

The implication is that respondents in such studies were " 'coached' or 'terrorized' by parents or other authority figures" [18] into giving the responses they did. The further implication is that "terrorized" children are the handiwork of the left. Such an assertion "seems untenable," in the opinion of Jerald Bachman and an associate, Greg Diamond. Diamond and Bachman have conducted a sophisticated reanalysis of the *Monitoring the Future* data, with the intention of achieving a greater understanding of young people's reactions to the nuclear issue. On the basis of their data they believe that nuclear fear or anxiety is more aptly seen as two quite different feelings or sets of feelings and attitudes: concern and despair. But "neither measure correlates with political orientation, party affiliation, or most measures of attitudes toward military policy." Moreover, they found that young people surveyed in the last several years tend to be more conservative, but at the same time more concerned. Furthermore, the number of students who react with despair, as opposed to concern, has remained more or less constant over a decade, contrary to what a "brainwashing" or "terrorizing" hypothesis might predict on the basis of increased attention from the media to the nuclear issue and increased teaching about it.

There is a further implication to Adelson and Finn's work. In repudiating the validity of self-report they would seem to favor some perfectly "objective" investigation of attitudes and feelings, thus in effect giving carte blanche to every sort of expert (except those who conduct opinion polls). Perfect objectivity hopes to abolish context, but perfect objectivity is a dream. An objective approach is itself a kind of context. Moreover, as Mack suggested, silence about a particular issue, if it is one that is taboo, can be a context. When it comes to the study of feelings and attitudes researchers would do better to realize that they are likely to be in the position of the three blind men and the elephant, each getting hands on a part of the truth but not necessarily the same part.

However, the issue of the validity of self-report is a matter of particular interest with respect to children: children are not in a good position to defend or promote their views. Moreover, adults are inclined to use children's views for their own purposes, as we shall consider in more detail in a later chapter. Thus Adelson and Finn point out, in this case quite rightly, that many antinuclear activists have made children the icons of their political message. But other adults—a far greater number—fail to give credence to what children have said they feel and think because it confounds their conception of childhood innocence.

Faced with these complex issues, how does one make sense of the nuclear-fear research so far? I believe that the best approach is to say what one might have said to the blind men after they had explored the contours of the elephant, and to conclude that despite the methodological limitations of some studies, the best are very persuasive and each piece of research reinforces others. Cumulatively, the work done so far presents a convincing portrait of the presence of the nuclear issue in the minds and imagination of a large proportion of young people.

It would be strange if this were not so. Although the public —including the youthful public—is in general far from knowledgeable about international politics and the arms race—let alone the intricacies of military strategy or nuclear-weapons development and deployment—nevertheless, there is a far wider and deeper public understanding today of the dangers of nuclear weapons and of the arms race than when Mike Seely was a boy (and today the weapons and their delivery systems are infinitely more dangerous). This understanding can be seen in part as a response to efforts to educate the public, spearheaded for the most part by a concerned minority of activists, which began almost at once after Hiroshima. These efforts have intensified in recent years, attempting to bring home the increased costs of the arms race and the fact that general nuclear war means annihilation.

The changes in public opinion over a thirty-five-year period are remarkable. Whereas in 1949 59 percent of respondents to a Gallup poll thought it was a good thing that the atomic bomb had been developed, in 1982 only 24 percent thought so, and 65 percent thought it was bad. Another Gallup poll in 1955 asked respondents if they thought all of mankind would be destroyed by an all-out nuclear war between the Soviet Union and the United States; only 27 percent answered yes, while 59 percent said no. A not identical but comparable question in a 1984 poll asked respondents if the Soviet Union and the United States would be destroyed by an all-out war. Eighty-nine percent answered yes. At the same time, individuals' sense of their own vulnerability has changed over the years: in 1961 40 percent of respondents to a Gallup poll believed that their chances of living through a nuclear war were fifty-fifty, and 43 percent thought their chances were poor—but by 1984 only 17 percent thought they had a fifty-fifty chance and 77 percent thought their chance was poor. In another 1984 poll, 55 percent of those interviewed found themselves thinking about the nuclear issue more than they had five years earlier.[19]

These figures put findings about children's concern in perspective. Although a young person's information about nuclear weapons or nuclear politics may not match an adult's, we can perceive that the growing presence of the issue in the consciousness of young people parallels increased adult understanding and a growing consensus that the issue is part of the public agenda.

But to say that an apocalyptic vision is present in the consciousness of many young people says nothing about the impact of this vision. So far, psychologists and psychiatrists have approached the question of impact in the following terms: how is the impact different for different socioeconomic groups—if it is? How is it different for young people from the way it is for adults? How is it different for different age groups? Finally, what is the nature of the impact, if any?

THE QUESTION
OF IMPACT

RICHER AND POORER

There has been considerable controversy about the impact of concern about the threat of nuclear annihilation on children of different backgrounds. This controversy has pitted what one might call "activists" against a number of researchers who question the validity of the nuclear-fear research conducted along the lines suggested earlier. The child psychiatrist Robert Coles has been an outspoken member of the latter group. He has argued that concern about the nuclear issue should be seen as class-influenced. It is, he asserts, primarily characteristic of children from well-off families, particularly those whose parents are themselves concerned about the issue. Moreover, he asserts it is certainly not a burning issue for working-class and minority groups. After interviewing more than a hundred children on the subject Coles stated, "I simply do not hear children of poor families mention the threat of nuclear war as a major worry for them."[1] Although he is not condemnatory in the manner of Adelson and Finn, his implication is that those investigators who have found widespread concern about nuclear war in responses to the surveys have found what they wanted to find, and that the concern expressed by young people is the result of the type of questions asked.

Peace activists who are teachers and researchers and who are interested in children's responses to the nuclear issue have been angered by Coles's position. Some of their anger has its roots in their not always explicit desire to use the image of the child—the fearful child—as a way of galvanizing public opinion. The image of the child has less credibility from a political point of view, they sense, if it cannot be shown that all children are concerned. Their point of view is marked by a certain longing for what has been called "credibility by class origin," which one commentator calls "one of the most debilitating pieces of prejudice" to which the left, or, for that matter, liberals in general, is prey.[2] Put another way, such a prejudice makes it very hard for liberals to feel comfortable if the poor do not join them in concern about an issue. Their response is to insist that the poor really do feel the same way, or failing that, to insist that they should. This position can end up making liberals vulnerable to derision from the conservative end of the political spectrum—or to the criticism of someone like Coles, himself a liberal, whose professional life has to a great degree centered on an exploration of children's feelings about their racial, economic, political, and class status.

Diamond and Bachman's reanalysis of the *Monitoring the Future* data does not provide much support for Coles's contention that children's concern with the nuclear issue is class-based: "We find concern to be uncorrelated with father's and mother's educational level, projected income level, and satisfaction with standard of living, job, neighborhood, and property security."[3]

But they do note that "Coles seems to be right in contending that some segment of the population is more disposed, for some reason, toward greater concern about social issues . . ." but their surveys do not provide them with the information to characterize this "segment" more fully.

To suggest the complexity of the issues involved in answering the question of the impact of the nuclear issue on young people from a range of backgrounds—and incidentally to suggest the grip of the liberal "credibility by class origin" prejudice—let us turn to a workshop that Maya Gillingham and Jody Lester held, soon after the workshop they gave at the Y, in the office of *New Youth Connections,* a newspaper run by New York City high-school students.

The office of *New Youth Connections* is a cramped, low-ceilinged space, quite the opposite of the spacious gym at the Y. On the afternoon of the *Changing the Silence* workshop it was crammed with some twenty teenagers, plus Maya and Jody and four adults. One of these was Donna Lawson, at that time the adult adviser to the newspaper; the other three were John Burt, producer for the *Changing the Silence* tour; Ernest Drucker, a psychologist and antinuclear activist; and Tom Roderick, a teacher and the New York director of Educators for Social Responsibility, a teachers' organization interested in nuclear-age education.

It was quite a different sort of workshop from the dance class at the Y. For one thing, Drucker and Roderick both gave brief factual presentations, one about the nature of nuclear weapons, the other a capsule history of the arms race. But what really made it different was the mood and responses of the participants. The dancers at the Y were all female, middle- or upper-middle-class, and (with one or two exceptions) white. The *New Youth Connections* young people were boys as well as girls, and multiracial: nearly half were black and there were several Orientals. Moreover, there was not the same protected air of privilege about them: their socioeconomic background was much more mixed. And whereas the dancers were docile and eager participants, many of these teenagers acted as if they had been dragged there. (And Donna Lawson subsequently told me that she had had to cajole many of the participants to come.)

The workshop began with a few warmup, get-acquainted exercises and then moved on to Drucker's presentation about nuclear weapons, which included photos of Hiroshima victims that assaulted the emotions. There was silence at the end of his presentation. Then one young man asked a question that would have been unthinkable in the polite, feminine atmosphere at the Y: "Why does anyone care?"

There was another silence. No one seemed ready or able to answer him. For a minute he had shattered the unspoken conventions on which the workshop was based—interested young people will agree to learn what concerned adults come to teach them; nice young people will agree to feel what other nice young people feel. I wondered what the question really meant. Was he asking: will these honkies pack up their show-and-tell and let folks get back to what's really on their mind? Or was the speaker protecting himself against the impact of the images of the victims of Hiroshima? Or both?

At last a young woman ventured, "I don't think we live just to die."

The answer somehow enabled Maya, who looked close to tears, to go on. She suggested going around the room, giving everyone a chance to say what he or she loved.

"There are so many things I love to do," a young man said.

"I love people," a girl in a blue and yellow sweater said.

"I'm not going to say I love my life or that everything is going wonderful," a tall young man said, "but I love the right to change things."

"Love will be here after we die," said the young man who had said, "Who cares?" He added, in a confused sort of statement, that he didn't mind the idea of "excessive force"—presumably the force of atomic weapons.

A girl changed the subject somewhat, saying, "I know that

people can change what's been started, but do you ever just get scared?"

Maya said she loved the idea of being ninety and that she wanted her grandmother to be ninety.

Now Roderick made his presentation. He started as Drucker had, with the premise that his audience knew nothing about World War II, nothing about the arms race, nothing about terms like ICBM and MIRV. It became clear that the historical and current-events background of the group was scanty at best, but everyone was very attentive.

After Roderick's presentation there was a coffee break. Then the group formed a circle once again—or rather an oval cramped in the confining space. Referring to Drucker and Roderick's presentations, Maya said, "We've heard all this information, but how does it affect our feelings?" She had her wind back and seemed willing to run the risk of another "Who cares?"

No one said anything. Not a word. In a remark that appeared to protect the *New Youth Connections* kids as much as it endeavored to facilitate, Donna Lawson said, "Ghetto kids find it embarrassing to talk about the nuclear issue."

Jody stepped into the silence and taught the group a song in which two youngsters, one American, one Soviet, express their concerns and conclude, "It's you and me and all our friends who've got to set things right." Two girls did not join in the singing and sat on the couch giggling.

Following the format of their workshop, Maya and Jody showed their tape of *Changing the Silence.*

When the lights came on, two young men—one the author of the "Who cares?" remark—had left the group and were sitting in a back room at the end of a corridor. Donna Lawson went to talk with them and coaxed them back, but they sat on the outskirts of the group, observers, not participants.

Maya passed her mask around, and asked, as she did at the Y, what peace meant to people.

A girl who said she had aspirations to be a writer said, "When I was thinking about peace, I realized I equated it with happiness, and yet things we do are often the opposite of what we want." Then she paused and took another tack. "I think peace is something collective," she said.

A boy in a plaid shirt said that he believed personal peace and peace in the world are "not really separate."

The girls giggling on the couch passed, but another girl said,

"It definitely has to be people with one thing on their mind—unity and equilibrium. Peace is not this," she added pointing to Maya's mask. Then she shifted again. "Peace is learning that you've got your own thing to do on this earth and I don't want to stop you."

Then the unexpected happened. One of the "observers" on the edge of the circle—not the fellow who had said "Who cares?" but his companion—said, "There's no peace in this room. There are people in this room who are silent because they're afraid to be ridiculed and there are people here who are talking because they're afraid to be silent."

Now floodgates were opened by a burst of talk and emotion. What "Who cares?" had not accomplished, this remark did. Maya talked about the "scariness" of touring with Jody across the country. "I want Jody to be safe," she said. Donna Lawson reiterated how hard it was for someone who is black to care "up front" about the nuclear issue. At one point Maya said, "I think acknowledging conflict is the beginning of peace."

One young man confronted the "observer" who had boldly opened up the discussion. Why had he bothered to come?

The "observer" retorted, "Don't tell us why we're here. Partly I came because I was invited and partly I wanted to learn."

Lawson suggested that they brainstorm the barriers to peace; now everyone contributed to a great tumble of words: "prejudice," "poverty," "the truth and the lack of it," "dominance," "pessimism," "ignorance," "insecurity," "oversensitivity," "language barriers," "family abuse," "pretense," "fear of not knowing," "the unknown itself," "fear and fear of fear," "rabble-rousing," "reluctance to try."

Next they brainstormed the ingredients of peace, both great and small: "a job," "control of the media," "acceptance," "a mansion," "equality," "free expression," "worldwide nutrition," "a ban on advertising of stupid products," "no violence," "a better subway system," "love and respect for diversity," "safety," and "all kinds of green stuff."

For a moment, when the brainstorming was done, the high lingered in the room. Then a young man who had not spoken until now said, "I've been here for a while and no one seems to be very realistic. God gave us one more chance and we blew it. We have snowballed to this point. All the talk, all the singing, it's very beautiful and we can have it in our family, but we're not going to get it any other way. It's got to the point where I just live day by day and if I can go to college and become a journalist—"

He broke off.

It was time to end the workshop—at the point that it might profitably have begun.

The differing responses of the young people at *New Youth Connections* and at the Y reflect differences in style and differing degrees of comfort and discomfort with the style of Maya's presentation. But I believe these differences reflect differing concern with the nuclear issue as well. Robert Coles has suggested that moral involvement, such as is called for in the antinuclear movement, must be preceded by "moral notice." He notes that "each of us seems to have the time, the inclination, the disposition to regard only certain matters or issues as morally compelling." He further notes that those who have daily survival taken care of—such as the young women taking a late-afternoon dance class at the Y—have substantial "leeway for moral reflection."[4]

The young people at *New Youth Connections* had leeway for moral reflection, too; otherwise they would not have had the time and energy to work on an after-school newspaper. But they did not find the nuclear issue as compelling as Maya and Jody did. When Donna Lawson suggested that they brainstorm the "barriers of peace," the subjects they did find morally compelling emerged, and they included poverty and prejudice. There would have been a variety of ways Maya, Jody, Drucker, and Roderick could have made arms-race issues more specifically relevant to the issues that were compelling for these young people; but time was limited and they were constrained by the tendency, often characteristic of those in the peace movement, to disregard differences in style and angle of vision on the world.

I believe it would be false, however, to conclude that because the *New Youth Connections* teenagers found the nuclear issue less compelling than Maya and Jody (at least in the terms in which it was presented) that it was therefore not present in their consciousness. The ability to take "moral notice" or the interest in doing so does not necessarily determine the presence of an issue in the imagination. "God gave us one more chance and we blew it. We have snowballed to this point," said one of the participants in the workshop at *New Youth Connections.* In two years of talking with young people I never heard a young person make a more pessimistic remark with respect to the nuclear issue.

The findings of Sibylle Escalona, Diamond and Bachman's

reanalysis of the *Monitoring the Future* data, and the work of a psychologist, Scott Haas, are useful in making sense of the discrepancy between this remark and what in general seemed to be morally compelling to the *New Youth Connections* group—and between the most reliable survey findings and Coles's position. Fewer children from very low socioeconomic backgrounds, Escalona found, spontaneously brought up issues of war and peace than children from lower-middle-, middle-, or upper-class backgrounds. One can assume, using Coles's concept of "moral notice," that given the full context of their lives these issues did not press to the foreground of their consciousness. But Escalona also found the poorest children to be the most pessimistic about the future.[5] Although they specifically refuse to make such a connection on the basis of their data, I believe Diamond and Bachman's reanalysis may offer some support for Escalona's finding. They found a slight but significant negative correlation between despair (as opposed to concern) and "mother's education, satisfaction with respect to the student's neighborhood and with personal safety"[6]—indices that one might assume bear some relationship to social and economic status.

The psychologist Scott Haas has attempted to establish how different groups rank concern about the nuclear threat compared with other issues. In the course of his research he interviewed teenagers from upper-, upper-middle-, lower-middle-, and working-class backgrounds. When he asked respondents to rank the following concerns—economy, employment, energy, marriage, and nuclear conflict—upper- and upper-middle-class teens ranked nuclear conflict as their primary concern, followed closely by employment and the economy. In contrast, lower-middle- and working-class young people ranked employment first by far. But in response to a question about whether they expected to see a nuclear war during their lifetime, 82 percent of working- and lower-middle-class teenagers answered in the affirmative, in contrast with 29 percent of the other groups.[7] These young people may not rate the nuclear issue high among their concerns, but this did not mean they were unaware of it or that their view of the future was optimistic—in fact, quite the opposite. Escalona and Haas's findings suggest that the nuclear threat is a factor in shaping the imagination of a much wider group of young people than those who rank it as primary concern, let alone those who are activists with respect to the issue. For the poor, the presence of the threat of nuclear war is one more dark element in a picture of the world already made dark by their position in society.

YOUNG CHILDREN

A nursery-school child came up behind his teacher with a construction made of Lego blocks, poked her in the back, and said, "This is an atom bomb and I'm going to kill you."

The same teacher told the following anecdote. She had created a Valentine calendar for the month of February featuring many hearts pierced by arrows, and had hung it on her bulletin board. Above the Valentine calendar was a large photo of an airplane, part of a quite separate display about transportation. One day she noticed a boy gazing at the bulletin board in a reverie while the other children ate their snacks. At last he said, "Those are the missiles the plane is dropping, aren't they?" He meant the arrows that pierced the hearts.[8]

In relating these anecdotes his teacher took them as proof that the child knew about nuclear weapons and nuclear war. But what did she mean by "knew"? What does a young child understand of war? What can a young child understand about the conflicts and rivalries that lead to war? These are questions that need answering in order to build a framework for understanding what a child may feel, or not feel, about nuclear war—and to begin to answer the questions posed earlier: is the impact of nuclear fear on young people different from what it is on adults? And is the impact different on younger children from what it is on older children?

At four or five children do not have the same conception of war as adults—or even children of eleven or twelve. Their thinking is very concrete, and they have a very modest supply of information at their disposal about the "big world" beyond their family. Nevertheless, their imagination is already being furnished with the vocabulary and images of their culture's aggressive and destructive forces. They can easily draw on this vocabulary or these images to express feelings of aggression or hostility—for instance, a strong feeling they may have about a teacher at a particular moment. In this, children today are no different from the way children have ever been. Even young ones have always picked up the images of power, danger, and vulnerability pertaining to the society in which they live, along with images of the adult means and strategies of defending against danger. In this sense making an atomic bomb out of Lego blocks is no different from a kids' bow-and-arrow game in a Neolithic village. What is different is the power of the weapon—and it is the increasing power of weapons in modern times that has turned some parents against war toys and war play and, as we have seen, made it difficult for them to accept the fact that images of such destructiveness have entered their children's consciousness.

Learning about war and the instruments of war is colored, like everything else, by the context of learning. Is the child's learning the result of direct experience or does it come from books or television? Learning about war in Beirut is different from learning about war in Scarsdale. Context includes the more subtle experience of picking up the tone with which adults or older peers convey information. To illustrate the latter with a personal example, my first memory of the "big world" beyond home, neighborhood, or community was a radio broadcast of a speech by Adolf Hitler. I was five, living safely and peacefully in Connecticut, but I was alarmed. In retrospect, I realize that the anxiety of the adults in my family as they listened, and the very exceptional fact that the radio was on at all in the middle of a perfectly ordinary afternoon, contributed to my feelings as much as Hitler's ranting voice speaking in a language I could not understand through the static of the short-wave reception.

As the child absorbs the vocabulary and images of power, destruction, and vulnerability, he learns who talks about them, who does not, and how they talk. He may learn that the men in his family talk one way and the women another, or that nuclear weapons, for instance, are just about never mentioned by anyone in his family yet are referred to on the nightly television news. As a preschooler he will feel less bound to abide by the rules implicit in the behavior he observes than he will a little later, when he is six or seven, but they are still part of the context of what he learns.

He may receive different and conflicting messages about war from members of his family and from playmates—but also from sources that are less personally connected with his life. If his parents participate in an antinuclear demonstration he may learn that "nuclear weapons are bad," but at the same time he may learn that Spiderman, to whom he is devoted, derived his power from a radioactive spider's bite. Or a peace-activist kindergarten teacher may give him a worksheet with the following xeroxed message at the top: "Peace means taking loving care of ourselves, each other, and our earth. I want to help keep the world peaceful by . . ."—and then blank lines for him, or the teacher writing for him, to fill in. Influenced by a set of messages about war that in all probability reach him through television—messages his teacher would no doubt find upsetting—he may dictate that he wants to keep the world peaceful by "calling eight army without their guns and explosives and ask

Peace means taking loving care of ourselves, each other and our earth. I want to help keep the world peaceful by _calling eight army without their guns and explosives and ask_ . them to catch 8 bad spies.

a t z,

Isaac DL

By

Peace means taking loving care of ourselves, each other and our earth. I want to help keep the world peaceful by _making a friendship circle of love around the world, everyone in the whole wide world_

By

them to catch eight bad spies." It is likely that the spies and armies of television are a good deal more exciting and glamorous than anything his teacher has had to say about peace in the world. But with the ingenious creativity of young children he has found a way to please the teacher by disarming the army—and in doing so he demonstrates that in a way consonant with his development he has grasped the point of view she has tried to convey. (She might well prefer the "answer" of another child who wanted to keep the world peaceful by "making a friendship circle of love around the world with everyone in the whole wide world," accompanying it by a fine drawing in which the "friendship circle" has become global man and the world, his mouth or navel.)

These drawings suggest the way in which young children begin to grasp key issues associated with war and peace, power and vulnerability. Their understanding is in one sense rudimentary but in another, as Robert Coles has demonstrated in his companion volumes *The Moral Life of Children* and *The Political Life of Children*, breathtakingly accurate and to the point. It is important, however, to remember what young children don't know or comprehend. They do not possess a body of information about war or weapons in the same way that adults or older children may. Nor do they have an intellectually well elaborated understanding of political institutions or the politics of nation states. Moreover, their world is still primarily their family. All of this means that if they feel anxious about war or nuclear war, it will not be because they understand the consequences of war in a way comparable with an adult's. They will be made anxious by what they pick up of the tone and mood of their parents' comments or perhaps something of the tone of a television newscast or feature (or, less likely, of a teacher). Moreover, they may be anxious to the degree that the images of war symbolize emotions they are struggling to handle—among others, their own aggressive impulses and their fear of separation from their families.

By the time they are seven or eight, however, children are capable of thinking about war in a much fuller and more organized way. However, in line with the still concrete character of their thinking they will focus, especially in the case of boys, on the "things" of war, weapons and equipment—as anyone familiar with the drawings of boys this age is well aware.[9] Their view of war is still shaped by their personal experience of "fighting"—particularly experience in play—but this experience is nevertheless shaped by the culture's messages about power and vulnerability conveyed by many sources, including sports, toys, comics, and television.

Young children are more inclined than adolescents to think that war has no justification. An early 1960s study found that 70 percent of eight-year-olds felt this way, in contrast to only 10 percent of fifteen-year-olds.[10] However, their lack of information concerning specific weapons may incline children this age to attitudes that adults would find surprisingly bellicose. In a study of student opinion during the Vietnam war, 41.2 percent of eight- and nine-year-olds, as contrasted with only 11.8 percent of twelve- and thirteen-year-olds, said they were willing to use atomic weapons.[11]

Differences between boys and girls are evident among elementary-school children in their attitudes toward war, as they have been at a younger age and continue to be as the young person matures. Unsurprisingly, research has found that girls are less inclined to mention weapons and other "concrete aspects" of war and more inclined to mention "fighting, dying, and killing." They are less inclined to support one adversary at the expense of the other and less inclined to see war as justified, although they are more "provokable" if confronted with a threat to family.[12]

Concurrently with their learning about war, children begin, starting at the age of six or seven, to develop a political attachment to their country; an attachment that Robert Coles, among others, has suggested may be qualified depending on their family's status in the society. They feel that there is a "we" of which they are a part and that other countries are "they," although compared with adolescents their assessment of "them" is relatively undifferentiated.[13]

They understand government in terms of persons, chiefly the president. Institutions are still shadowy to them, and their exposure to and absorption of attitudes is far in advance of their acquisition of the information that might flesh them out. They are disposed to view the government as good, a source of the benevolent control they still need in their own lives—unless, of course, they are members of a group—South African blacks, for instance—that has suffered at the hands of the government. The average American child will be inclined to feel a strong, idealizing patriotism, which is likely to be focused around and reinforced by symbols such as the flag and the Statue of Liberty as well as the figure of the president.

Learning about nuclear weapons can make it hard to see the government as good, but a child will go to some lengths to preserve a sense of a trustworthy adult world.

A fourth-grader wrote President Reagan:

> *Dear Ronald:*
>
> *I hate Nuclear Bombs. In fact I hate any kind of violence! Please you have to stop it! I'm serious! If you want to see your great grand children and grand children, stop it! You may think I'm just another face in the crowd but I'm not! I'm Sarah Harris! And I think you're o.k. But you make a lousy President!*

The president is the embodiment of government for Sarah, and she endeavors to separate the man who is "o.k." from the "lousy" president, suggesting that she does not want to demolish Reagan totally as someone in whom she can believe.

For a young child, his own impulsiveness can have consequences in the form of punishment; this fear of consequences, which is part of his moral order, may be reflected in the political positions he espouses. A classmate of Sarah's wrote:

> *Dear president,*
>
> *I think that you riely shodn't mes a ronde with nuclear disarmament becase it can be danderis becase if you drop a bomb on Japan a lot of people can get hirt then they might diside to drop a bomb on the unitid statse then you'll no how it feels.*

Nuclear arms, not disarmament, is what he means but his point is clear: What you do unto others may be done unto you.

Another fourth-grader's views about our nuclear strategy suggest the way in which personal experience continues to shape his thinking. He translates to the sphere of international politics a rough-and-ready set of rules that might be instructions to his "side" in a playground game of war:

> *Dear Ronald,*
>
> *I think we should make as much as we need to fight. If the Russians start we start. Don't start until they do.*
>
> *But don't make too much cause the more we make the more they make.*
>
> *The last move I want you to make is five atomic bombs at Russia.*
>
> *Your fan,*

"Your fan," suggests the patriotism and strong attachment to the president characteristic of a child this age. (It may also indicate loyalty to a parental viewpoint.) But the awkwardly phrased last sentence, which would read better if "fire" replaced "five," may hint at an undercurrent of fear.

Yet another child from the same fourth grade phrased her sense of political opposition or outrage in terms that were exceptionally mature, but essentially personal:

> *Dear Ronald Reagan,*
>   *Why are countries always trying to be the most powerful? Why couldn't you and other presidents be satisfied with the terrible weapons we already have? I think that if you don't stop people in this country from making nuclear weapons no one else will. You're the president. Are you sure you understand the responsibilities of being president? It's a big job. Nuclear weapons are dangerous. Think of all those speeches you make. You say you are going to do something about this but you don't! You get all the glory and applause and you feel like a big shot but of course, you don't do anything! What you're trying to say is "I don't care about anyone but myself. As long as me and Nancy are okay I don't care about you" that's what your saying. I think you're dumb for just sitting back and doing nothing when thousands of people are worried stiff. If I were old enough to vote I wouldn't vote for you. I hate you.*

The letter begins with a speculative question suggesting interest in a generalized and more abstract kind of inquiry than is usual for a child this age. But this inquiry is not sustained and by the end of the letter the writer is speaking to Reagan very much as she might feel —but probably not say—if she felt her parents were selfish and irresponsible.

The tie to parents is still very strong for elementary-school children and the fear of being separated from or losing them is the fear that has the deepest sense of reality with respect to fear of nuclear war. But this fear may be expressed indirectly as well as directly, as in the following letter.

> *Dear President Reagan,*
> *I am sure that my parents don't like knowing that I may*
> *never reach twenty-one or even twelve since I'm only eleven. You*
> *may not be causing it but you can control it in the U.S.*

Speaking of what he is sure his parents don't like is as close as this child could come to articulating his anxiety.

Children's concepts of peacemaking are as personal as their concepts of war. They are likely to think in terms of "making friends" and "making up"—and they do not like the idea of lingering conflicts.

While her fourth-grade classmates wrote the letters to President Reagan quoted above, one girl preferred to write her mother:

> *dear mommy,*
> *I think that we should have a nuclear freeze, but I am*
> *scared that Russia will take over America. But I hope that Russia*
> *will be friends with America and not fight with us.*

Within her framework, "being friends"—something her own experience had probably taught her a good deal about—would mend the rivalry and suspicion of the superpowers.

YOUNG ADOLESCENTS

Most researchers have found that young adolescents aged between twelve and fourteen are more apt to be intensely concerned about the threat of nuclear war than are younger children or older adolescents. It is easy to imagine that they are more afraid than younger children because they know more—about nuclear weapons, about the intractable nature of international politics, about the nature of war. Greater knowledge leads to an intensified emotional response. But why are young adolescents more afraid than older adolescents?

We can approach this question first of all from a cognitive point of view. One of the key changes of adolescence is the development of a capacity for thinking more abstractly. This capacity enables the adult, in the words of Sibylle Escalona, to "schematize the way you look at things," that is, to fit perceptions and experience into a highly developed intellectual framework. In such a framework, Escalona noted to me, "you don't see a new fact so clearly. It becomes enmeshed and embedded in the scheme." This cognitive step begins in pre- or early adolescence, but it does not develop all at once or at the same rate in every individual and may not be fully evident until the later adolescent years. I believe that the fact that it is not fully achieved in early adolescence contributes to the young teenager's greater fear of nuclear war. He cannot schematize the way he looks at things and therefore distance himself from their impact. Mike Seely's experience is illustrative. Conelrad broadcasts, which within an adult intellectual framework would probably be seen as formalities, were far from mere formalities for Mike. (Moreover, his father's reply to his question, that some day nuclear weapons would be outlawed "like mustard gas," suggests the way in which an adult's "schematized way of looking at things" may be an inadequate reply to a young person's concerns.)

Let us look at the differing ways in which two adolescents describe their feelings about the threat of nuclear war and the arms race.

A fourteen-year-old, Tom, wrote:

> The idea of nuclear war scares me. I'm only fourteen years old and I have no wish to die or even to be a survivor in a post-nuclear world. I have my whole life ahead of me and I don't want my world to be turned upside-down.
>
> I can find only one good thing about the effects of preparing for war. When the Russians build newer and better weapons, we have to develop newer and better weapons to counteract theirs. This is causing a fast increase in all technology, giving us better stuff until, of course, war happens.
>
> Another thing I don't understand is the nuclear freeze. If we freeze our weaponry and the USSR freezes its weaponry, some other country will build lots of bombs and decimate our countries.
>
> I feel that we have way too many weapons. We could start dismantling warheads at the same time as Russia. We could then only keep enough to deter attacks and sign treaties with many other countries stopping the advance of nuclear technology.

Compared with the letters and essays of fourth-graders quoted earlier, Tom's essay represents a big step toward maturity in the range of topics tackled, the grasp of issues or problems, and in the writer's ability to express himself. But let us contrast it with an essay written by a young woman two years older, Serena.

I basically felt all the emotions depicted in the play [*Changing the Silence*]; however, instead of self-disgust, I felt helplessness. Why should I be angry with myself for my government's actions? I do believe they're very irresponsible in handling our futures, that they will never cast away their masks, so I find myself thinking that things are virtually hopeless.

I strongly disagreed with one boy's "script." He said that what's the use of loving, of working, of trying hard for something when the next day it will be all gone. Well, it was no different before the threat of nuclear war became a big issue. Even when we weren't faced with nuclear war, we still didn't know when we were going to die. It's a cop-out to use nuclear war as an excuse not to *try* to live a full, productive life. We didn't use to know when we were going to die, but now nuclear war makes it seem much worse because we know the deaths are guaranteed to be ugly and grotesque. Our *knowledge* of the effects of nuclear war on human beings and our *envisionment* of the ugliness *promote* the fear, not the "unknowingness" of when our deaths will come. We never really have known when our lives will end, and that's normal, but ugly deaths scare us even more.

It is hard to imagine Tom using words like "helplessness," "envisionment," or "unknowingness" (he doesn't use the word "proliferation," for instance, although he is clearly concerned about the problem), and it is difficult to imagine him mounting an argument of the sophistication of Serena's. In contrast with her, Tom still handles topics very concretely, although his grasp has expanded far beyond a younger child's. He is still some distance from being able to do what his older contemporary can do so skillfully—move easily from the concrete to the abstract, carefully orchestrating an argument based on history ("Even when we weren't faced with nuclear war, we still didn't know when we were going to die") with a psychologically based argument about motivation ("knowledge" and "envisionment," not "unknowingness," determine nuclear fear).

The two passages—and those quoted in the earlier section on younger children—illustrate the enormous steps in cognitive development the majority of adolescents take in the course of a few years—in Piaget's terms, from concrete to early formal to fully formal thought.

A young adolescent like Tom has acquired a considerable knowledge of the world, and this knowledge may in the case of some young people include information about the nature of nuclear weapons, their delivery systems, and the arms race in general. But he may not yet be capable of "schematizing the way he looks at things." He may not yet be able to cushion or distance himself with the kind of thinking that leads to the use of words like "helplessness," "envision- ment," and "unknowingness." In the words of John Mack, young adolescents have "a kind of raw vision" of the danger and conse- quences of nuclear war. Like the younger child they still see "face to face"—but with more information at their disposal.[14]

The emotional vulnerability of younger adolescents may be further exaggerated by another consequence of their still limited cognitive development. The psychologist Joseph Adelson, whom I quoted earlier, has argued that

> the child's adherence to the personal and the tangible makes it difficult for him to adopt a *sociocentric* perspective. Since he cannot easily conceive of "society," or of other abstract collectivities, he does not take into account, when pondering a political action, its function for society as a whole. . . .
>   To put it another way, at the threshold of adolescence the youngster gives few signs of a sense of community. Unable to imag- ine social reality in the abstract, he enters adolescence with only the weakest sense of social institutions, of their structure and func- tions, or of that invisible network of norms and principles which link these institutions to each other.[15]

Adelson gives an example from his research. In order to explore the political understanding of young people in three different countries, he and his associates devised a story about a group of a thousand people venturing to a Pacific island to found a new society. Young adolescents read the story and then replied to questions based on it. One question concerned the 20 percent of the people on the island who were farmers and their fear that new laws might damage their interests. At the beginning of adolescence respondents "could do very little with the question." They might deny the problem, or worry about the farmers, or urge that the farmers take matters into their own hands, but it was not until a little later in adolescence that "the idea of negotiation or communication takes hold," and later still, toward the middle of adolescence, that "youngsters acquire an understanding of the nature of collective institutions and of repre- sentation."

    The young adolescent's still limited sense of social institutions increases his sense of helplessness and therefore his anxiety and pessimism about nuclear war: his still quite concrete way of thinking does not allow him a very developed understanding of the way people can work together to prevent war. Nor does he have a very developed understanding of the way in which the individual leader is, at least in a democratic society, restrained by social institutions and their representatives.

Yet another factor contributes to the potential vulnerability of the young adolescent. As he matures cognitively, a young person becomes capable of examining "the logic and consistency of existing beliefs" in a fashion he was incapable of earlier.[16] By the time he is a young adolescent he can wonder why man suffers if God is indeed good and loving, and conclude that there is no God. Or he can conclude, as he discovers that parents are fallible, that they are not worthy of respect. Such thinking has many implications for his moral and religious outlook and, applied to the political sphere, it makes it much harder to take the position of the fourth-grader who wrote about President Reagan, "I think you're o.k. But you make a lousy President." Her remark implied the ability to maintain at least an uneasy peace between very different ideas: "Presidents are good" and "Bad things for which leaders have responsibility can and may happen." An adolescent, on the other hand, might be tempted to conclude: "If bad things for which leaders have responsibility can and may happen, then one cannot be certain a leader is good," or, more pointedly, "A leader who is not preventing bad things from happening is bad."

The fact that such a conclusion is not likely to be alleviated by a very evolved understanding of the political process may contribute to the pessimism and fears of young adolescents.

THE IMPORTANCE OF THE FUTURE

An issue important to understanding older as well as younger adolescents' concern about nuclear war is the particular significance to them of the future.

The characters in *Changing the Silence* suggest adolescents' urgent relationship to the future when they say:

> I want to grow my hair to my knees.
> I want to have a baby.
> I want to deliver your baby.
> I want to play the saxophone.

I want to climb the Pyramids in Egypt.
I want to build a house in the woods.
I want to be a potter.
I want to sail around the world.
I want to grow up . . .

The developmental changes of adolescence bring the future into the foreground as it is not for a child. With their maturing bodies, their discovery of sexuality, their new self-awareness and their concern with self-definition apart from family, adolescents make their future as adults their agenda in a way that is more explicit and impatient than is true for younger children. But I believe that the fact that younger adolescents feel "further" from that future than older adolescents, and far more untested and unsure in relation to what it promises, aggravates their concern that it will be taken away from them. One young adolescent wrote: "There isn't even a middle to my life yet so how can there be an end? And I want to have lots of babies and become a grandmother and an actor." The wistful bravado of her conclusion suggests how deeply she needed to believe in the future: "And anyways," she concluded, "the Beatles said, 'Nothing's going to change my world.' "

At the same time, adolescents, both older and younger, need the future as people of all ages do to underwrite intention, purpose, and commitment, to give weight to the reality of the present—but they need it more than adults because their goals and commitments —and their sense of who they are—are not supported by habit or achievement to the same degree that is usual for an adult. The promise that there will be time to build a house in the woods has a quite different significance if you have never built one and are not yet ready to do so than if you already have. One adolescent struggled with these issues:

> I'm angry because I feel I won't have a future like most people and
> I ask myself why do I take classes I hate, such as science and math
> when maybe I won't live to use my knowledge from those classes
> in college. I feel helpless. I keep trying to kid myself and forget
> about any possibilities of a nuclear war.

The need for a sense of the future is made especially important in our culture where at least among middle class young people adolescence is an "aging vat" in the interest of an educated work force. In another time and culture adolescents might already be potters, mothers, fathers, or carpenters, but today in our society they must wait if they want to "get ahead," and this makes confidence in the future vital to their sense of purpose.

GOING IN AND OUT OF CONSCIOUSNESS

If an adolescent lets in the nuclear vision in a deep and vivid way he or she is confronted, as Maya was, with death anxiety, a sense of meaninglessness and helplessness, a feeling that life is out of control—and often rage at the possibility of being cheated of a chance at adult life.

Despite natural resistance to feeling such feelings, for a number of adolescents, older as well as younger, intense awareness does break through. It may be triggered by many factors—a personal confrontation with death, as in Maya Gillingham's case, or something that makes the power of the weapons concrete, such as photographs, or a film—for one young man it was a picture of a watch that stopped at the time of Hiroshima that pierced his defenses. Awareness may also be triggered by something someone says—a teacher, friend, or parent—although this is less likely, given the general disinclination to talk about the subject. But for most young people who become aware, awareness is a gradual process in which knowledge from a variety of sources—their own development; the influence of parents or teachers; the emotional impact of a book or film; and a certain inner readiness to let go of resistance—combines.

A high-school sophomore described this process:

> Ever since I have been aware of world matters, I have known about nuclear weapons. I was never really scared of the thought of nuclear war before; I think that is because I never really knew what nuclear war would mean.
>
> Just in the past year I learned what a nuclear reaction was. Then I started becoming more and more aware of how much damage nuclear weapons could do.
>
> After hearing a speech on nuclear weapons in my English class I was really moved. I thought about how much one bombing could do.

Vali Rajah, a young antinuclear activist, echoed these words. "I think I was aware of the issue for a long time, especially because my older sister was interested. I can remember having talks with her about it all the way back to fourth grade. But I was like the rest of the public, I hid behind my little shield. I wanted to know my few facts but I didn't want to know any more. I've just realized this."

When the "little shield" is pierced or dropped, awareness can be intense and painful, as Maya's experience suggested. For a few the subject becomes all absorbing. "I came to the point where I couldn't just not think about it," Maya said.

"I listened to the radio a lot for early warning," another said, and Mike Seely remembered the importance of Conelrad and *Lucky Lager Dance Time* during his teenage years.

Many who become aware feel confused, as if the ordinary framework of reality were all at once called into question. A student who had seen the videotape of *Changing the Silence* wrote:

> During the movie I felt a great deal of things. Complete confusion was the main feeling. Should I feel sorry for myself? Should I worry for the rest of my life about what kind of future I'll have, if any? It seems as if each day I worry about things like crossing the street safely, passing a test or turning this paper assignment in on time. Isn't that what we really worry about, day by day, week by week?

Imagining the threat of nuclear war exists in another dimension, quite different from the ordinary, day-to-day, week-to-week world. Isn't the day-to-day world the real one? If sudden apocalyptic awareness breaks through, it suggests there is another reality and the result is confusion.

Feelings of helplessness and being "out of control" are also associated with a breakthrough of awareness. A high-school student noted in the journal she kept for a course taught by Roberta Snow, an educator who has been in the forefront of the move to teach young people about the nuclear issue:

> Last night I watched *The Day After* on TV and it brought about many questions and confusions. I felt extremely helpless during and after the film for I feel as though I really have no control over my life. Of course, I have control on a day-to-day basis, yet at any time a nuclear bomb could be launched and destroy my home and myself.

Such feelings of helplessness and of being out of control are not tolerable for more than a brief period. Confronted with them a young person must in effect choose activism—Maya's choice—which helps the individual maintain some degree of awareness without being engulfed or paralyzed. Or, after a period of intense awareness, he or she can mend the "little shield" and in one way or another "manage" awareness. (Psychiatrists and psychologists have used various terms—none entirely satisfactory—to describe this "management." "Numbing" is the term Lifton has used and Mack has used "resisting awareness.")

One teenager wrote:

> I probably first thought about nuclear war when I was in about sixth grade. I remember that I used to think about it a lot. I probably stopped thinking about it because it was too depressing.

But for many of those who have experienced an intense period of awareness, it does not disappear entirely. Many describe it as going "in and out" of consciousness: "I don't want to think about a nuclear war because it scares me. I try to put it out of my mind but it comes up over and over again and I can't deny that any second I could die."

For many, awareness becomes a kind of internal secret segregated from daily life. They use the word "inside" to describe where it "sits" in their consciousness: "The film [*Changing the Silence*] did get the message across. It does somehow deal with the inside terror and horror we young people walk around with."

Another teenager wrote:

> Sometimes, I get some of these feelings [feelings similar to those portrayed in *Changing the Silence*] to express my concern. But also at other times it makes me feel better to keep these feelings inside. This may sound weird but I would rather live my life in joy rather than live it in constant fear.

In describing an awareness that is kept "inside," these young people are describing a state of consciousness very like Mike Seely's "life at two levels."

For some, awareness is relegated, as it was for Mike Seely, to the world of dream and nightmare:

> I'm scared, but I know that unbridled, unreasoning fear is destructive. I have had nightmares with the alert coming over the television and hordes of blackened people screaming to the sky.

But the dreams of children do nothing positive. We must join together to change the present situation. We must have both attainable and ideal goals. We must never lose hope.

Setting boundaries on a sense of helplessness and paralysis is an important part of managing awareness. An interchange between a student and her teacher, Roberta Snow, suggests this process. At first awareness overwhelmed the student and she wrote in a journal that she kept for a course on the nuclear issue:

> I can't even finish my homework, the reading I mean. I'm just too tired of war and pain. Why do we have to deal with it? We are only kids. It's so hard to think about.

After reading the entry Snow tried to reassure her in a written comment. Responding, the student wrote:

> I think I should reassure you. I'm really not that depressed as a person. Most of my fear and even pain come out in writing. I read a whole bunch of my work to my father and I think I really scared him. This is good because he saw me or rather a new dimension of me. Not his free-for-all, devil-may-care kid but a person with fear and pain and thoughts about what was going on. Even if I don't know what exactly is going on.

The writer puts boundaries on the inroads the depression and paralysis associated with a feeling of helplessness can make in her life— but she does not repudiate awareness. She makes a contrast between what "comes out in her writing" and herself "as a person," that is a person who keeps intense awareness within bounds so that she can live "as usual." But in describing her feelings after reading what she had written to her father she makes plain the difference awareness has made, and that it is a deep and authentic part of herself.

ACTIVISTS AND SURVIVALISTS

Given the intense awareness of some adolescents and the tendency of a far greater number to resist awareness, how can one assess the impact of concern about the nuclear threat on adolescents, particularly those who are no longer at that early adolescent moment of great vulnerability?

Thinking within the framework of their disciplines, psychiatrists and psychologists have hypothesized that the threat of futurelessness should make it more difficult for young people to be hopeful, to feel in control of their lives, and to develop the capacity to delay gratification and work toward long-term goals. They also propose that the fact that the arms race continues and nuclear weapons still proliferate undermines the trust between the generations—and such trust is closely connected with trust in the future.

So far they have not been able to prove their thesis. There is anecdotal evidence that many adolescents are far more impatient with the idea of delayed gratification than those of a couple of generations ago, and some connect their impatience with the possibility of nuclear war. "It's not that I can't plan," one young woman told me, "but the possibility of nuclear war makes it impossible for me to do something that I don't like doing at the time." Or they may question the commitments they do make in the light of an uncertain future. As a young woman quoted earlier put it, "I ask myself why I take classes I hate, such as science and math, when maybe I won't live to use my knowledge...."

However, it is difficult to believe that research will ever prove that the capacity to pursue long-term goals is limited specifically and exclusively by the threat of nuclear war. It is next to impossible to assign a single cause to the need for short-term gratification demonstrated by some adolescents or to a certain bleakness of emotional tone just below the surface that one can detect in many more. The nuclear issue is "but one of several complex, rapidly changing forces operating in our modern industrial society" which include "the growth of technology itself, the changing patterns of family structure, broad disillusionment with the political system as evidenced by decreasing rates of voter participation, declining American prestige and power in foreign relations, and economic woes." [17]

All of these can be construed as inspiring a sense of pessimism about the future, a tendency to live in the present, and a sense of personal powerlessness.

There is another reason, and a deeper one, why research will not discover that the nuclear threat has limited the ability of young people to pursue long-term goals. This is the overwhelming human need for a sense of being in control and for some sense of "forward motion," especially once adult roles and responsibilities are undertaken or in view.

Recent research supports this interpretation. A team of Canadian researchers surveyed two samples of students between the seventh and thirteenth grades, more than two thousand students ranging broadly in socioeconomic background.[18] The researchers' aim was to discover if young Canadians worried about the threat of nuclear war, and beyond this, "how those who worry a great deal might differ from those who worry very little or not at all." In the first part of the questionnaire were open-ended questions about hopes and worries along the lines of those Escalona had asked twenty years earlier. In the second part students were asked to rank a list of hopes and worries.

To the open-ended "worry" question, 51 percent of the first sample and 55 percent of the second mentioned concern about nuclear war as among their three greatest worries (29 percent in the first sample and 32 percent in the second ranked it first)—but virtually the same percentage (51 percent of the first sample and 41 percent of the second) mentioned future work and employment— an indication that at least some respondents, like Mike Seely, lived life "at two levels" or, put another way, that they had a "double vision" of the world. In the second part of the questionnaire, among the questions asking the students to rank worries, concern about nuclear war ranked second—63 percent—behind fear of parents' death—75 percent.

The third part of the questionnaire asked specific questions about job or career plans, the prospect of employment or unemployment in the future, and the threat of nuclear war. The answers to these questions further confirm the presence of a life "at two levels" or a "double vision" of reality and begin to suggest how this may operate among young people. Respondents were asked how often they had thought about job or career plans or nuclear war in the last month, and how often they had felt anxious or fearful about future work or future war. "Not at all," "at least once," and "almost every day" were the categories offered. Whereas 37 percent thought about job or career plans "almost every day," and 14 percent worried about these issues almost every day, only 10 percent thought about the threat of nuclear war almost daily and only 8 percent worried about it almost daily. (Twenty-three percent claimed never to think about the nuclear issue at all, as opposed to only 2 percent who claimed never to think about their employment or career future.)

But among those who thought or were anxious "at least once" about employment or the nuclear issue, the contrasts are less marked. Whereas 98 percent thought at least once about job or career plans and 70 percent were anxious "at least once," 77 percent thought about the nuclear issue at least once and 63 percent recalled being anxious. The researchers conclude that " . . . high concern with personal job/career plans suggests that thoughts about nuclear war have not led these students to 'foreclose' their own futures." But clearly the nuclear threat is present in the imagination of many of these young people as well.

Awareness of the nuclear issue, as we have seen, is not accompanied by the same feelings or intensity of feeling in every young person. The Canadian investigators' analysis of their data allowed them to discern differences between those who worry a great deal and those who don't at all. They found that "the more often students were fearful and anxious about nuclear war, the more often they thought about personal job/career plans." In other words, the 8 percent who worried about the threat of war almost daily tended at the same time to be intensely concerned with their own future plans. Moreover, the researchers found that "the more frequently students felt fearful and anxious about nuclear war, the more likely they were to feel they had some personal influence."

One might call such young people "activists"—and the Canadian study found that many had indeed taken action against the arms race. "Activists" were a small percentage of the Canadian samples—8 to 10 percent—and they would certainly be a similarly small percentage of any American sample. They are capable of tolerating "the strong negative emotions associated with the threat of nuclear war" while still feeling efficacious—or perhaps it would be more accurate to say that they can tolerate "strong negative emotions" because they feel efficacious. Maya can be thought of as a member of this group. So can another young woman, Hannah Rabin.

In 1981 Hannah was the founder, with her sister Nessa and several friends, of the Children's Campaign for Nuclear Disarmament. She was fifteen at the time and already exceptionally articulate, forceful, discerning, and—with her long blond hair, blue eyes, and high pink-and-white coloring—beautiful.

One summer day in 1983 at her family's home in Vermont, she recalled for me the founding of CCND. We sat at the kitchen table and between us stood jars of jam which Hannah had just finished sealing when I arrived. She had picked the raspberries for the jam. "There weren't enough cultivated," she said, "so I found wild."

Hannah began by telling me what she and her sister and friends had felt when they started CCND. "We were mostly concerned about the kids who are afraid," she said, "and we were really, really angry, just furious that a government could do anything so incredibly horrible and disgusting as have an arms race and endanger kids' lives. We talked a lot together. I remember hanging out and talking about the issue. We were just outraged. We had known about it and we'd been talking about it with our families forever, and our parents were all very active in the antiwar movement in the sixties. In my family we'd sit around this table at dinner and talk politics, talk everything. So much happens around this table.

"I think that we were really aware two years ago. Not that many people were so aware then. It's not so surprising now for a group to start, but two years ago I think people were shocked that we decided to start a group because people just weren't thinking about the issue so much."

Hannah described the purpose of CCND as "sort of a twofold thing: we wanted kids to be able to get rid of some of their fear and anger, to feel they could be doing something, and we wanted to actually do something, make a difference."

They started with "the crazy idea we wanted to have a kids' big peace march, a huge peace march, thousands of kids who would walk one hundred miles to the Pentagon, or walk a hundred miles from anywhere and stage a demonstration. We talked to our parents about it and they all said, "You've got to be kidding! Just kids marching a hundred miles down the highway, it's silly!" So we started to think about ways we could organize large groups of kids without having them leave home, because it really is difficult for kids to travel, and parents don't want their six-year-olds running off about the country."

A letter-writing campaign was the answer to their needs and they announced it with a leaflet which they circulated to "newspapers and magazines, mostly radical newspapers and to peace groups, some of the old-time peace groups, and we asked these groups to include something about CCND in their newsletter or have some leaflets available in their office, or send them out in a mailing, whatever, just to get the word out as much as possible. They did that."

As we have seen, the public was ready to listen to children's nuclear concerns at the time Hannah and her sister and friends started CCND. "We started to get requests for a hundred leaflets from somebody who wanted to do a big mailing," Hannah said. "And we started to get some press coverage. Newspapers called up and said, 'Who are you? What are you doing?' "

In their original leaflet Hannah, Nessa, and their friends had promised young people that they would "read aloud in public" every letter addressed to President Reagan they received and "present them personally" to the president. On October 17, 1981, they made good on the first part of their promise, but were foiled in fulfilling the second.

"The seventeenth, the day of the letter-reading, came around and at eight o'clock in the morning we were at the White House lined up on the sidewalk," Hannah remembered. Reinforced by about thirty young people, the original members of CCND proceeded to read aloud the 2,832 letters they had received by that date. (By the spring when the second letter-reading took place, they had received more than eight thousand in all.)

Meanwhile they had requested a meeting with President Reagan and been refused. "Then we started to call around different offices in the White House. We tried to meet with Bush. We tried to meet with Weinberger. And everybody was either out of town or busy, or whatever, but they didn't want to meet with us." But up to the last minute Hannah persisted, finally contacting a White House staffer who said "he would try to find somebody who would meet with us." Hannah kept calling him once she was in Washington. "He

Barbara Zahm

finally admitted that the White House had no idea what to do with us, everybody was completely baffled about how to handle this, a group of kids reading letters in front of the White House."

She made her last call while the letters were being read. "I made one more call from a pay phone across the street from the White House. The staffer I had been talking to said that Thelma Duggin, Liaison for Youth at the White House, would meet with us. She would come out at one o'clock, which was perfect for us because we had a press conference scheduled for one. So we kept reading letters and at just two minutes before one there were tons of TV cameras and newspapers and radio people; there was a big, big press turnout. At two minutes before one, a messenger came out of the White House and said that nobody would be allowed out because it was White House policy not to allow officials outside when there were cameras present—which is garbage, because they do it all the time."

Hannah had offered the White House a photo opportunity, but it did not match policy. That left CCND to make it their own.

"We were furious, and we said so for the press. 'This is ridiculous,' we said. 'Here we are, we're asking a very simple thing, couldn't one person from the White House come out and meet with us?' We realized that it was probably because they were afraid. They backed out of it at the last minute because they didn't know what to do. We were asking a very simple thing, the right to grow up in a world that is free from the nuclear threat, the right to grow up in any world at all. And when they're building as many bombs as possible, what could they say to us? You know, they knew we were right."

Both of Hannah's parents, Helen and Jules Rabin, have been active in the civil-rights movement, against the war in Vietnam and against nuclear weapons (her father filmed the San Francisco–to–Moscow Peace Walk in 1961). Like many young activists she was raised to be concerned. But she was also raised to feel empowered, and I believe this sense of being empowered made it possible for her to sustain her concern. In later chapters we will look more closely at the sources of empowerment, but here briefly we might detect them first of all in the information her parents gave her. "When we asked them questions," she said, "you know, just about numbers of bombs, about the difference between a nuclear bomb and a conventional bomb, they could tell us. They were able to answer us when we asked about the Soviet Union: why are we in this? What is the Cold War? They believed that it's right for kids to know everything."

Second, Hannah's parents offered her support but a lot of independence as well; this combination, discussed more fully in a later chapter, helped foster her sense of empowerment. Her parents and the parents of the other founders encouraged their children to create CCND as an entirely independent endeavor, but they provided advice and support as needed.

"They supported us. They didn't say, 'You kids are crazy. You shouldn't be talking about that stuff.' But also they didn't push us. CCND was definitely our own idea. If anything, they said, 'Take it easy. Don't go so fast.' "

Moreover, in an explicitly political sense Hannah's parents raised her not only to think about current issues but to be aware of strategies for expressing and influencing opinion. "We knew what to do," Hannah said at one point while describing the founding of CCND. "We were outraged, and we knew that the next step from that was to say something about it, to make ourselves heard, find out what other people were thinking about this. And I think because of our parents' backgrounds, we knew that we should start a group."

Hannah did not always feel optimistic but she did not feel politically helpless. Moreover, in a general way she was sustained by a sense of responsibility as a citizen—and a sense of what the government owed her as a citizen. These convictions emerged when she spoke about her calls to the White House: "I felt that I was making an appointment. I mean, I'm a citizen and I have as much right as anybody to speak with the president. The president is supposed to be listening to me, the president and everybody else in the White House and everybody else in the government. They're our servants, in a sense, and they are serving the country. As a citizen, I have a right to call up the White House and say, 'Hi, I'd like to meet with you because I have a big complaint.' It's not only me, it's about three thousand other kids that I know of. I felt, in a way, like I was representing those three thousand other kids. It wasn't just me calling up and lodging a personal complaint, it was me backed by three thousand kids."

Whereas the Canadian researchers concluded that those, like Hannah, "who were most often fearful and anxious about the threat of nuclear war were also those who felt the least helpless," they also concluded that "those who said they had not felt fearful and anxious also expressed the strongest feelings of helplessness." Yet although this latter group claimed not to be anxious, "25 percent mentioned nuclear war as one of their three greatest worries, and half of these students mentioned it as their first worry." This group can be thought of as "survivalists," although not necessarily with the connotations of preparing for disaster or hoping for divine rescue sometimes associated with the term. This group was far larger than the "activist" group and comprised about a third of the Canadian sample. I believe at least this proportion of American young people would fall into the same category. Not much attention has been devoted to understanding them: activists more easily attract the attention of adult antinuclear activists, the press, and researchers. But the "survivalists" are important to listen to because many factors associated with the nuclear issue—and, more generally, the thrust of much of contemporary life—make their cast of mind increasingly prevalent.

Let us listen to several of these "survivalists" and note the numbing or restriction of their feelings, their sense of helplessness, and their pessimism or resignation in relation to the future.

One girl said: "It's weird, I'm kind of scared of all that nuclear stuff, but I think, If it's going to happen, what can be done? So I just take it as it is. I'm not against any of this [the videotape of *Changing the Silence* and Maya and Jody's workshop], but I can't honestly say I am for it either. I just live one day at a time. I don't worry about too much."

Another girl said: "To me nuclear war is not a problem. That is, I don't really worry about it. I realize there is a threat of nuclear war but I feel there is nothing I can do about it. I think it's important for people to realize the danger of nuclear weapons but not to fear them. The only strong feeling I have concerning nuclear war is that I'd like to die of the first blast instead of radiation."

Some "survivalists" are wary of being forced to feel. One girl wrote: "But even now I do not admit to my own emotions because I am scared and I do not want to have to think about it. It is too much of a hassle. It takes too much energy. So still I remain in the silence like many others. But then there are a few, those few people who are trying to change the silence. But why? Why do they want us to feel? Why do we want to hurt?"

Some are openly hostile to the challenge of feeling. In response to the *Changing the Silence* workshop one teenager wrote:

You people are far too pessimistic. My God it is absolutely
ludicrous for you to think that you yourself can prevent a nuclear
war.

Don't dwell upon the fact that you will all die. Stop thinking
about the extremes and live your fucking lives.

I myself think that there is no conceivable way to stop arms
production here or in the Soviet Union. If we don't violate the
treaty the Soviets will.

Please stop pushing your beliefs on everyone. Next time
you choose to perform in front of a group please make it on a
come on a voluntary basis. Do not take my valuable class time.

I think about nuclear war as little as possible. It seems as if
just as I get it closed out of my mind people like you re-enter it.

I don't want a nuclear war, but if it is going to happen it
will I guess.

The effort to maintain a life unaffected by a threat to the
future is developed even more explicitly by another young man.
After he had seen a videotape of *Changing the Silence,* Ken, a high-
school junior, wrote:

My reaction to the film we saw yesterday was profoundly negative.
In common words, I thought it stinks. The way it was written was
so that it would seem as if people were doing normal things such
as New Years and Thanksgiving and then suddenly stop and start
thinking about the horrors of nuclear war. That's ridiculous. A
person would have to be seriously insecure and in an abject,
constant terror of an impending nuclear war to be thinking about
it and moaning how terrible it would be in the middle of New
Year's for Christ sake. In fact, the main reason I don't like it is
because (a) it is too overdone, and (b) because the feelings
expressed in it are in direct opposition to my own feelings of how
one should deal with the threat of nuclear war. I feel that
wandering around going "Oh, how terribly awful would be nuclear
war and, oh goodness, it could happen tomorrow and wouldn't
that be awfully terrible" is sick. If one spends every day worrying
that the roof might fall on his head and kill him, one is not going to
have very much fun in his house. Of course I agree that the arms
build up is idiotic and that nuclear war would be mutual suicide,
but I really don't feel that I can do very much about it on my own
without the expenditure of a great deal of effort and time (and
even then the results would be questionable as to effectiveness).
Thus I really don't worry about it too much. Sure, I would die in a
nuclear holocaust tomorrow, but the odds are that I could just as

easily be knifed in the street or run over by a truck; do I then live in constant fear? No. I don't worry about it. I'll die someday somehow and when I do I'll be content knowing that I did all that I had time for. I don't worry about it. Worry and fifty cents will buy you a cup of coffee. How can I worry about atomic destruction? If it happens, it happens and everybody will die horribly. If it doesn't it wouldn't have done any good to have sat worrying, would it? And wouldn't you look silly then, too, having spent all of that time of your precious life worrying about death because you haven't lived enough?

Ken is the sane man struggling to maintain sanity in the face of insane circumstances—to preserve the psychological life-space or "house" in which he can live his "precious life." He is determined to "manage" awareness, to live at the level of "ordinary life." He sees "abject, constant terror" as being incompatible with the sane living of "precious life," symbolized by Thanksgiving and New Year's—and he's right, it is not compatible. "Precious life" is his primary agenda—as it should be for an adolescent—and he specifically rejects those feelings associated with a sense of futurelessness that would threaten the quality of that life, "fun in his house." (Thus, implicitly, he recognizes the way in which the present needs the guarantee of the future.)

But nuclear weapons are not compatible in themselves with precious or sane life. Ken more or less acknowledges this fact ("everybody will die horribly"). Thus he tacitly admits a degree of "double vision," but he distances himself from it, not only by means of his matter-of-fact tone, but through his attempt to equate nuclear death with "ordinary death." One can manage life well enough if death is ordinary (that is, presenting no extraordinary assault on the defenses), so the trick is to see nuclear death under the same guise. But he doesn't quite succeed: "How *can* I worry about atomic destruction?" implies that it is beyond the scale of ordinary death. He ends on a fatalistic note: "If it happens, it happens," accompanied by his caution about squandering "precious life" on worry, a word he nevertheless uses seven times in the course of his essay.

Ken's tone—his brittle offhandedness, if not quite cynicism —and his pose as an emotional pragmatist (you don't worry about things you can't affect) suggest a restriction of feeling. This restriction of feeling is akin to the bleakness of emotional tone and the wariness that is noticeable in many contemporary adolescents.

*   *   *

Ken's attitude brings to mind the mentality of the "survival artist" that the historian Christopher Lasch identifies as characteristic of our times. Lasch argues in his recent book *The Minimal Self* that the unprecedented evils of the twentieth century—the Holocaust and other contemporary decimations, and the fact that we can now exterminate ourselves with our own technology—are seeping into consciousness along with the intractable environmental and economic problems of the world and a kind of declining faith in "political remediation" of our ills. As this happens, he argues, we come to feel personally embattled, fatalistic ("if it happens, it happens," Ken wrote), determined to "survive the general wreckage or, more modestly, to hold one's own life together in the face of mounting pressures."[19] The result, Lasch argues, is a "beleaguered" sense of self. It is this beleaguered self that one hears in many young people, perhaps a majority, determined to survive but surviving because of what they keep out of mind and heart. One can see how true this is by rereading the words of the "survivalists" quoted earlier, and Ken's in particular, in the light of Lasch's description of the "survival artist," who

> takes bad news for granted; he is beyond despair. He deflects reports of fresh disaster, warnings of ecological catastrophe, warnings of the probable consequences of the nuclear arms race by refusing to discriminate between events that threaten the future of mankind and events that merely threaten his peace of mind.[20]

The condemnations of *Changing the Silence* I have quoted are brought to mind by the "survival artist's" effort to protect himself from "various kinds and degrees of bad news" by

> dismissing those who bear it as prophets of gloom and doom— misanthropes and killjoys embittered by personal disappointments or an unhappy childhood, left-wing intellectuals embittered by the collapse of their revolutionary expectations, reactionaries unable to adjust to changing times.[21]

That is, dismissing anyone but the man who in the face of an insane situation stays sane by restricting thought and feeling.

I believe that the most serious impact of nuclear awareness on young people is its encouragement of the "survival artist" mentality. This seriousness lies in what the survival artist will *not* feel and therefore not do. Ultimately he runs the risk of not being able to react adequately to danger. His restriction of feeling, although in the good cause of combating helplessness, makes him more privatist and leads him to withdraw from the democratic process. In other words, I believe that the presence of the nuclear vision in young people's consciousness, and the fact that many do not believe they can make themselves heard by those in power, will have greater impact on public life and policy than on private. But it may affect private life as well, although in ways that will always be hard to measure: it is hard to restrict feelings in one area and not in others. What will the survival artist grow up *not* doing on his own behalf or on behalf of those he loves?

As we consider the impact of the nuclear issue from this point of view, we would do well to keep in mind these words of Sibylle Escalona's:

> There is ample evidence to show that personality characteristics developed during childhood are predominantly those best suited to the adaptive requirements of the particular culture and society in which children grow. For one well-known example: children who grow up in chronic urban poverty usually end up as excellent survivors in ghetto life. They have skills and strengths to adapt to that setting which those raised in middle-class environments cannot match. But these same children often do not have the motivation, the perseverance, the style of problem solving and reasoning that are best suited to achieve success in academic learning or in vocational careers in a technological society. The same principle operates across nations and continents.[22]

In this light we can be very sure that we are raising children who meet the "adaptive requirements" of living in a world with nuclear weapons, who are, like Ken, "excellent survivors" in such a world—but who may not have the "motivation, the perseverance, the style of problem solving and reasoning" to live in another world —that is, a world not so dominated by the arms race.

The questions then become these: is this the sort of child we want to raise? Are we protecting our children by raising them this way? Are we insuring that in the long run they will be able to protect themselves?

I believe that the answer to the last two questions is no— although protection is our dearest wish. And I believe that if we were clear about the adaptive requirements of living with nuclear weapons we would not want to raise children who meet these requirements.

ADAPTING TO THE IMAGE OF FUTURELESSNESS

Diminished emotional responses to the nuclear issue such as Ken's can be thought of as an adaptive requirement for living in the nuclear age. This is the approach not only of "survival artists," but in a somewhat different way of "survivalists" in a more specific sense—those religious fundamentalists who believe in the "Rapture," the belief that in the event of a nuclear holocaust supernatural intervention will carry the "saved" to heaven. I feel that their religious beliefs, although of ancient historical lineage, are in large measure a reaction to the image of futurelessness created by nuclear weapons and to the threat of a sense of personal powerlessness that is the result of rapid change and the large scale of modern institutions.

Let us look more closely at this image before considering the ways in which young people adapt to it.

The threat of nuclear war is a message about death that goes beyond ordinary death. This message was there from the very beginning of the nuclear age but it has intensified and ramified beyond anything that could have been imagined when Mike Seely was a boy. The reasons for this intensification are the proliferation of nuclear weapons in the world, their enormously increased power, the development of delivery systems that did not exist forty years ago, and the increased understanding of the threat of nuclear winter.

As described earlier, the vision of the possibility of futurelessness is one that increasing numbers of young people grapple with. Although many, if not most, are ignorant of specific facts about the weapons, their delivery systems, and the risks of conflicts escalating into war, more and more are aware that nuclear war is not like conventional war. This awareness involves a difficult act of the imagination.

A thirteen-year-old, Karen, struggled to portray the problem of thinking about nuclear annihilation in a sketch she drew with colored markers. Three bubbles rise, as in a cartoon, from a carrot-topped head. The first, at the top, is relatively small and contains a conventional mushroom cloud drawn with restraint in black. The second, below it, is filled with fire. The third and largest, to the right, is colored solid black.

Karen was not pleased with her work. "Everything came out

very abstract," she said. "I thought if I wanted people to understand, like in a slide show, I'd have to make it clearer. I wanted to show what it would be like for a person thinking about nuclear war but it's not serious enough." I suggested to her that the very nature of the subject makes it hard to render and think about. But she responded, "Or maybe it's not that hard to think about, but it's hard to describe, even in words."

There were other young people present, members, as Karen was, of a chapter of the Children's Campaign for Nuclear Disarmament. We had all gathered at the home of an adult peace activist who was an adviser to the group. I asked these other young people what words they associated with nuclear war. "Mysterious," "sad," "empty," they replied.

When they were done, Karen herself seemed to find the words she wanted to describe the solid black balloon in her drawing. "It doesn't show you a specific thing," she said, "but it shows you everything. It leaves it up to you. We know what a mushroom cloud looks like, but the blackness shows that it's bigger than that. It has more magnitude."

Her black balloon was the darkness of the void, of annihilation so total that there is no one left to perceive it. It portrayed the end of the "imagined infallibility of the world,"[23] an imagining that is essential to our ability to deny death and therefore live our lives meaningfully. It was a portrayal of futurelessness.

To understand the link between this and the survivalist's belief in the Rapture, one must understand that the vision of futurelessness threatens our ability to believe in God's concern for man. If man can threaten creation, will God save man? Or, pushed a little further, if man can threaten creation, did God ever exist? Very understandably, such a threat to essential meaning is insupportable to many, leading to attempts to counter the erosion of belief with fervent assertions of religious faith, including an assertion of the reality of salvation in its most literal-minded form, that of the "Rapture." Such religious belief provides a rationale for the restriction of fear about the threat of nuclear war.

Many children learn such an approach to the "management" of nuclear awareness from parents who are members of certain fundamentalist churches, and through their own church and Sunday-school participation. But before we listen to these young people, let us attend to others who do not come from a fundamentalist background. Their words demonstrate that even quite young children may intuit the spiritual or philosophical problem posed by nuclear weapons.

Jan Fullenweider, pastor at St. Peter's Lutheran church in New York City, reported to me the following conversation with her Sunday-school class of elementary school–age children.

"I said to them, Let's put away all these books," she said. "I want to ask you what your understanding of nuclear war is. One said there won't be anything left. Another said maybe a monster would evolve. Then I asked them what do you see God doing? One guy piped up and said that God will still be around but we won't."

For this child the image of extinction—the black balloon—seemed to break the link between man and God. Something about the enormity of man's invention jeopardized the idea of God's intervention on man's behalf, as if the child instinctively felt that the balance between man's propensity for evil and God's mercy had tipped too far.

A teenager, Eric, saw the troubled link between man and God in this way:

> My general reaction to nuclear war is to shove the whole idea into the back of my mind and look it up in my subconscious. I sincerely dislike the prospect of having my insides dissolve while I wait.

I begin to philosophize about what I would do with one wish. I believe I would make a barrier—a thought barrier—to humans so that whenever someone came close to developing a weapon as deadly and foolish as nuclear weapons, they would be able to go no further.

I always wonder about God. If there really is a God, which I'm not sure there is, would he let this happen to civilization? Would he let us destroy his earth? Or is this his way of saying, "You blew it!" Maybe he thinks this is the best way. Is Reagan a sign? Is Watt a demon sent to destroy us?

In a world from which God may have withdrawn, Eric suggests, man must rely on himself for his salvation; unable to count on grace or the possibility of redemption, he must try to find within himself a "thought barrier" against his capacity for evil.

Then again, Eric goes on, leaning toward a millennial vision, God may exist, but as a result of human evil he may have decided to punish rather than save.

Karen's black balloon and Eric's words suggest an important consequence of the presence of the threat of nuclear war in young people's consciousness: it threatens to conjure up the individual's deepest fantasies of destruction. Speaking of these fantasies, Sibylle Escalona has written:

Psychologically speaking, one feature of the nuclear danger, which spreads throughout the social fabric in subtle ways, is especially important. Children respond with sensitivity to anything that is surrounded by a feeling of the uncanny and mysterious, a feeling such as that attached to our thoughts of nuclear disaster.... The thought that virtually all people in a huge area might suddenly die and sicken, and that survivors would have no life supports, leaves us with the prospect of something like a black hole or a vacuum. The fact, well understood by many children, that plants, water, and all organic life can at the same time be destroyed, touches upon deep and primitive fantasies of world destruction. Psychiatrists as well as poets know that such fantasies lie dormant in all human beings. It is as though a bizarre and for the most part unconscious fantasy that had been safe enough, because understood to be totally impossible, had become a fact, turning our perceptions and expectations inside out. This connection between the thought of nuclear war and a primitive inner dread lends an air of the uncanny and almost supernatural to much that is said about the topic.[24]

In the light of Escalona's thinking, Karen's black balloon, her friends' use of the word "mysterious," and the Sunday-school pupil's suggestion that a monster might evolve in the wake of nuclear annihilation take on new meaning. In "leaving it up to you" the black balloon gives you dark permission to approach mysterious or uncanny feelings that usually are not conscious—a sort of monster within. Escalona commented to me on this turning of the inside out, "In mythology the idea of the end of the world has always been there and in each human being some vague, deeply rooted idea of the end of the world has been present. Those who are not fundamentalists can live with it precisely because it is a fancy. Now all of a sudden what was a fancy is part of outer reality. One result is that inner reality is made to feel like prophecy."

Escalona's words illuminate what Eric had to say. He did not want the "inner to become outer"; he preferred to keep the nuclear threat in the "back of his mind," relatively safe on the far side of a "thought barrier" in his subconscious. But the difficulty of keeping the inner from becoming outer is suggested by his rhetorical question, "Is Reagan a sign?"

If the inner threatens to become outer without the brake and solace of religious belief, it threatens to bring to the surface primitive feelings of chaos and abandonment, feelings that psychoanalytically oriented thinkers would associate with the most anxiety-laden infantile terrors.[25] A hint of these terrors is suggested by Maya's dream in which she was enveloped in darkness but "wasn't able to scream"—an infant's only form of protest. Such feelings were also suggested by the climax of *Changing the Silence,* in which the actors tear off their masks, fall to the floor, and writhe there, suggesting in their bodily movements that letting in the vision of nuclear death means letting in the most regressive emotions—emotions that are normally kept unconscious.

When developments in the "big world" make inner reality begin to feel like prophecy, a fundamentalist religious stance is very appealing, almost a necessity: the worst may happen but you, the individual believer, will be saved.

Thus a young member of a fundamentalist church wrote:

The first time I thought about nuclear war probably occurred when I found out about the bombing of Hiroshima. It made me wonder what happened to those people. But I know that we aren't going to blow up this planet, because God didn't plan it that way (read your Bible). I am not afraid of this so-called "threat" on the earth. God is in control and I've no reason to question.

Another wrote:

> As a Christian I believe I will go to a perfect place after I leave earth. If the planet blows, so what? My only concern is for those who won't go to a better place. The unsaved souls.

However, fundamentalist faith is not always an iron-clad defense against anxiety for young people. One boy wrote:

> Personally, I am a Christian. I don't know what religion you belong to or if you have one. In the New Testament of the Bible in the book of Revelation, it says that in the Rapture, when Jesus Christ comes back to Earth to take the believers of him to Heaven that one man will go and another will stay. If there is a Nuclear Holocaust before he comes back, there won't be two people left for one to go and another to be left behind. I plan to go up in that rapture. It also says that after the rapture there will be great wars and the world will be blown up and God will make a new earth where all the people in Heaven will live for all eternity. Even if I was killed in a Nuclear War I plan to go to live with the Lord for all Eternity and I am not afraid. I do feel that we need to bring more people to the Lord so that if it does happen, we will know where we are going. I don't feel I am ignoring this subject because I know there is a great danger and I also know there are a lot of crazy people in the world. But I also know what I believe in very strongly and anyone can go to the Lord through a religion that has been around for a long time. Still even with the way I believe *I am still scared.*

ADAPTING TO A SENSE OF POWERLESSNESS

Ken, the "survival artist," suggested in his essay an association between diminished feeling and a sense of political powerlessness: "Of course, I think the arms buildup is idiotic but I really don't feel that I can do very much about it on my own without the expenditure of a great deal of effort and time. Thus I really don't worry about it too much."

A similar sense of powerlessness is expressed by one of the

characters in *Changing the Silence:* "My parents tell me, 'Now you're responsible for your life, make it what you want it to be.' But I can't. I'm not in control. People I don't even know, who don't even know me, are controlling my future, planning my death and I'm letting them." Such expressions of powerlessness occur frequently in young people's remarks about the nuclear issue.

This sense of political powerlessness—and its opposite, some degree of confidence in potential political efficacy, such as Hannah Rabin demonstrated—is influenced by many factors in a young person's life. Important among these is his perception of his family's economic and social position and the constraints, leeway, or opportunity it entails. He assesses their situation relative to their political power in the "big world," and this shapes his sense of his own potential empowerment or political efficacy. Thus, with respect to the issue of nuclear weapons, it is more likely that young people from middle- and upper-middle-class families will feel that they can make some effective contribution to stopping the arms race than young people from poorer backgrounds. (Children from a poor background can, however, grow up with a sense that they can be politically effective about causes they care about, if family members of moral energy and conviction guide them and act as models.)

But a young person's perception of the "big world" itself and "big world" issues is another factor influencing his sense of empowerment. Learning about the way in which technology is shaping our lives is an increasingly important aspect of this perception of the "big world," and in many ways it is inseparable from political learning: as a young person learns about technology he learns about those who control it, the opportunities control gives them, and the constraints that exist on those who don't control it.

Learning about technology is not simply a matter of facts and figures gleaned from books or television, although these matter too. This knowledge enters a child's life through his parents' experience: his father or mother loses a job because technology has made that particular job obsolete, or a parent lands a job because of his or her skill with some new aspect of technology. Often the older adolescent begins to assess his own future employment chances in light of his technological skills and his access to such skills through education (access to education itself, of course, may be strongly influenced by his socioeconomic position).

Moreover, the role of technology is communicated to children—boys in particular—through some of their favorite imaginative works: comics and science fiction and the toys and films derived from them. Power and powerlessness are at the core of science-fiction dramas, as well as sharply drawn conflicts between good and evil. Superheroes are continually threatened with situations of total powerlessness in their struggles with their enemies. They triumph because they have the latest technology—or an imaginary equivalent of it—at their disposal, often incorporated into their bodies. Laser beams issue from their eyes, they can "phase" through solid substances as if they were X rays, and they are equipped with robotlike claw hands. But their antagonists are almost equally well equipped; it is the evil of their intentions that most distinguishes them from the "good guy" superheroes.

From what they learn of technology and of those who control it, children gradually become acquainted with the problems and unanswered questions inherent in the role of technology in our lives: does our very advanced technology make the individual more powerful or less? Which individuals does it make more powerful and which less? Finally, can man exercise ethical control over technology? Although educators are beginning to urge that reflecting on these questions be made a part of the high-school curriculum, so far popular imaginative works, principally comics, have for the most part done a better job of presenting these key issues to young people than schools or television.

In a sense the questions associated with technology are age-old. Today's "smart" weapon is yesterday's crossbow, and the issue of power versus powerlessness that control over an era's most powerful technology conjures up has always had great psychological resonance, particularly for boys and men. But the accelerating impact of technology on our lives has given an entirely new urgency to the ancient, still unanswered questions with which it is associated. Nuclear weapons are only the most grotesque example of the problems this acceleration has created for us.

A technological revolution almost as encompassing as the Industrial Revolution was just beginning in the years immediately before Mike Seely was born. It has brought space travel, unparalleled advances in medicine and communications—and enormous advances in our ability to kill each other on a vast scale and with great accuracy; to snoop on each other's lives; to further degrade the environment; and to consume resources. Today's children take advanced technology for granted and find it deeply intriguing and gratifying: a cornucopia of consumer goods and an alluring source of power and fascination. At the same time the arms race, the rapid consumption of resources, and environmental pollution inspire fear and anxiety in them—as indeed they do in adults. Earlier quotations from the American Psychiatric Association Task Force study suggested the extent of young people's conflicted feelings about nuclear power and its ability to provide useful energy as well as dangerous wastes and dangerous weapons. The technologies associated with space travel and communications in space pose a similar conflict. When Mike was a boy, space travel was a science-fiction fantasy just beginning to be a realistic gleam in technology's eye. Today it is a full-fledged reality, and, for the child, a last frontier of adventure—literally and in the imagination. But "star wars" is a possibility too—and not just at the movies. Expressing this dilemma, a child once told me that one of the things wrong with nuclear weapons was that they had "ruined space."

There are two poles to children's reactions to technology. One is an intense fascination and sense of identification; the other is a longing for escape from a world that advanced technology and man's inability to control it has made dangerous. Expressing the latter feeling, a sixth grader wrote:

> When I grow up I would like to live on another planet. Sometime soon this planet will come to an end because of man's greed. I would like to live on another planet because not only would it be more interesting but it would be safer.
>
> When I grow up I think and I hope we will have discovered other livable planets. We are very close to discovering them now.
>
> I'm sure that by then we will have discovered better ways of space travel.
>
> The planet I want to live on will be full of wilderness. It will have a warm, pleasant climate.
>
> It would have taken a long time to settle the planet. The space ships will not be able to carry many passengers.
>
> When the other people in the exploration party and I land on the planet we will have a celebration party.
>
> In the morning we will explore the planet's surface.
>
> About a month later the crew of the spacecraft will leave to take the craft back to earth. We all will wave farewell. On the way to earth the spacecraft will have an accident.
>
> We will wait and wait for it but we will finally give up.
>
> The people on earth will think the mission was unsuccessful and will not bother with the planet.
>
> Meanwhile we will develop a prosperous civilization on the planet.

The author of this composition was identified by her teacher as the member of her class most overtly concerned about the threat of nuclear war; certainly in my observation she was the most outspoken on the subject in class discussions.

Using the conventions of science fiction, she found a way of imagining an escape from anxiety. The "wilderness" of the new planet suggests the dream of escape from a world dominated by technology man has not learned to control. Although escape is not permanent (eventually a "prosperous civilization" is developed), she dreams of a reprieve (it will take a long time to settle the planet) and of a fresh start (the accident of the spacecraft on the way back to earth means that no one from earth can come to "contaminate" the—presumably pure—first exploration party).

Her classmate conjured up another version of escape from anxiety:

> I want to live in an underground city with my family, like my mom, dad, sisters, uncles, aunts and cousins. The city would be small for a city, but it had room for four big houses. There wouldn't be many other underground cities, and the ones that were around, only rich people or governors living in them.

The writer eliminates the problems of the aboveground world (including the problems of poverty) from his underground city. But I suspect that it was a perception of the world as a dangerous place that drove him underground, just as it drove Mike Seely to explore the abandoned mines of Paradise, California.

Another classmate had a similar dream. His words are a good example of the way in which personal and global issues cohabit in a child's consciousness:

> I would want a job at a camera store to sell cameras. And the world to be free to work and to play. And the world don't smoke and don't drink alcohol.
> That we would live under water in golden cities.
> That there's no wars. And my mom and I will get along better.

People have always longed for "golden cities," underground, underwater, or in the sky, offering surcease from the anxieties of this world; but the thrust of technological and social change, the dangers of the arms race, environmental problems, and the individual's sense

of his own powerlessness—which is one result of these changes—
make them a more tempting vision than ever.

In contrast with this escapist point of view—and with the
point of view that totally identifies with technology—are the
thoughts of another sixth-grader who was presented with a "dilemma" as a class assignment in a unit on ecology. According to a
capsule "case study," or "dilemma," the owner of a small factory
manufacturing plastic bags used during blood transfusions has been
ordered to install an expensive filtering process to reduce wastes
presently dumped into a nearby river. The cost of the installation
means that half the workers may be laid off. A request for a government loan is turned down. The student wrote:

> If I was the owner of a small factory making plastic bags and the
> government came to me and said I was polluting I would do
> something. I would try and cut down the prices of my paper bags.
> When I saved the money needed for the filters I would go back to
> my normal price. The reason I would do this is so I would not
> have to lay off workers but still help with life.
>
> Another thing I would try would be not throwing waste
> into the river. I would try to gather up all my waste and make
> more product of my waste. I would try and recycle it.
>
> But I would never give up my grandfather's factory that was
> handed down to me. On the other hand I would *really* try to save
> the environment. Without creeks, animals, plants, and air we could
> not live!!!!!!!!!!!!!!!!!!!!!
>
> So I have come to a conclusion, I will do something about
> my pollution.

The exclamation points suggest the intensity of the writer's
feelings about the natural world and his sense that it is at risk; but he
has a strong sense, too, of technological resources, which he thinks
of as a heritage. His words suggest that he does not feel powerless
and that he has some degree of confidence that he can find a way of
coping with even a very complex situation in accordance with his
values.

This student's pragmatic appraisal is an example of the middle
way, probably most characteristic of American thinking; but his confidence is not shared by all young people—and it is not at all certain
that he will feel as confident when he is older and has more information at his disposal. In general, a sense of confidence in the individual's ability to control his future has not increased along with
technological innovation and its bounties. This has been found to be

particularly true with respect to working- and lower-class young people. Summing up his findings in a study referred to earlier, the psychologist Scott Haas wrote:

> Technology appeared to have a life of its own in the imagination of the working and lower-middle-class adolescents. It is felt that once a new scientific development is implemented, human control of it is necessarily diminished. There is scant belief in any benefits to be gained from technological progress. And yet, many were convinced that technology will soon play an increasingly major role in most people's lives.[26]

Working- and lower-class young people fear that increasing automation and the use of computers mean future unemployment. If they had to answer the question, "Does new technology make us more or less powerful?" they might well reply that although it may make those who control it more powerful, they personally will become less powerful.

Moreover, they are unlikely to have had any direct contact with those in control—the result of the large size and scale of enterprises in which most people work, far increased, in many cases, over the size and scale of enterprises in which their grandparents and great-grandparents worked. This change in scale is linked to a shift in the "balance of power" among the institutions of the society.

The accelerating impact of technology on our lives has occurred at the same time that the institutions to which the individual traditionally had strong ties—neighborhood, church, and family—have declined in power relative to the larger, less personal and bureaucratic institutions of society: government, large corporations, even hospitals. (Needless to say, the defense industry is a prime example of one of these large, complex, and—in its relationship with the government—interlocking institutions.) One result of this shift is that the forces that control an individual's life have tended to become harder to understand, and more "invisible." This is true for adults but even truer for younger children, whose information and analytical capacity are limited. It is hard for a young child to understand the workings of such large-scale institutions accurately—harder, for instance, for an eight-year-old to understand how the MacDonald's corporation operates than it is for him to understand how the corner luncheonette is run.[27] If he hears his teacher or parents talking and asks why "they" don't "just stop" building a certain weapons system, since it seems to be "bad"—or stop medicating the feed of cattle if it is making people ill, or improve the storage of toxic wastes—he may be told—implicitly if not explicitly —about interests and powers that are so complex and interrelated and so nearly invisible to the ordinary person that they seem beyond influence or accountability. With respect to the nuclear issue, this sense of the complexity and invisibility of the forces controlling society, in combination with his still immature sense of social and political institutions and of the possibilities of collective action, adds to the child's feelings of vulnerability and lack of control. It underlies phrases frequently used by teenagers, such as "nuclear war can happen any time," or, as one of the dancers at Maya's Y workshop put it, "I might go poof at any moment."

What the child learns of these large institutions through his parents' encounters with them—chiefly their employment—is often a lesson about complexity, institutional constraints within them, and the inability or unwillingness of those in charge to respond. This lesson may be reinforced by an inadequate portrayal in schools and by the media of the way in which change is accomplished and goals attained in the society; or by a focus on exceptional individuals with whom a young person has difficulty identifying. The overall message can lead him to feel that he is dwarfed in relation to the "big world" and to a sense that once he steps outside the sphere of intimate life there are limits on his effectiveness on his own behalf or on behalf of those he cares for. Those young people who come from lower socioeconomic groups, for whom powerlessness is usually an entrenched expectation, are more likely to believe that this is so; but there are many middle- and upper-middle-class young people who share the same belief. One such was Ken, who was the son of a lawyer prominent in his community. Another was the author of these remarks:

> As much as I am negative about the movie [*Changing the Silence*] the movie was negative about death and our future lives. When I left the room I didn't feel like I was going to go out into the world to get world peace, but I felt like there was no way that I'm going to lose sleep over what my future life is going to be like. When and if the time for war should come I hope that death is quiet for everyone because at this point we can't just sit and *hope* because nobody's listening to anyone's prayers and we've already developed the knowledge to rebuild what we've already created. And the people holding the power to set them off have become so power happy, stubborn and silent that it has been left on their

shoulders to communicate with the other end of it all so that
nobody has to be forced with the fear of misfated death.

The writer is as much of a "survival artist" as Ken, as determined not to "lose sleep" as Ken is not to worry. Her attitude is
clearly shaped by her political perception of the "big world." Implicitly, the "people holding the power" are beyond the reach of popular, democratic action, yet they hold—or carry on their shoulders—
the power of life or "misfated death for us all." Their inaccessibility
and their supreme powers have emotional consequences for ordinary people: hope becomes a foolish emotion, since it presumes
someone who responds. The "sensible" course is the restriction of
emotions—this is the implication of a decision not to "lose sleep"—
and a kind of resignation, which goes as far as imagining a sort of
"easeful death."

The restricted feelings of the "survival artist" are akin to the
behavior known as "learned helplessness."[28] This term was coined
to describe phenomena first discovered in animals; a dog, for instance, that has had no previous experience with an electric shock
will learn to avoid it by jumping over a barrier in a box or enclosure
specially designed for experimental purposes. But dogs "that first
received shocks they could neither avoid nor escape"[29] became passive, and did not learn to avoid shocks even in situations where they
could do so. Analogous experiments with analogous results were
later conducted with humans. For instance, people who had been
subjected to noise they could not control failed to control it in later
experimental situations where they did have the means to do so.
Encounters with large bureaucratic organizations in which one's responses and sense of responsibility seem to count for nothing can
teach a very similar kind of helplessness. Even when individuals may
not have had specific experiences that lead them to feel helpless,
they may conclude from what they know of the society's scale and
complexity that they are indeed helpless, or would be if they tried
to effect anything outside the immediate sphere of their private lives.
Lack of models of collective action accentuates this feeling.

Helplessness is the motive for the restriction of emotion for
another student:

We are the members of a generation in which talk of nuclear
power, weapons and war is commonplace. We are for the most
part casual and blasé about the whole subject. This return to the

sixties type movements of peace and flower power is useless in the 80's. As I see it if "they" don't set off the bombs, wonderful; if they do set off the bombs, we're all dead anyway, so who cares?

The "they" whom this would-be blasé writer puts in quotation marks are the "power-happy, stubborn and silent" people of the earlier quotation.

Another high-school student also rejected activism, but with a less cynical tone:

About a month or two ago I became very concerned with the issue of nuclear war. I thought about it almost constantly but I felt helpless. I became very scared and I didn't like the way I felt. But what can I do? What can anyone do? Petitions, rallies, demonstrations, they don't work. They haven't yet. I don't think they will.

In contrast with the student quoted previously, this writer admits to intense emotion, but the fact that she uses the past tense to describe her fears suggests that helplessness has led her to "manage" her awareness.

Yet another emphasized the insignificance of the individual's feelings in relation to the invisible "them" who control policy:

It doesn't really matter what I feel if they want to have one [a nuclear war] they will no matter what I feel. I don't want to have one but I can't stop it. No one can.

One sophisticated eleven-year-old with a strong interest in antinuclear activism had a somewhat different interpretation, which he portrayed in two drawings. In one, a human figure tried to keep the world and nuclear weapons apart, suggesting his commitment to activism. (Whether the picture suggests a sense of empowerment I am less sure: there is something powerless about the way the figure floats in space.) In another, cartoonlike picture, President Reagan, against the backdrop of the seal of office, force-feeds a baby an MX bottle. Taken together, the pictures seem to say that political action by individuals is possible, but they act against great and dwarfing odds.

The young person's perception of the scale of modern society adds to the sense of being just one among millions or billions—a

mere "face in the crowd," to borrow the phrase of a girl quoted earlier. This feeling is a repeated theme in adolescents' writing about the nuclear issue:

> Although nuclear war does seem imminent yet I don't see what I can do about it. I am merely one person among billions. People say I can make a difference, but just how I haven't figured out.

Or:

> Being one person amongst millions of others it really won't do much good for me to go out and voice my opinion because no one really seems to listen.

Another, who had seen the videotape of *Changing the Silence* and referred to Maya's imagery of masks, phrased his sense of being dwarfed a little differently and very astutely:

> I often see a mask of apathy on the face of a friend and sometimes feel that I am wearing one. I feel that if a person does not speak out for himself, he should speak out for others. Unfortunately, the mask is strengthened and solidified by an individual's feeling of belittlement, of being so infinitesimal as to not matter. If only people would communicate in small groups, these could affect larger groups, and we could act more as one than as four billion.

Television, which can be viewed as an institution that is very much a part of the "shift in the balance of powers" in our lives, can contribute to a sense of powerlessness among both young people and adults.

The average preschooler watches television for nearly four hours a day, nearly a third of his waking hours. The average child aged between six and eleven years old watches more than three hours.[30] But the mere toting up of hours does not suggest the significance of television in children's lives. This significance can be suggested in terms of what watching television keeps a child from doing: in many cases activities that might encourage a sense of competence and mastery that is the very opposite of a sense of powerlessness. With respect to the content of television, as opposed to the passivity that watching encourages, its significance can be seen first in terms of information and then in terms of imagination—although the two are, in fact, not separable, either on the screen or in the child's consciousness.

In a study of the effects of war on children conducted during World War II, the children questioned affirmed that their parents were their chief and primary source of learning about the war.[31] In contrast, a 1971 study of children's knowledge of and attitudes toward the Vietnam war found that 43 percent of the sample of children aged between seven and fifteen rated television as their biggest source of information about the war. "Parents," concluded Howard Tolley, the author of the latter study, "exercise considerably less influence than do the media about what children *know* about the Vietnam conflict."[32] Sometime between these two studies a profound shift in sources of information took place in children's lives. In general, children today are more likely to garner *information* (as contrasted with attitudes) from the media—chiefly television—than from their parents or teachers.

For all its unquestionable flaws and failings, television provides young people with more and better information than all but the best informed and dedicated of parents and teachers could offer; it is essential to educating young people for life in the contemporary world. But television is often inclined to present information about the world in a sensationalized, oversimplified, and at the same time impersonal fashion. The lurid and the gory make the best news (and always have), but the commentator cannot respond to individual questions or anxieties. He cannot tell if the viewer has not understood, nor will he ever know of the viewer's nightmares. This leaves a need for response, interpretation, and sometimes reassurance which in most families is largely unmet. Families, it has been pointed out by many students of political socialization, for the most part do not transmit their opinions and feelings about specific political issues very clearly, if at all. (Indeed, they may not have clear opinions, and may feel uninformed or presumptuous pronouncing on issues far beyond the ken of their daily experience.) The lack of parental cues and clues about political issues leaves what have been called "empty psychological spaces"—into which nonfamily influences, preeminently through television, flow. Most of the time it would be wrong to think of these "spaces" or what fills them as either good or bad (although parents may be surprised to find that as their children grow up they may have different political opinions and different political priorities from their own). But when the information and images that fill these "spaces" provoke fear, there is a real risk that this fear will be exacerbated by the lack of interpretation or response. It is absurd to imagine that already overburdened parents can find the time or energy to become news analysts; but I believe that they should be aware that the flood of information and images with which children are confronted creates a need for interpretation and guidance that is greater than in earlier generations.

We cannot be sure of the effect of the shift in sources of information brought about by television, or of the effect of the usually insufficient interpretation of the world by adults on the child's concern about nuclear war and other world issues, but it seems reasonable that these two factors collaborate to intensify anxiety and at the same time drive it underground.

Television is far more than a purveyor of information, however. It is

> the first mass-produced and organically composed symbolic environment into which all children are born and in which they will live from the cradle to the grave. No other medium or institution since preindustrial religion has had a comparable influence on what people of a tribe, community, or nation have learned, thought or done in common.[33]

Television has much in common with myth and ritual, and as "today's central agency of the common culture" it generally maintains and reinforces the culture. George Gerbner, co-author of the passage just quoted, has argued that violence, which is such a key part of the "symbolic environment" of television, is critical to its role in maintaining the culture. From one point of view, television violence is a "cheap industrial ingredient" efficiently delivering the viewer to the advertiser, but from another point of view:

> Violence plays an important role in communicating the social order. It provides a calculus of life chances in conflict and shows the rules by which the game is played. It demonstrates the relative distributions of power and the fear of power. The few incidents of real-life violence it incites may only serve to reinforce that fear. The scenario needs both violents and victims; both roles are there to be learned by viewers.[34]

Thus Gerbner suggests that the effect of television violence is not only the encouragement of aggressive attitudes and tendencies

—proved by 90 percent of the flood of research in the last twenty-five years—but the "tranquilization of the vast majority." Fear is scarcely matched as an instrument of social control, and fear of violence, in world that television by its nature portrays as more dangerous than it really is, encourages dependency on and acquiescence to the established order—feelings that have a certain kinship with "learned helplessness."

It's a far cry from the storylines of prime-time television that are the chief focus of Gerbner's concern to young people's perceptions of the threat of nuclear war. However, it is likely that what the child learns about power versus powerlessness while he is being entertained colors his political imagination as well as what he learns from the news. Thus the "mean world" that a child sees on television, with close to ten thousand television murders by the time he graduates from high school, together with the generally sensationalist portrayal of the news, may mold his eventual understanding of international relations along these lines: "It's a dangerous world and we need all the protection we can get"; and "I feel pretty helpless, so I'd better not question people who seem to know best."

The desire for "all the protection you can get" can foster the decision to take matters into one's own hands in troubled times, even if doing so involves violence and the sanctioning of violence. It is also an important psychological basis for the fundamentalist belief in "the Rapture" and, it goes without saying, a basis for the continued escalation of the arms race and for popular support of attempts at pseudoinvulnerability like the Strategic Defense Initiative. That children are not immune to such thinking is suggested by a nine-year-old's advice to President Reagan:

> *Dear Mr. President Ronald Reagan,*
>   *I really think that you are stupid if you are thinking of a peace conference or thinking of throwing nuclear arms away. I think that you should send a laser satellite over Russia.*

A PACT OF SILENCE

DARA

Over the phone, Dara Peterson told me that we would have a better chance of talking if she got out of the house, away from her energetic boys, Sean and Adam, aged seven and three. By five-thirty her husband, Steve, would be home and would take care of them. We agreed to meet in a bar–restaurant on one of Paradise, California's two main streets. But when we did meet, happy hour was under way with a vengeance and it was very hard to talk.

"I've never been here at this hour," Dara said. "If I had I would have suggested someplace else."

Looking at her across the table, I was convinced not only that the setting was a disaster, but that I was wrong in talking to her. She seemed the traditional dream of the perfect, pretty wife and mother insulated from the cares of the world by a protective husband; she would not have thought about nuclear war.

But it was too late—I could not pretend that we had made a date to talk about some other subject. I asked her what she thought her boys knew about nuclear weapons. Her answer was not what I expected—except that I had no clear expectation beyond the innocence I imagined her to have.

"The thing I don't approve of—" she said, then paused and began again. "There's this commercial break with an explosion, then the screen goes black. I thought, Is that for kids or is that for adults? I thought of little kids seeing that. I'm sure it's more scary than they would let you know."

Television, in the form of a public-service ad, had brought the "big world" into the "little world" of Dara's home—and, she imagined, into her children's consciousness.

In fact, Dara did not know what her older son, Sean, knew or thought about nuclear war. So far the subject had never come up between them. Unlike many parents, however, she did not say that it was improbable he knew or felt something about them. "It may not dawn on you that your kid is interested in things," she said, "until he comes home and talks about it."

Dara felt that she herself was held back from talking with Sean not only by his youth but by a feeling of helplessness. She saw helplessness in spiritual rather than political terms. "I think," she said, "I really should sit down with Sean and explain my feelings about what's going on in the world, but I don't know how to do it. If you're religious you have your rationale, and if you're not you have a completely different rationale. I think if we were to sit down we'd have to say that this is what may happen, without any sugar-coating. It's easier really if you're religious, because you have a little out."

We talked for a few minutes about the fundamentalist notion of "the Rapture"—the "little out" Dara had in mind. Then I asked her if the school Sean attended or the parents' association in which she was active had considered sponsoring a program to help parents understand what their children might be feeling about the nuclear issue.

"We've talked about a program about talking to kids, but where do you begin and where do you end?" she replied. "How do you give them hope for something that may not even be?"

Then we both backed off from the somber intensity of what she had just said and talked about the community of Paradise. "People here like things to go nice and calm," she said, adding, with reference to the large retired population of the town, "This is a place people come to die." She was bitter about the prejudice of the retired against young families: "You get these stigmas from people who have retired—this is their dream." She added that she and her husband, dissatisfied with Paradise as a place to raise their children, were hoping to move to a more remote place, "where there's hunting and fishing without driving to it the way we have to do now."

The noise in the bar had increased, and our conversation, perhaps in reaction to it, or perhaps in a continuing attempt to cool down our discussion, remained on safe topics. We talked about a forthcoming school book fair. What is a better reassurance of everyday reality than a book fair? Then we talked about the way parenthood changes a person. "If you decide to sleep in an hour on Sunday, something that small, you wonder," Dara said. We talked about the pressures on contemporary parents. It was an easy transition to the particular pressures on women. Housing is very expensive in California; even in a smallish town like Paradise more and more women go to work to help meet the mortgage payments. "My husband and I often talk about it," Dara said. "There's pressure to be a good mother and to contribute economically. The pressure is expanding and expanding like a big balloon."

We came back to the problem of presenting the nuclear issue in a school setting. Would Dara agree to her son's participation in a course about the history of the arms race if he were, say, an eighth-, ninth-, or tenth-grader?

"Yes," she said. "Someday there will be a course like that for all the things people don't want to talk about."

A few minutes later she recast the issue of what people don't want to talk about in a very personal light, when I asked her what her own early memories of the nuclear threat were.

"I was staying with my grandmother in Portland," she said. "Chet Huntley and David Brinkley were talking about World War III. I cried and cried. I was afraid I'd never get back to my parents in California. My grandmother asked me what was the matter, but I never told her. I never told anyone."

But this was not Dara's only memory of the threat of nuclear war. "During the Cuban missile crisis—I was eleven—we were on vacation in Sacramento. There was a radio in the car, and my sister and I said, What's going on? But our parents never told us. That was one of the times in my life something could have happened and I wouldn't have known anything."

Silence was the protection Dara's parents offered her, but in keeping silent they furnished her with a model that she followed with her own children. We talked about the parental desire to protect a child—and then about the times when to protect a kid you must make him anxious.

"You could burden them with so many things," Dara said. She paused and then added, "There's a cement truck working in our street. Just today I told Sean he could die and be bloody and never see Mommy and Daddy again if he didn't stay out of the street."

Now it was Dara herself who came back to the nuclear issue. A desire to protect their children is not the only reason people don't talk about it—they just don't know enough. "If you took one hundred adults," she said, "and asked them what would happen if three bombs were dropped in the western states, you'd get fifty different answers."

By now it was getting late. Dara had to get home to her family.

Both of us were weary of the noise in the bar. But I had a last question, one I should have asked earlier. Had she and her husband let Sean watch the film *The Day After*?

They had not, but she added, "I could have let him watch it, it wasn't realistic." Once again she paused, and went on, "How can you be realistic about something like that?"

The waitress brought me the bill. While I paid it, Dara said, "What we're doing is gambling. It's like going to Reno with thirty dollars and you saying I could lose it all, but more than likely I'll double my money. That's what we're doing."

Early in our talk she had used the phrase "what I feel about what's going on in the world." At the time I had felt I should have stopped her, asked her exactly what she felt, but here was at least part of the answer.

We got up and went out into the parking lot, said goodbye, got into our cars, and drove away.

THE DESIRE TO PROTECT

Dara Peterson kept silent with her sons about the nuclear issue, as her parents had kept silent with her. Mike Seely's father kept nearly silent: all that Mike could remember him saying was that some day atomic bombs would be outlawed, "like mustard gas." Silence between the generations has generally been the rule on the subject of nuclear weapons. It has many sources—a sense of helplessness, a feeling of being inadequately informed, the distance of the issue from daily life. But when it is parents who are silent, another motive is at work as well: a desire to protect children, that is, to keep them psychologically strong by sparing them feelings of helplessness, hopelessness, and vulnerability.

In one sense parents have always offered psychological protection to their children, not only through the care they give them but by introducing them to the rites, rituals, and religious beliefs of their culture. But in another sense psychological protection has taken on a special meaning in modern times. As the private, intimate world of the bourgeois family, imagined as "apart" and "safe" from the "big world," became an ideal, shielding children from this "big world" came to be seen as a way of realizing this ideal, and parents —at least middle- and upper-middle-class parents—saw this newly conceived form of psychological protection as part of their role. Such protection was viewed as important to religious and moral training, particularly in the nineteenth century; with the aim of rearing a "pure" and "right-thinking" child, parents aimed to protect their offspring from a knowledge of the corruption, suffering, and dangers of the world beyond the home, including the dangers of war. The advent of nuclear weapons, and the acceleration of the arms race over the last forty years, has meant that the desire to protect children against a vision of futurelessness has been added to this list—even if silence is the only form of protection offered. But, as already noted, during the same forty-year period there has been a remarkably accelerated shift in the "balance of powers" among institutions, including, most importantly, the advent of television. This shift has made the family's ability to offer any form of psychological protection that is conceived of as "filtering out" the big world far less plausible, if it ever was. Dara worried about the public-service ad on television that brought the mushroom cloud into her home; she was only too aware that she could not think of her children as "apart" and "safe" from the big world, much as she might have liked them to be. Her own memories of Huntley and Brinkley and of the Cuban missile crisis indicate that she herself had not been "apart" or "safe" as a child.

LEARNING SECRETS

The silence of parents means that young people tend to learn about the nuclear issue as a kind of secret. They "learn secrecy" at the same time that they "learn nuclear." This, in effect, is what Dara learned when her parents did not reply to her questions at the time of the Cuban missile crisis. Mike Seely learned partial secrecy when his father remarked that some day atomic bombs would be outlawed, but added nothing more. "Nothing more" was an important part of his father's message.

"Learning secrecy" can be thought of in terms of the parental model of silence presented to the child, but the "systems" interpretation of family therapists is an intriguing alternative view. According to this interpretation, silence or secrecy is a response on the part of the child to a need perceived in the parent. A family therapist, Stephen Zeitlin, has argued that young people, intuitively aware of their parents' sense of helplessness about the issue, keep their own nuclear awareness silent and secret out of a desire to protect their parents as well as themselves. Zeitlin, who has interviewed a number of families, notes:

> Our interviews . . . suggest that the large majority of parents feel
> overwhelmed by the nuclear issue, and that many children, al-
> though troubled, are protecting their parents by not bringing up
> their concerns, by saying they are not really bothered, or even by
> reassuring their own worried parents.[1]

Zeitlin's perspective as a family therapist leads him to note
that typically "children respond to their parents' chronic helplessness" by attempting "to maintain the family balance with a variety of
protective maneuvers." Zeitlin's interpretation is supported by the
memory of Hayat Imam, one of the authors of *Watermelons Not War,*
a handbook for parents about the nuclear issue. Imam was an eleven-
year-old in Iraq at the time of the Suez crisis. She recalled to me not
only the silence of adults, but the way in which she felt obliged to
participate in that silence. "It was an incredible crisis between the
U.S. and the U.S.S.R.; for a few hours anything could have happened.
Around me all the adults were frightened; fear oozed out of them, I
could smell it, but they didn't say anything, the risk of war was a
nonsubject. I wanted to protect them from their knowledge; it felt
impolite to bring up such things; you don't bring up deformities. I
didn't feel the permission to bring it up."

Whatever its dynamics, intergenerational silence about the
nuclear issue is confirmed by most research. One study of Californian
children, for instance, found that only a modest percentage of respondents talked "quite a bit" with their parents about the nuclear
issue; 10 percent talked with their mothers and 8.5 percent talked
with their fathers. The large majority "hardly ever" talked about the
issue—74.3 percent in relation to mothers and 72.6 percent in relation to fathers. Yet when these same children were asked "how much
do you think about nuclear war?" 41.6 percent answered "quite a
bit." Asked "How much are you afraid that a nuclear war might
happen?" 55.7 percent answered "quite a lot."[2]

But however much intergenerational silence is the rule, a
secret held within a culture will nevertheless be "broken." If the
secret is part of official policy—and in this case it is—then the
"break" can come more easily in the subculture. In this respect a
comic book series is interesting. Marvel Comics' *X-Men* sells more
than 400,000 copies a month. The X-Men are superheroes who are
mutants as a result of radiation released into the atmosphere through
the aboveground testing of nuclear weapons. In asking the reader to
identify with heroes who are mutants, the story conveys the message
that in some sense he too lives in a world shaped by nuclear weap-

ons. Not only are the X-Men mutants but new mutants, depicted as children or young teenagers with whom the reader can identify even more directly than he can with the heroes, are discovered in the course of various episodes. One can interpret their "mutant" nature as a portrayal of the nuclear vision as part of young people's consciousness. But among the mutants' enemies is the clean-cut, sinister, all-American evangelical minister William Stryker, whose intention is the extermination of every mutant. Stryker's vendetta is portrayed as a warped and agonized reaction to the birth years earlier of his own child, born a monster as a result of radiation damage. The message is that nuclear weapons are not only dangerous in themselves but a dangerous issue between the generations. Stryker's planned extermination is a fictional portrayal of society's battle against nuclear consciousness—a battle in favor of silence, secrecy, and taboo between the generations.

Secrets have a fascination all their own, and the authors of the *X-Men* series capitalize on this. The allure that surrounds the X-Men and the young mutants is not only the allure of power—the power of nuclear weapons—but the allure of the mystery and secrecy connected with the weapons. Power, mystery, and secrecy drew Mike Seely up into the cottonwood tree before dawn; and in a study of the beliefs and feelings of a group of people born between 1940 and 1950—Mike's generation—the historian Michael J. Carey found that mystery and secrecy were themes that characterized their memories of their first perception of nuclear weapons.[3]

Continuing and intensified public attention to the nuclear issue in recent years has not entirely changed the intergenerational silence surrounding it. Whatever the context in which they have learned about the power of the weapons—home, school, church, or television—young people tend to speak of coming to consciousness as an essentially private and solitary experience.

Vivian, who graduated from high school in 1984, said: "It just suddenly got me. Uh-oh, I'm not going to grow up, I'm not going to have kids."

Asked when he first became aware of the nuclear threat, Jared said:

"That would be hard to pinpoint exactly. Around fifth or sixth grade I did a lot of reading about Hiroshima and Nagasaki. I guess I'd heard of the atomic bomb. In the back of a history book there was a picture of a watch that had stopped at the time of the blast. That was when the destructive potential of the weapons struck me, but I didn't begin to connect it with my own life until seventh or eighth grade, when I read *Last Babylon* and *Fail-Safe*. In the end of *Fail-Safe* New York City gets blown up. That was when I discovered that there were systems to deliver the weapons. For quite a while after that I used to get scared every time I heard a plane. At that time I believed planes would be the delivery system. I learned about ICBMs later. I listened to the radio a lot for early warning. I didn't talk to anyone."

Jared's silence is particularly interesting, since, like Maya, he grew up in a family where the nuclear issue was much debated, and was not a forbidden or secret topic. It may have been evidence of an effort to protect himself. For many young people, keeping the nuclear vision a secret is part of a nearly instinctive effort to keep fear at bay, to make the unthinkable less of a possibility by withholding the degree of reality that comes of speaking aloud one's thoughts and having them responded to. Vivian was explicit about feeling this way:

"I couldn't talk to people about it because I was afraid they would say, Yeah, you're right."

Sometimes even explicit encouragement to think of the nuclear issue is scarcely picked up. A woman now in her thirties said:

"I remember being about thirteen or fourteen. I remember the day in my parents' living room with the wall with books and the picture window. It was almost as if it was a rite of passage that my father went to the bookcase and gave me John Hersey's *Hiroshima* with a tone of sobriety that I didn't understand. He said I was old enough to read it. I picked up his tone, but I didn't understand it. I read it and put it back on his desk, and I guess I decided it was a story—I read a lot of fiction at that age. I decided it was not true on any deep level."

Her father took her into the secret, but she found it easier to keep the subject a secret from *herself,* that is, to resist full awareness. Interestingly, however, she remembered no discussion with her father about *Hiroshima*. If he had discussed it with her, could she have so easily seen the book as fiction? Was he keeping a partial secret from her, as Mike Seely's father had from him? Was he teaching silence at the same time that he was "teaching nuclear"?

An almost clandestine quality can characterize the experience of even a committed activist. A teenager very active in the peace movement said:

"Logically, in the last ten or twenty years we could have had a nuclear war, but I can't imagine myself being blown up. I'm quite thick that way, not that imaginative. I don't go home and worry at night." She paused, and then went on:

"But I did have one dream. I was in history class. The teacher was going to detonate a bomb so we'd see what it was like, and we discovered that New York was going to be destroyed. There was one plane that was going to escape, and naturally I was a VIP and had a seat on the plane, so here I was grabbing these women's babies to save them. There was an explosion at the end of the dream and we were wondering if all the oxygen was going to be sucked out of the plane."

She herself was involved in teaching other young people about the nuclear issue through her participation in a New York group of high-school activists, Kids' Outreach. Her dream suggests not only her feelings about nuclear weapons but her sense of the danger of awareness itself, that is, of "teaching oneself" about the issue.

THE SOCIETAL MESSAGE OF SILENCE

The protective urge for silence within the family is reinforced by social factors that foster silence and secrecy about nuclear weapons. The fact that they are an invisible and largely secret presence in the society encourages the individual to keep silent about them. The ordinary person does not see or touch them. Nor does he know when they are being trucked through town. No matter how much they are in the news they do not have the same immediacy, vividness, and concreteness as crime and traffic accidents, nuclear power plants or toxic-waste dumps. (The fact that fallout from aboveground testing could be measured—making the threat tangible—helped arouse the public pressure that led to the Limited Test Ban Treaty, one of the handful of agreements concluded on nuclear weapons with the Soviet Union.)

Other factors encouraging individual secrecy or silence are attitudes that have their root in "assumptions . . . held in conformity with what the society regards as its essential political and economic purposes, values, and ideologies."[4] These assumptions both reflect and reinforce individual impulses toward silence. At the same time, the elite groups that manufacture weapons and make policy welcome, if they do not explicitly encourage, public silence, so that they can proceed relatively unhampered—and often in ways that are markedly at variance with public perception of national policy.[5] Moreover, the complexity and relative "invisibility" of their decision-making add to the remoteness and secrecy of the weapons in relation to the public.

Children cannot understand the social context in which nuclear weapons and the arms race are embedded, but they begin to take in the "signposts" of this context, thus laying a foundation for understanding that will be refined as they develop.

Ellen, a high-school senior in 1983, said, "I wasn't aware of the reality of nuclear bombs' actually going off until eighth grade. But when I was a kid and we lived in Princeton, there was this field, a plain field, but no one could walk on it. There were atomic things underneath it, and trillions of dollars poured in, and people with long, famous names worked there, and it would be the first to go. I was seven years old when I first thought of the field as secret and dangerous."

In the choice of phrases—"plain field," "atomic things," and "people with long, famous names"—the seven-year-old still seems to speak within the sophisticated young woman talking. In these phrases one hears an echo of a child's early learning—in this case about an essentially invisible power: "atomic things" hidden under a "plain field." As a child Ellen had the beginnings of an understanding that this power was associated with the elite of the community where she lived, and that this elite was in turn connected with money and technology. She also began at an early age to associate this power with danger and vulnerability—the "plain field" would be the "first to go."

The fact that Ellen lived near the "plain field" meant that nuclear weapons were less "invisible" to her than they are to most members of the society; but in less explicit and dramatic ways, most children gradually absorb the same societal messages concerning them. These messages are usually well learned by the time a young person reaches junior high.

BRINGING HOME A MESSAGE OF SECRECY

Families in which one parent works with nuclear technology or in a military- or defense-industry setting are particularly adept at absorbing messages of silence. The parent "brings home" silence and secrecy from the workplace, and family loyalty and dependence on him or her as a breadwinner tend to mean that the issue is at least a half-secret within the family. Yet, as we shall see, under the surface of silence there may be considerable variation in viewpoint.

Nuclear submarines have been an important part of Richard Grant's navy career. When I met with him and his wife, Meg, I asked if they ever talked with their two teenage daughters about the nuclear issue. Captain Grant replied, "We don't say much about it and I don't worry about it. Anything I've ever had to do with them has been with tactical weapons, not strategic. A torpedo would still do a lot of damage. Mostly, I've been so busy keeping a nuclear reactor going or training people or working in the shipyard that I haven't had time to philosophize. I get so busy doing what I'm doing that I don't think about the political or ethical ramifications."

He began with an outright denial of concern. He then proceeded to make a distinction between tactical and strategic weapons, associating himself only with the former. But as if he was at heart aware that his distinction was a dubious one (since it took no account of the highly charged and probably escalating circumstances in which any nuclear weapon would be used), he made another point: torpedoes do a lot of damage, too. Thus he attempted to blur the distinction between nuclear and other weapons. Then he became more personal—he was so absorbed in his work that he had no time to "philosophize." But *philosophize* is a subtly pejorative term, and, as Richard Grant used it, a near slur on people (including presumably, members of the antinuclear movement) who sit around thinking and talking about political and ethical issues while other people do the "real work" of society, including the job of defending it.

I asked Meg, his wife, what she felt. She began by saying that their elder daughter had told her that in the case of a nuclear war she did not want to be a survivor. She contrasted this point of view with her husband's: Richard, she said, would include a fallout shelter if they built a house.

"I guess I have more hope," he commented. "I guess I feel you keep struggling through, whatever. I guess I think that even if it's an airburst you try to survive."

Meg's point of view did not entirely match her husband's. "I guess my main hope is that you might as well be optimistic and hope it won't happen," she said, and then went on, with less confidence, "but I guess that's not too realistic." She paused again, then continued, "I think we should do something to protect ourselves instead of just this threat to retaliate. I think the ABM is a good idea. I think if we could do something to protect ourselves we could say we were peace-loving."

I asked the Grants about their early memories of nuclear power and nuclear weapons. Meg said very little: "In grade school we had those drills; I don't remember being particularly frightened."

Richard said, "Initially I thought it was impressive we could develop the bomb. Nuclear power was going to be a source of clean fuel. It was one of the wonders of technology. I still think it's good in submarines." Then he added, "But one thing I've learned, the higher the power, the more complex the technology."

Later I asked if I could meet with the Grants' daughters, Tina and Sue. Their mother said she would ask them but that they were shy "because we've moved so much." Tina, who had said she did not want to be a survivor, refused to talk with me—the only young person in two years of interviewing who did so. I will never know the reasons why she refused, but given the way she felt about the chances of surviving nuclear war, I have wondered if she didn't wish to avoid appearing disloyal to her father in front of a stranger.

Her younger sister, Sue, agreed to talk with me. Slightly built and as shy as her mother had said she would be, Sue sat at the other end of the couch in the family living room. The picture window we faced framed a lovely semitropical garden. No, she had not seen *The Day After.* Yes, she recalled that there had been "a lot of talk about the film" at her school, but she was unable to be more specific. I could not decide which of us was more uncomfortable. We chatted for a few minutes more about other subjects and finally I said that I had really taken too much of her time.

I was baffled. What was I hearing? A genuine lack of interest or curiosity, a genuine lack of concern? The silence of a loyal daughter? The careful "management" of awareness?

After Sue rose from the couch and went back to her room I joined her parents in the kitchen. Meg asked me somewhat suspiciously what the viewpoint of my book would be. I told her as best I could and then found myself talking about the silence that surrounds the issue. I felt irritated with myself as I spoke: put on the spot, I was somehow making things all right for the Grants, not at all what an inquiring journalist should do. But to my surprise my words acted as an open sesame to a great deal that had not been said so far.

"Our problem," said Meg, "is that we have trouble just getting together for a meal. That's when we would talk."

"I often think," said Richard Grant, "that working for the navy must be like being a manager in a large corporation. You're expected to stay until eight, eight-thirty. The problem is maintaining standards."

What did he mean by "maintaining standards"?

He was referring to the careful checking and rechecking of the submarines' nuclear reactors so that they met the navy's stringent safety standards. "We have an impeccable record," he said. "The point is to keep it that way; you've got to do everything you can so that things are perfect, perfect."

He went on to say that he felt it was hard to find enough good people to draw on in the upper ranks of the navy—too many, in his opinion, retired after twenty years, seeing that they were not going to make flag rank. He himself was doing the work of "two-and-a-half" men; he had had five days' leave in a year and had not been home before eight or eight-thirty in longer than he (or his family) could remember. "I get stressed," he said.

Meg reminded him of a recent occasion. "I was trying to get repairs done," he said. "We call the guy in charge of the yard the Darth Vader of the Pacific. I get so frustrated I come home unable to eat or speak. I go to bed and sometimes I'm still angry when I wake up in the morning."

Then he shifted the course of the conversation to his "dream." In four years he too was going to retire. He was going to build his "dream house." It was going to be in Vermont, with "passive solar heating," "the perfect wood stove"—and a fallout shelter. Meg was going to have her chance at last. "I'll stay home," Richard Grant said, "and she can go to school."

Here was a set of messages that, except for the fallout shelter, suggested at the very least ambivalence about the life Richard Grant was leading now; it was a flight from high technology—"the higher the power, the more complex the technology"—and the demands it made—"doing everything so that things are perfect, perfect"—and a search for the American pastoral dream of the simple life. Grant passed no explicit judgment on nuclear weapons any more than he did on nuclear power (beyond saying that he still thought nuclear power was good in submarines), but to the degree that the weapons were powered by the same technology as the submarines, and to the extent that working with this technology had exacted a high price from him and his family, there was an implicit verdict in his "dream."

Sometimes a parent's "dream" is as important a message to his children as the life he lives or his day-to-day official "line" about his life. When I asked Sue what her sister was planning to major in at college, she replied, "Russian." And when I asked her what she herself was interested in she said, "Plants—you know, landscaping."

THE "REALISM OF STRENGTH" AND THE "REALISM OF VULNERABILITY"

To a greater degree than her husband, Meg Grant thought of nuclear weapons in terms of total vulnerability. In contrast, Richard Grant's thinking was shaped by a desire to stay strong at all costs. Strength in this context meant technological strength as well as the ability to "struggle through whatever." Although he did not put it into words, his conception of strength also clearly had connotations of national allegiance and loyalty.

In many families, "learning silence" is inextricably connected with learning a conception of strength very similar to Richard Grant's and this conception is apt to be most clearly associated with the men in the family.

Lenore Stewart greeted me at the door of her house in a town in southern Oregon. I entered and we sat at the dining table at one end of the living room. While we talked family life continued around us. Penny, aged ten and the youngest member of the family, returned from school, wearing a still spotless party dress—it was her birthday. Ted, aged fourteen, came into the living room and made a copy of a cassette, using the family's elaborate stereo equipment.

Lenore told me that Will, her nineteen-year-old, was getting ready for a job interview. When we began a few minutes later to talk about the nuclear issue, she said, "I feel afraid, and in fact I took Penny out of the house when they showed *The Day After.* Will and Ted saw it but I didn't want to see it or know about it. I don't even read the newspapers. My husband came from L.A., but I had a very sheltered life when I was a child. I think that affects me. Even going to college and seeing colored people was a cultural shock for me." She paused a moment and then went on, "I was brought up here in town. My dad owned a store and my mom did volunteer work. It was a small town then; it's too built-up now. It was a real fun way to grow up. There was a bowling alley where the hoods went and a drive-in movie and a skating rink. We had fun."

I asked Lenore if she had any early memories of the atomic bomb.

"I remember movies of the bomb when we would go to the show," she said, "but I don't remember ever being afraid. I just thought it was terrible."

What did she feel about school programs about the nuclear issue?

"I suppose basically I want to see children protected," Lenore said. "I imagine there should be more in the schools about it, but without scaring the kids. I feel the children don't have any idea of what we're getting them into."

Then Lenore changed the subject. Her husband, Robert, was worried, she said, that the country's nuclear plants were becoming obsolete very fast. "He thinks they should be put out of business until we have fusion," she said. "But I don't think they have any idea what to do with the waste. That's what I worry about. When I see people sitting down and blocking power plants I think that's good, we should stop it. But I don't know if I had an opportunity whether I'd do it. I'd be afraid of what people would say. I just think with my heart about it. I don't know enough about it. I don't have enough information. It's funny, you just want everything to be rosy."

"But you joined Educators for Social Responsibility," I said, referring to the teachers' antinuclear organization.

"Like everything else, I went into it to learn. I read the national literature they send, but it tends to frighten me more than it makes me aware."

She paused and then went on, prodded perhaps by the theme of fear. "The house up the road where my mom lives has a kind of half-assed bomb shelter, just a wall in the basement, you know. I wonder if I'd go up there if anything happened. There's no food there." After another pause she said, "I don't know that I'd worry too much about what would happen to me as long as I knew my children could carry on and survive."

Ted finished copying his tape. As he approached the table Lenore told me that at school his class had just completed a unit on the arms race. In reply to a question from his mother he said he had found the content scary but that he had not talked about it to his friends.

His mother asked him, "Do you think the grandmas and grandpas of the world really messed things up for you?"

"They did what they thought they had to do," Ted replied. "You can't call that messing things up."

I asked Ted what he thought of *The Day After,* which had been aired some months earlier. He replied that he thought it was scary but "underexaggerated." Then, as if to introduce the opinion of a more reliable authority, he said, "Dad thought it was accurate."

Now Will, Ted's older brother, joined us at the table. He was on his way to his interview, his teenage energy temporarily restrained in a coat and tie and his hair carefully slicked back. His first remarks echoed his father's thinking about fission-based nuclear power plants.

Then Ted pressed Will about safety factors. The plants were "getting safer," Will said. He wouldn't demonstrate against the plants; he would rely on legislation to ensure safety.

I asked Will what he thought about the arms race and the threat of nuclear war.

"I'd keep going," he said. "I don't think I'd prepare for it in any way. You can get your big bomb shelter, but how long can you stay in it?" He went on to speak about public attitudes toward nuclear weapons. "People are just accepting them," he said. "They know they're not right but they know they're here to stay. Some of them could be cut back, but you see, like in business these days, if you cut back, the quality cuts back."

"I never would have thought of that," Lenore interjected.

Would he consider protesting against the weapons, I asked?

"The way I look at it there's not much I can do except write legislators, but I'm not going to do much about it until it gets much worse." Then he concluded aphoristically, "The right to swing your fist comes at the very tip of my nose."

His mother reached out a hand to him. "You're a real good kid," she said, "You know what you want."

And he was off to his interview.

When Will had left I asked Lenore what her husband thought about the nuclear issue—beyond his opinions of power achieved through fusion rather than fission, should it ever become feasible.

"He's not afraid," she said. "He's more realistic. He's not like me, but I think being afraid is realistic."

Lenore contrasted two "realisms": one might be called the "realism of strength" and the other the "realism of vulnerability." Both attitudes are present in men and women, and boys and girls, but the former is more characteristic of men and boys and the latter of women and girls.

Some months later, when I met Robert Stewart for the first time, I recalled the distinction his wife had made.

On a Sunday evening, Lenore, Robert, and I sat drinking coffee in the Stewart living room. I asked Robert about his first memories of nuclear weapons.

"When I grew up in L.A.," he said, "every time they'd test a bomb there'd be a map in the newspaper with a circle saying this much would be wiped out. They'd interview civil-defense officials, and it was clear we had no defense. Then three weeks would go by and everyone would forget about it." He paused and went on, "I remember when the first Nike interceptors for long-range bombers were tested. You'd see them go up."

What did he remember of civil defense in the schools? "We didn't get under our desk, we'd go into the hall and lean against the wall."

He went on to recall seeing factories still camouflaged against the possibility of Japanese air raids during World War II: "War talk and talk of bombing was something you grew up with; you didn't think about it."

Lenore asked him if he had been scared; if he was scared now.

"If you live with that kind of fear when you're growing up," he replied, "you'd better not worry about it, because you don't have any control over it. Only the man in Washington counts." Thus, very succinctly, he described the "survival artist" strategy that many young people follow. But he went on to suggest that he had thought a great deal about fear in relation to U.S.–U.S.S.R. relations.

"Maybe I'm cynical," he said. "We've been at each other's necks for forty years. You know how many wars we'd have had without nuclear weapons? You want to scare a general, you tell him he'd have to fight the Russians. It's part of his training to figure out his probable casualties. That's exactly what keeps us from each other's throats."

I asked him if he thought we could go on as we had been, relying on a strategy of deterrence and inevitably escalating the arms race.

"That's the danger," he said, "if we go on one-upping each other, we'll be in trouble."

But he didn't believe that one-upmanship would go on exactly as it has, and his opinion suggests the public appeal of the Strategic Defense Initiative. "Defensive systems will improve," he said, adding, "Right now we have too many warheads. Someday nuclear weapons will end up like surplus military supplies, being taken apart."

However, Lenore pressed him again. Wasn't he bothered at the idea of their children and grandchildren living with this threat?

"Nuclear war is going to go on hanging over our heads," he said. "But it may be the strangest thing that ever happened. It's so scary it may never happen as long as it never gets in the hands of a madman. I wouldn't like to see an atom bomb in the hands of someone like Khomeini or Qaddafi. But if a madman got it, how long do you think he'd be in power? The Russians and we would get together and get rid of him. You make the risk high enough and we'll risk our necks.

"It's got to the point where war is unacceptable to the Russians, just as it's unacceptable to us. There's been peace in Europe for forty years. There are standing armies with the best equipment on both sides. But there hasn't been a war because everyone's scared to death."

Robert admitted the reality of risk and vulnerability, although he was more reluctant than his wife to do so. Moreover, he worried less than Lenore about the possibility of nuclear war, in part, perhaps, because the realism of strength and "playing the game" of deterrence according to rules derived from the realism of strength were more convincing to him than they were to her. But it may be, too, that he worried less because, as a man, a feeling of vulnerability was less tolerable to him—or more avoidable—than it was to Lenore.

Robert and Lenore now turned to the subject of nuclear power, and here too the contrast between the "realism of strength" and the "realism of vulnerability" was evident in their attitudes.

Lenore stated her concern about the disposal of nuclear wastes.

The wastes were a problem, Robert agreed, but added that "the people who work on these things believe in advancing things. They're not mad scientists." He noted, "The Germans put nuclear wastes in salt mines. I agree with that. I don't really like the idea of putting it on ships and running it out to sea, but that's the only thing that's politically acceptable to us to do now."

"What happens if the ships leak?" Lenore asked.

"You know how big the ocean is?" Robert asked her. He rose and left the room, returning a moment later with an encyclopedia. He looked up the deepest dive made by man to date—437 feet with scuba equipment, the encyclopedia said. The ships holding nuclear wastes would be sunk far, far below that, he said. Ninety-eight percent of the containers holding nuclear wastes would be concrete, he added, and would last a thousand years.

It seemed for a moment that facts were going to serve him well in keeping anxiety at bay (you mustn't worry if you can't control what you fear), but then he undercut what he was saying by adding that the radioactive wastes would have a half-life of thirty thousand years.

"That's what I mean," said Lenore. "It makes me sick."

"That's why I think the Germans are better, putting wastes in salt mines," Robert said, making a quick recovery. "Because by that time we'll know what to do with it."

He reiterated his belief in technological progress. "I think we'll find a use for the waste. It might take a hundred years before we do. Till then we have to keep them someplace where we can keep an eye on them. It's a new technology; it will take us a while to handle it."

"You're understanding the mechanics," Lenore retorted, "but I'm not caring about that."

"What does nuclear power mean to you?" Robert asked her, somewhat exasperated.

"It creates waste," Lenore replied.

"It eats water," Robert retorted. "It's a big steam generator. A regular generator would create more waste."

He mentioned his hope that fusion reactors would be feasible. "Uranium is a diminishing resource," he said, and summing up his point of view: "The problem is not to stop using nuclear power but how to use it correctly."

"So you admit it's a hazard?" Lenore asked.

"Oh yes, it's a hazard," he said. "Everybody agrees."

Once again, in this discussion of nuclear wastes Robert could admit the reality of risks inherent in advanced technology, but his words on the subject made it even clearer than when he had spoken about nuclear weapons that he wanted to ward off too great a concern with these risks, lest it hinder the pursuit of strength—which in this case he conceived of as technological progress. One might guess that he found very hard to tolerate the feelings of vulnerability associated with the discovery or admission that strength as he conceived it was jeopardized. In order to stave off such feelings, he minimized the risks associated with nuclear wastes and, with respect to nuclear weapons, downplayed the risk of war. His attitude suggests the subtle and not so subtle ways in which the realism of strength is implicated in the perpetuation of silence or near-silence about the nuclear issue.

Lenore's focus was essentially the opposite of Robert's in a way that was even clearer than in the case of the Grants. The maintenance of strength did not have the same resonance for her that it had for Robert; for her the sense of risk was a more pressing or less avoidable issue. She was more explicitly concerned with care and the long-term protection of the generations than her husband. He was also concerned, but their emphasis was different. I did not think to ask them to spell out what protection meant to them, but everything they said implied that to Robert protection meant staying strong, while to Lenore it meant keeping in mind the risks and consequences of the assertion of strength.

Robert and Lenore were engaged in a now worldwide debate about what constitutes real strength and what constitutes unacceptable risk—a debate that involves environmental as well as arms-race issues. In a sense it is an ancient argument that has often pitted men and women against each other (except that women's views were mostly unheard), but it has new urgency today, given the power of our technologies and their impact on our lives. It is a debate, moreover, which led Lenore and Robert to convey differing messages to their children.

I did not talk at any length with Penny, their daughter, but it was clear that their sons, particularly Will, the elder, had absorbed their father's message concerning the realism of strength. This would mean that they would be likely to downplay concern about the risk of war, minimize concern about nuclear wastes, and in general do little to break silence about the nuclear issue. Thus although Ted began by saying that he thought *The Day After* was "underexaggerated," he quickly corrected himself to bring his views into line with his father's "downplaying" attitude: "Dad thought it was accurate."

In line with the "realism of strength," Ted's older brother, Will, used a business analogy to talk about nuclear power plants and weapons. Doing so allowed him to "talk strong," to leave out the emotional dimension, to make nuclear power and nuclear weapons sound manageable, and, by relating them to business, to ally them with an ethically acceptable arena of strength. To be competitive, he asserted, a business requires the latest technology; less specifically, he asserted that some nuclear weapons could be dropped, but "you see, in business these days, if you cut back, the quality cuts back."

He supported his decision not to do anything against the arms race "until it gets much worse" with the remark, "The right to swing your fist comes at the very tip of my nose." The metaphor is that of one-to-one physical threat and combat, but it alludes as well to a principle of equity.[6] Those interests propelling the arms race had a right to pursue their goals as long as they didn't hit his nose. By extension, the Soviet Union could pursue its interests—swing its fist —unless it hit him directly. This principle of equity can be associated with the realism of strength: if you want to be strong, the other guy will want to be strong too, and you will have to work out ground rules for the exercise of your respective strengths—or spheres of influence. In crude form, "the right to swing your fist stops at the tip of my nose" is such a rule.

Lenore's reactions to her son are of interest. When he made his business analogy, speaking of the arms race, she said, "I never thought of that." When he asserted that "the right to swing your fist stops at the tip of my nose," she said, "You're a real good kid. You know what you want." Both of these remarks could be considered acts of acquiescence, or at the very least failures to assert her own point of view. It is probable that in her heart she had not let go of her own convictions, but several factors may have combined to make her support her son: a desire to support him simply because he was her son; a feeling of inadequacy because she herself lacked information and experience; a less clearly articulated sense of her own views; and a tendency to find his show of strength attractive or reassuring despite the fact it was basically at variance with her own outlook. However, by supporting the "downplaying" tendencies he had learned from his father, she, in effect, added to the silence that made her so uneasy.

Acquiescence like Lenore's, if acquiescence is the right word for it, is characteristic of many women; it is often linked to a tendency to retreat from discussions of world issues.

Two forms of realism, each with ethical and political implications in relation to nuclear power and nuclear arms as well as to other issues of the day, were available to the Stewart children— indeed they are in many families. But for Will and Ted, identifying with their mother's point of view—much more overtly colored by fear, much less clearly asserted, less well informed, and not supported by their father—would conjure up feelings of helplessness that would have a strong and unacceptably "feminine" cast. One is tempted to say that of course boys identify with their father, and it is true they do; but in the next chapter we will see through the experience of another family that the assertiveness of a mother and the support of a father can modify this pattern with respect to opinions about the "big world."

GOOD PROTECTORS?

We have seen how the silence of parents about the nuclear issue is at least in part related to a desire to protect their children. The desire to protect is a desire to foster and preserve strength, to see that young people grow up neither helpless nor hopeless. We have also seen that private silence is reinforced by social messages concerning silence and secrecy—messages that are themselves related to a certain conception of strength. Thus private and public visions of strength are inextricably linked in the consciousness of individuals—and in general the rhetoric of politicians does what it can to see that they remain so.

But does silence make children strong?

I believe that the answer is no. Silence at home does not protect a child from the nuclear vision. If he is afraid, it does not relieve his fear. But it does reinforce an inclination he may already have to keep his fears and concerns to himself.

For a young person, silence adds to a conscious or unconscious feeling that adults do not care about the nuclear issue. This feeling may be a misperception,[7] but if you feel you are alone with fear that is potentially overwhelming you must find some way to handle it. We have seen the ways recommended by a variety of young people—"keeping it inside," "locking it up in your subconscious," "not thinking about it very much." In the short term, such approaches allow you, like Ken, to have "fun in your house," and therefore in a circumscribed way to feel strong, but in the longer term they threaten to undermine the ability to recognize danger and act appropriately.

In saying these things I do not imply that parents should feel obliged to stage conversations with their children about the nuclear issue or feel guilty if they do not. Young people's questions do need answering if they come up, but staged, set-piece discussions are almost inevitably awkward. There are other ways of breaking silence that have to do with what one does, far more than with what one says. These may involve becoming informed oneself (and in the process bringing information into the home in print or on the screen), supporting teaching about nuclear and other current issues in the schools and churches, and, for some, taking steps toward political action. There is some evidence, to be cited subsequently, that taking such actions speaks more effectively to a child's concerns than anything merely said.

Few parents can take such steps without the support of others —after all, they, as much as their children, are subject to the social messages of silence and the need to control helplessness and anxiety. But changing public attitudes are making it easier for individuals to find support and speak out.

When silence is broken new questions arise. What is the best way to help children feel less helpless about the nuclear issue? How can parents help? How can schools help? Before we turn to these questions let us first listen to some parents whose intense concern about the issue and intense sense of connection with their children led them to speak out.

THE INSPIRATION OF THE CHILD

PARENTAL CONNECTIONS

Molly Scott, Maya's mother, described her reaction to Maya's breakthrough of feelings, the breakthrough that led to the creation of *Changing the Silence,* in these words: "The freshness of Maya's pain opened me to levels I had not realized before because there was no way I could block it."

Her words hint at the sense of vulnerability that is often part of the experience of parenthood. "It almost seems like your children are your permanent vulnerability," another woman said. "You know your own breaking point but when you have children you can't limit your vulnerability." Love for the child is the prime reason for this feeling, but awareness of the child's dependence and therefore of one's own responsibility is another. Yet another is recognition that the life of the child whom one loves and on whom one has lavished care will be shaped by circumstances over which one has no control.

This parental sense of vulnerability can be so visceral that it is a strong inducement to silence, but it can also overcome defenses against vivid awareness of the dangers of nuclear weapons. For a few this sense of vulnerability is linked with the reawakening of nuclear fears they felt as children. Mary Brett Daniels, a child-development specialist at the Booth Maternity Hospital in Philadelphia, and her colleague, Joan Sand Reivich, found this to be so among the young mothers who participated in a workshop they held called "Parenting in the Nuclear Age." Some of the workshop participants had questioned whether they should become pregnant in the first place because of the threat of nuclear war; others became aware of the threat once they had given birth. But over the weeks and months of their participation in the group many of these women rediscovered long-buried anxieties from their own childhood, anxieties that were first aroused during civil-defense drills in the Fifties and during the Cuban missile crisis. Could their parents really protect them? was the question that underlay their anxieties, a question with new urgency now that they themselves were parents.

For these women, discussion made explicit a link between awareness in the present and awareness in the past—a link that is only hinted at in the experience of other parents.

Ellie Deegan is one of the authors of *Watermelons Not War,* and one of the motives behind her contribution was the desire to equip other parents to respond to their children about the nuclear issue in a way that her own parents were not equipped for. Deegan had been active politically in the Sixties, but much less so throughout much of the Seventies. But with the birth of her daughter in 1976 world events acquired a new resonance for her. Deegan is handicapped, having inherited a congenital skeletal deformity from her father. There was a risk that her baby would inherit the same deformity, but she was born normal—"hard won," as Deegan put it, and doubly precious for being so. It was a moment of victory and sweetness, but before long "the real world came crashing into our small, safe one":

> It happened on a rainy autumn evening. I was sitting in the living room, nursing Deirdre, listening to the soft rain outside, half watching the news, half lost in the reverie of nursing. Tom [Deegan's husband] was in the kitchen fixing supper. Everything was warm, cozy, safe. The real world intruded through the voice of the six o'clock newscaster. I was looking at Deirdre, at her intense little face, feeling her soft, warm mouth on my breast, adjusting the shawl that was slipping off my shoulders, when I heard that the soft autumn rain that was falling so gently, so reassuringly outside the window was no ordinary rain. This rain, in the month of my daughter's birth, in the days of our golden possibility, was dangerous, radioactive, potentially deadly rain that was falling from a huge killer cloud that had made its way to us from halfway around the world: a birthday present from the People's Republic of China. Best to stay inside, the newscaster was saying. Best to drink bottled water. Best to ... best to ...[1]

It was not the first time she had felt such vulnerability. "I was afraid of being bombed as a child," she said, "because when I was in first grade the Korean war was going on. I remember being very frightened, but the few times I did crawl out of bed I was told the president was taking care of that. And I just remember having the sense that I was the only one in my house who really understood that this bomb was different from other bombs and that I might not grow up. But my parents seemed blissfully unconcerned. I don't think they fully understood the difference between an atom bomb and another bomb or the firebombing of Dresden or any of the things that they as a generation had witnessed. I don't think they understood that everything had changed."

She paused and went on, "My parents' unconcern made me even more scared. It made me feel crazy, and when I tried to say something, I was told I was morbid—that was one of my mother's favorite adjectives."

Despite changes in child-rearing patterns women are still more closely connected with young children than men. It is no surprise, therefore, that children inspire more women than men to break silence about the nuclear issue, to see "political action as a part of mothering," as Deegan put it. But a sense of connectedness with children inspires more and more men. One new father, Roger Wilkins, wrote:

> One morning recently, I was at home reading a newspaper argument about the uses to which the MX missile can be put in arms control maneuvering and the proper way to interpret Andrei D. Sakharov's most recent writing on nuclear arms, the Soviet Union and the United States. I was also trying to rock my ten-day old daughter to sleep. As I wondered whether a super weapon based in vulnerable silos could ever be considered useful for any purpose other than a first strike, the thought crossed my mind that it was obscene to read and think about such things while holding a person who is one foot, nine inches long and weighs about seven pounds.
>
> Then I realized that that was the exact circumstance in which I *should* think about nuclear weapons—while the image of my daughter emerging from her mother was still fresh. As an old father, I did not have to imagine the future; she was at hand. Her helplessness put a sharp point on the feeling of responsibility as an adult of this generation that I had developed in a more general way in conversations with my older children. That responsibility was, quite simply, to wrestle with the nuclear problem right now, in my time.[2]

Intimate contact with his child, as much as the fact of becoming a parent, brought Wilkins to a deeper awareness.

Glenn Hawkes, the director of Parents and Teachers for Social Responsibility, an antinuclear group based in Moretown, Vermont, described a similar breakthrough.

I met Hawkes in a Montpelier, Vermont, restaurant. He has fading ginger-colored hair, a ginger mustache, and green-blue eyes.

"I just happen to have my flag in my pocket," Hawkes said after we ordered a lunch of soup and bread. From the back pocket of his pants he took an infant's white knit undershirt, the kind with overlapped sleeves. On the table between us the undershirt looked out of place, an almost flagrant reminder of vulnerability.

"I was always interested in social causes," Hawkes said, "but it wasn't until I was caring for my own child at home that the arms race got home enough so I decided to do something about it. My wife was out at school and I was taking care of Elijah. I was sitting in the rocking chair, rocking him on my shoulder in the afternoon and watching the soaps, and suddenly I was transported—I don't know how to describe it, I don't need to—by the thought of war."

It is easy to guess that Hawkes's sleeping son conveyed a sense of preciousness and vulnerability that was intense, concrete, and inescapable, and that the quiet activity of rocking, which helps one let go of the daily round of thoughts and activities, with their strong defensive aspects, facilitated this awareness.

Sometimes closeness to children can deepen a commitment already made. Alan Rozycki is a pediatrician at the Dartmouth–Hitchcock Medical Center in Hanover, New Hampshire, and an active member of Physicians for Social Responsibility. "I think it's difficult," he told me, "for anybody to say they're a nuclear virgin. But making that subtle transition from knowing to feeling is hard and this is where people take refuge in denial."

Later he told me the story of his own "subtle transition." He had been concerned about the issue in the Sixties, "but then I was dormant until '79. One weekend I was building a stone fence with a friend of mine, Tom Powers—he has been writing about the issue for ten years. Well, he and I were talking about a lot of things, as we are wont to do. I asked him why he thought Americans were obese. I was hoping for a literary answer, and instead he asked me, "What do you think kids think about nuclear war?" I think his question was one factor that led me to do the march from Washington, Vermont, to Moscow, Vermont, with my sons in 1981. It was twenty-six miles and it took two days. When you're in that kind of situation you think a lot. One of my kids got sick. He was vomiting. It was a shambles in the tent. When you're tired, your defenses are down. It was sort of a personal conversion in a sense. I'm a fairly nonemotional person, but this issue is awfully close to the surface for me. I like control and the nuclear situation is completely out of control, and I'm angry at having to feel this way. That's what keeps me active."

Closeness to his sons in a situation where Rozycki was directly caring for them, and time away from his busy routine, parted the membrane between knowing and feeling that for some people is impregnable.

Experiences such as Rozycki's, Hawkes's and Wilkins's may be made easier by the changes in child-rearing that are bringing men into closer contact with young children. However, such experience is threatening to most men because it arouses feelings of vulnerability and, as Rozycki implied, feelings of loss of control. For this reason it may be a type of experience that only a few will ever let themselves feel. But the feelings of even a few may be important in gradually changing attitudes.

Even when a breakthrough of awareness is not associated with close contact with children it may be linked to an individual's sense of himself as a parent.

Tom Schmitz, a Roman Catholic and member of Pax Christi in Syracuse, New York, came to the peace movement slowly. During the Vietnam war, when he was in his early twenties, he first considered becoming a conscientious objector, but conversations with his pastor and his father discouraged him. "My pastor said, 'You can't be a conscientious objector, we have the just war theory,' and when I talked to my father about it, his response was just real clear: if you ever become a conscientious objector, don't ever come home again. It was the ultimate in rejection. I couldn't deal with that."

Despite his misgivings, Tom joined the army, thinking of it as a career. Vietnam was "a God-and-country kind of issue. People went and I went too." But his experience in Vietnam transformed misgivings into convictions: "I was a platoon leader. I had responsibility for a bunch of kids. Their average age was nineteen. They just did what they were told to do. I saw them get blown up, their legs and arms shot off. None of them was politically aware. They had no idea they could do anything about it."

His experience in Vietnam led Tom to leave the army in 1976, sacrificing his financial investment in his military career. He went to law school and became involved in peace issues. (He now earns his living working in a runaways program sponsored by the Salvation Army in Syracuse.)

"For me it's only been very recently that I've been able to appreciate the whole nuclear issue at all," he said early in 1984. "I was unable to differentiate between nuclear war and conventional war. When I thought about war I thought about Vietnam. There was no significant difference between killing one person and killing a million people. But there is a difference. I've come to understand it: you're talking about perhaps the elimination of all life. It's like reversing creation. I've only just come to realize that in the last year or so. For a long time I focused on what had happened during that time in Vietnam—not so much the killing aspect, as the responsibility I had. I think they're sort of tied together."

For a man like Tom, responsibility is an evolving sense. He thinks back painfully to an occasion when he was interrogating a prisoner in Vietnam whom he hit when the man reached toward him. Only later did he realize that the prisoner was pointing at the crucifix he wore and trying to tell him that he too was a Christian.

An evolving spiritual commitment brought Tom to a point where, late in 1983, he was involved in a civil-disobedience action at the Seneca Falls Army Depot, where cruise missiles are sent before their shipment to Europe. He and a group of similarly committed protestors entered the depot and broke bread—seventy-five loaves —with anyone they encountered. He was arrested; a second attempt would bring arraignment and perhaps a jail sentence. The basis of Tom's action was first of all spiritual. "It was less a question of civil disobedience than of divine obedience." But it was connected to his role as a parent as well—Tom and his wife, Cheri, have two children, Melissa and Jeremy. Once he "took in" the real nature of the nuclear threat, "parenthood added a sense of urgency" to his response. "The ultimate responsibility is to provide a safe, nurturing atmosphere for children." It was, in fact, the issue of responsible parenthood in these times that led him directly to his act of civil disobedience.

"I never really considered it until I went to the sentencing of Jerry Berrigan at the federal district court in Syracuse. He was sentenced for an action at the Pentagon. They asked him if he wanted to make a statement, and this was what he said. He said that people say, How can you do it. You have children, you have responsibilities. But he said, I've done it for my children. They need to have a model. They need to know they have a father who has values that are important."

For every Tom Schmitz or Jerry Berrigan there are hundreds of less articulate, less radically activist men and women whose role as parents—or grandparents—has moved them to join the grassroots antinuclear movement. One anonymous grandparent, for example, wrote during a workshop following the showing of the film *The Day After*:

> Today I am beginning to work to see that you will be, that the world will be here for you to enjoy as I have. It is a big job and I hope I have a bit of help from similarly minded people—we have to work together. The problems we face are all man-made, and therefore can be, and must be, solved by mankind; I intend to do my part. What I alone can leave for you will be small, but what we together can leave behind is the world.

Another grandparent participating in the same workshop wrote:

> *Dear Randy,*
>
> *You are thirteen and the world should look like a shining star to you. There should be no black clouds hanging over your dreams of the future and what you might do with your life.*
>
> *So today I pledge myself to use whatever skills or gifts that I might have developed over sixty-five years for the purpose of turning the threat of nuclear war around. Persistence and patience may not seem to go together but skillfully used they are a strong team. We of the older generations can't let you down.*

For parents who are not accustomed to speaking out and who lack a supportive environment, breaking silence can be an act of considerable bravery. This was the case for Patrice Centore, who is the mother of five children and publishes a yearly bridal directory in Syracuse, New York. In the early eighties Centore began writing letters to her local newspaper, the *Syracuse Post-Standard*, about the nuclear issue. At the same time she started a small mother's group for women who wished to discuss their feelings about the issue. It was not the first time she had struggled against the silence surrounding nuclear weapons.

"I wasn't active during the Fifties," she told me. "I was concerned, but there was no one you talked to. My brother enlisted right after World War II. He was with the medics and he sent us pictures of Hiroshima or Nagasaki, I don't know which. I was very upset but there was no one to talk to. I went to a parochial school and the nuns didn't let you forget about the bomb or the communists."

We were sitting by the picture window in the living room of her house in the suburbs of Syracuse. Outside on the lawn her sons and their friends were kicking around a soccer ball. The houses across the street, prim bastions of the American dream, were a backdrop to their play. I asked Centore if she felt that there had been a taboo attached to the subject. She replied, "It was like when my grandfather died. I was very upset about it but I didn't say anything. I thought it would upset my mother."

Here again in Centore's experience was a suggestion that young people protect the adults in their family from problems that evoke troublesome emotions.

In time Centore "kind of managed to get over" her concern. "I said to heck with it," she went on. "I'll get on with my life, and I got married and started to have kids. After the Cuban missile crisis I was under the impression that things would get better, although I always got very upset if people said 'better dead than red.' How could you feel that? I thought. Then I started getting really upset when Reagan was elected and he started spending more money on defense. I listened to *All Things Considered* on public radio, and it just seemed to me things were getting much worse. I wanted to talk to someone, but I didn't talk to anyone. One night we were out with friends, and they were all for what Reagan was doing, and I said, We'll all be annihilated. I was having a sundae and I was in tears before we left the place.

"Then I saw an ad in the *New York Times* about Ground Zero. I wrote them, and Roger Molander gave someone here—Phil Klein —my name, and he called me. It was so funny, I was so afraid. One reason is obvious: my husband's family—is extremely hawkish, some of his family, that is—I didn't want to stir up a tempest."

It was about this time that Centore started her mothers' group with a few friends. Hoping to add to the group, she appealed to other women in a letter to the newspaper. "The response could have been better," Centore said. "I guess I was disappointed. There had to be a lot of women out there. I even had an argument with the editor of the paper. He said there are too many groups already; why was I starting another?"

When I met Centore in 1983 it had been two years since she had organized her group, which had never had more than a few members. Few of the women she invited to meetings ever ended up coming. "I've had people approach me who've seen my letters in the paper and tell me how much they agree, but mostly I'm listened to but I'm not commented to." She added, philosophically, that her efforts had led to some "interesting conversations." "One woman said 'There's so little we can know,'" she recounted. "'I think we have to let the experts decide for us. I just don't think we can trust the Russians.'

"A man in the neighborhood said, 'I don't think we should add any weapons, but I don't think we can deal with the Soviets.' I said to him, It's our only hope, and he said, 'Patty, that's your thing.'"

One of her most interesting conversations was with her parish pastor. Centore found the bishops' pastoral letter a source of tremendous support: "So often I think we've gotten where we are because none of these moral issues were raised by the Church in World War II, but the Church is beginning to come back to the way you always hoped they'd be. If abortion is a moral issue then the killing of innocent people is a moral issue. It's the most moral issue."

But despite the fact that an anonymous parishioner had donated four hundred copies of the pastoral letter to the parish, Centore's pastor had confined his response to it to one sermon saying, in effect, that the bishops who had formulated the pastoral should not be seen as seditious. Centore went to talk with him. She told him she was going to start a mothers' group; his reply was "that the bishops are not in agreement with what those women in Seneca Falls are doing."

"I said I was in agreement with their feelings, although not their methods, and that I would never climb over barbed wire."

Her pastor then revealed his own difficulties in dealing with the nuclear issue. "When I offered to help him start a discussion group, he said he wasn't sure about anything like that because he was afraid of losing parishioners. I think," Centore concluded, "a lot of the clergy have had people threaten them and be real nasty, and that is hard to take." She knew how he felt: "I've had people—well, not exactly call me a commie pinko, but to that effect—and it really hurts."

Centore knew that her husband had mixed feelings about her involvement. "I know he agrees with me basically, but he was worried about my becoming involved, and one night he had to defend me to a family member. I think he's got the typical problem like not wanting to have it [the nuclear issue] there. One night he said, Can't you just forget about it, it's just getting you upset. I said it's not *working* on it that gets me upset, it's *not* working on it. I'd have to have a frontal lobotomy not to get upset. It's our children."

In fact her greatest source of support was her five children. "I don't think they're as indignant as the kids in *In the Nuclear Shadow* [a film showing children discussing their concerns about nuclear weapons that both Centore and I had seen shortly before we met], but it's been going on in this house for three years. I know they're proud of the fact I'm involved, and they're very supportive."

Unlike their father, they did not see concern as something that it was better to "get over" because it was "upsetting." One of her sons, Matt, came into the house while we were talking. Centore asked him to go to the store and gave him a grocery list. While she looked for her wallet I asked him what he felt about his mother's activities. He replied, "The reason my mother is this way is that she's scared, but any reasonable person would be worried."

Despite the subtle and not so subtle rebuffs Centore received, and despite times when she felt defensive, she felt stronger for having spoken out. "I don't know," she said, "but I feel better, I feel gutsier myself since I've written those letters and had the few little discussion meetings. And I've found that even if people won't join the group they're still my friends. Like this one woman I know; she doesn't want to think about the issue but she doesn't cut me off. But now I'm past worrying about it. If people are my friends, they're going to have to accept me the way I am, and I think my husband has got to love me the way I am, and I think he does. Like I say, I wouldn't jump over barbed wire, I wouldn't make a spectacle or embarrass my family, but I think if you do what you believe in people respect you."

LEARNING FROM THE YOUNG

The support that Patrice Centore received from her children hints at an interesting process: parents may be helped to break silence not only by their own parental feelings, their intense sense of connectedness with the next generation, but by encouragement— or a prod—from their own children. Adults—including social scientists studying the political socialization of children—have until recently usually tended to think in terms of a one-way transmission of ideas and information from adult to child. True as this concept is in general, it underestimates the reciprocal nature of influence, the "two-way street" between the generations, which is particularly notable in fast-moving times. In some cases, young people, especially the few who can be called "activists," can be "ahead" of the majority of adults—and sometimes of their own parents—in relation to an issue. They pick up the anxiety surrounding it which is unacknowledged or half-acknowledged by adults, but instead of numbing themselves to its presence they press for solutions. They smell it out and make it "theirs," and it becomes part of their search for self-definition and for ethical ground they can call their own.

Parents often feel confused or guilty when children prod them toward awareness. Norma Vogelstein, the mother of a member of the activist group Kids' Outreach, said:

"Lynne has taught us the nuclear issue in far greater depth, it breaks my heart to say, than the media. It was part of her work for Kids' Outreach to find out the facts.

"Literally, she was saying to us: you have said to me, as all good parents say, there are all these problems in the world, but it's all going to be fine; there have been serious problems in the past and we have overcome them; we're not going to die in a nuclear blast, no one is crazy enough to push that button—and then you disguise your feelings in doing this, you run from your fear.

"She made us come to terms with what we were disguising, with what we were dissembling. To a large extent, I think we came to realize a certain guilt that we had put aside, as if we finally had to confront it and say, Oh God, how did we bring a child into this terribly fraught world; how did we have the temerity to do that. How did we fail that we did not stop to notice potential holocaust within our young lives? You know, we sent our checks to SANE. I guess our greater interest during those years was the civil-rights movement, it had a greater emotional appeal."

Another mother commented about her sixteen-year-old daughter, "Sarah was very keen for us to take a stronger stand. She said it was not enough for us to march in the June 12 rally and give twenty-five dollars a year to Greenpeace. We had a long talk one weekend, and she accused us of being irresponsibile citizens. She pointed out how little the issue rubbed off on our lives." Sarah's father, an architect, said during the "long talk" that he was committed to making life better for others through his profession, and her mother, who worked for an environmental action group, said she was doing the same in her own way. But Sarah insisted that the nuclear issue was one on which everyone had to pull his weight.

It is hard for parents to be challenged by a child, but Sarah's mother said, "It happens a lot with my children. They feel very strongly about certain things that they want us to take a strong stand on. In many cases they're right. I like that. I like to have things pointed out to me. I'd rather have my children do that than probably anybody else. I'm interested in what they care about. I do feel a responsibility to respond to what my children feel strongly about. Sarah's challenge was pretty valid, particularly since we've taught our children that you don't want to be passive about life." She spoke with regret of the environment of her own upbringing: "My mother always used to say that I was famous for the ten-pound look, but my parents never talked about, much less came round, to my point of view."

I would guess that Sarah's mother's desire not to perpetuate the ground rules of her own upbringing facilitated Sarah's challenge —and helped keep her respect. At the same time, her parents' committed stance—although not to the issue that Sarah cared about— provided a model that helped her take a stand to a far greater degree than she may have been aware. Moreover, her parents' assertion of the validity of their own choices, while taking in the importance of what she had to say, may have helped her in her search to define her own ground.

The experience of a third mother, Jessica, is another example of the way in which the younger generation can prod the older with respect to the nuclear issue. Jessica's daughter, Annie, was active in her high school's branch of the student–teacher antinuclear organization STOP. I asked Jessica what she felt about her daughter's activism, but she began her reply by talking about herself:

"I'm a person who's never been particularly interested or active politically. I can't say why, but my parents were not, and I don't have much confidence in my ability to change anything. But I do know that what it feels like with your own children is that you become more interested, because it's going to affect their world. I think the nuclear issue actually affects a lot of parents. So far, all it's done with me is make me feel anxious. I haven't done anything about it. So I feel a little bit guilty but a little bit anxious at the same time. But maybe because of that I applaud Annie's efforts to do something. In a way I may feel that she's doing it for both of us."

In saying that Annie was "doing it for both of us" Jessica implied that Annie was the political or ethical "grownup" of the family. This was not the only area in which Jessica felt this to be true.

"I don't try to be a grownup for Annie very hard," she said, "I guess that's why she's getting pretty good at it."

A single mother who had gone to graduate school while raising her daughter, Jessica felt she had had to lean on Annie—"I've really needed her help." At the same time she felt that her own upbringing had been too protected, and she had made a conscious decision that it would be helpful to Annie in the long run if she were more open with her about subjects such as sex and money, which had been taboo in her own family. "I thought it would give Annie a head start to know about them; that way she wouldn't have to go through that period of finding her sea legs. In some ways it makes more anxieties for the child; in other ways Annie has fewer unknowns than I did." But she was not entirely confident that she had made the right decision in encouraging Annie to be something of a grownup before her time: "Perhaps in a way it's been an evasion of responsibility on my part."

Annie, she felt, had a quite different view of the adult world's ability to provide security and the "answers" than she had had at the same age: "I was a graduate student at Kent State in 1970. So by then I knew what was going on. My apartment was searched and the soldiers pushed my female roommate up against the wall. But when I was in high school, those were the Eisenhower years. I felt that the grownups took care of things. I don't think Annie has much confidence in the grownups."

However, Annie's activism and the complexities of the nuclear issue itself prodded Jessica to be more of a "grownup" with her daughter than she usually was. Jessica was particularly concerned that Annie not take a position in favor of rapid or unilateral disarmament—a position that some young members of STOP advocated. When the film *The Day After* was aired in November 1983, Jessica insisted that Annie watch the panel discussion on *Nightline*, moderated by Ted Koppel, that followed the film:

"She felt she'd seen the movie and the panel would be boring. I listened to a little bit of it, and I thought that it was probably a lot more important than the movie, so I dragged her back in here and said, You'd better listen to this. You're going to get some real opinions instead of just fiction. Afterward I asked her a couple of questions to see if she'd understood what they'd said. We went through it again and I think she understood the two sides a little better. Actually, there wasn't anyone on that panel who was saying we should just totally disarm. She got to where she understood that the focus on the panel was on choosing the best method of gradual reduction, trying to mesh it with what other countries were doing, and making sure that no one crazy decided to do anything extreme. The issue wasn't whether we had nuclear arms or not, that was a foregone fact, but how we handle dealing with them. I think that was a complication she hadn't thought about—I hadn't either. When she went to the next STOP meeting she realized some of those kids hadn't thought through these things either. So I think she's really operating on a pretty small base of information. But from what she says, the other students are operating on an even smaller base."

THE STEP TO ACTIVISM

A breakthrough to awareness or, occasionally, a child's prodding, often leads parents to take some action against the arms race or motivates a renewed commitment to action. In effect, they let go of a model of strength that calls for silence and feel their way toward a new model that involves learning, inquiry, and some degree of action, however modest. Annie's involvement with the nuclear issue made Jessica more assertive politically than she had ever been, even if her "activism" was confined to insisting Annie watch the panel discussion following the showing of *The Day After.* Glenn Hawkes founded Parents and Teachers for Social Responsibility, an organization chiefly devoted to public education about the nuclear issue. Alan Rozycki intensified his commitment to Physicians for Social Responsibility, and he pointed out that only by staying active could he hope to restore the sense of being in control that deeper awareness of the nuclear threat challenged.

Ellie Deegan and her friends, who had all come to a similar kind of awareness at about the same time, began by meeting as a group to work through their feelings about the nuclear issue, using consciousness-raising techniques familiar from women's groups of the Sixties and Seventies. Thus they drew on the women's movement to find a model of strength in relation to the nuclear issue.

"The first step," said Deegan's colleague, Hayat Imam, "was to get together to support each other in being parents, and the next step was to think, Well, maybe there are others who feel like this. We wanted to reach out to others. It was a very feminist experience. We stayed with the process at every step. We shared the feelings, we remembered together, we tested each other. And then we began to feel, yes, there was really something worth exploring here."

In time, still collaborating as a group, the five members of the group wrote *Watermelons Not War.*

Some of those who become active as a result of feelings about their children have a more or less articulate sense that the nuclear issue has changed and is changing parenthood. They believe that it challenges individuals to add a new dimension of political under-standing and action to the parental role. Paradoxical as it sounds at first, the global nature of the nuclear threat makes them feel called upon as individuals to respond in terms of one of the most intimate aspects of their lives.

In one sense parenthood has always encouraged a changed relationship with the world in the direction of a wider sense of responsibility. "I know that my feelings about myself and the world began to change once I began to extend my life beyond myself and my own life," Hayat Imam said. But our ability to annihilate ourselves challenges parents to expand responsibility further. Imam contin-ued, "Very close to a certain time period we all began to feel a certain way. I was beginning to feel that as a parent this issue is different for you. I think that we all feel that being a parent today is uncharted territory. It's different from any other period of time for parents. It's no longer sufficient to comfort and feed your child nu-tritious foods with this thing hanging over us, and there aren't very many guidelines for us as parents."

The "certain way" that Imam spoke of has to do with the fact that when generational continuity is threatened, parents are chal-lenged to become politically active—as parents. This was the chal-lenge that Hawkes, Centore, and Rozycki all met in different ways. In a more modest but nevertheless real way Jessica took a step toward meeting it when she insisted that Annie watch the *Nightline* panel discussion following *The Day After.*

When parents in some way break silence, they in effect take a position about the importance of examining conceptions of strength and vulnerability. Their spouse may not always be in agreement. As we saw in the Stewart family, men and women often have very different perspectives on the subject.

In an earlier chapter we met Jared, who was impressed by the photograph of a watch that had been stopped by the blast at Hiroshima. We noted that he did not tell his family for a long time how strong his anxieties about nuclear weapons were, despite their concern with the issue. Jared's mother, Alice, is studying for a doctorate in psychology; his father, Brian, is a child psychiatrist.

One evening I met with Alice in the "room of her own" she had made her study in their Cambridge, Massachusetts, house. We talked about a paper she was writing—the topic was patterns of women's friendships with other women. Finally, she told me about a still active food-buying cooperative she had organized in the Sixties. Then we turned to the subjects that had brought me to see her, and at that moment Brian joined us.

"Since I was a teenager I've been horrified and frightened by the possibility of nuclear war," Alice said. "I've had dreams of being a refugee, of surviving but being a refugee. I've been emotionally, murkily distressed, but I didn't feel I myself had any way to do anything about it except perhaps talk to the children. Talking to them was a conduit to activity."

"My wife and kids were several paces ahead of me," Brian said.

I asked him what his early perceptions of the nuclear issue had been.

"A mixture of being impressed and worried and frightened, but I turned to the peaceful uses of nuclear energy and I was stirred like a young man by a marching band. Nuclear power was cheap; it was the same thrill as hydro power. The third world could have electricity, places like Afghanistan, Pakistan. I didn't think very much about it but I was worried about the arms race."

Alice interrupted, "Once I started to know something about nuclear power I was concerned about nuclear waste and birth defects."

"I think there's a basic sex difference," Brian said. "I see that the male side of myself was taken in by the marching-band side, the use of power. I didn't think about the relationship side of the issue."

"But you didn't jeer," Alice said. "You never said nuclear power was the only answer."

"As a small boy," Brian said, "I was impressed by the massive solidity of buildings. My thought now is that there is nothing that can't be wiped out. There's no Blue Mosque for Yeats to write 'Byzantium' about. My whole life's work could be wiped out in fifteen seconds."

His words prompted Alice to mention an occasion when one of Jared's two brothers had made a metal bowl at school. When he had brought it home she had praised it and he had asked her if it would last through a nuclear war.

"It's an absolute given in our children's generation that anything they do may just evaporate," she said. "I admire them so much for getting up in the morning and going on, because I believe it's part of their consciousness."

I asked Brian and Alice about their relationship with Jared in relation to the nuclear issue.

"When Three Mile Island happened we were on vacation," Alice said. "We did turn to Jared as a resource. He knew what a meltdown was. He's an authority."

"He was obviously calling it right. He had the knowledge," Brian added.

I asked them whether they thought that they had reversed roles with Jared around this issue—a theme we shall return to.

"I suppose it really was passing on the responsibility to him by talking to him about Three Mile Island," Brian said. He paused, then added, "I had an interesting feeling about Jared. I was busy with other things. I used to say, I can't go on this march and risk being arrested. I can't risk not being able to work. I have responsibilities to the family and to my patients. Jared sort of carried the flag for the family. Like a medieval village where the monastery does the praying for everybody." Now Brian changed metaphors and concluded, "Jared was the ambassador for ethics in our family."

"But we always backed him," Alice interjected, "although we had major run-ins."

They had felt they could not support Jared in acts of civil disobedience, which for a while he contemplated. Breaking the law, even in a good cause, was not acceptable to them, and for Brian at least it carried a heavy—and unacceptable—taint of depression and even masochism.

"People have appetites for different types of knowledge," he said. "There's a certain confluence, a running together of concern about something like the nuclear issue, depression, and passive resistance—a wavelength band across all these issues. The mendicants and the prophets of this world are drawn to Shoreham."

But couldn't the arms race and the possibility of a ravaged environment be cause for depression? I asked.

"You mean a reactive depression?" said Brian, using the jargon of his profession.

I said I supposed that was what I meant.

Brian did not back off what he had said, but he added that he recognized that describing antinuclear activists as he had "knocked the veracity of the issue." Soon he got up, saying he had to get back to his desk.

I asked Alice how she felt the nuclear issue had affected her feelings about being a parent.

"It was another framework of immortality to be bringing up the children in," she said. "And it added a political component to the responsibility of communication about moral behavior. It's a terrible responsibility, one I would rather not have."

In his basic attitudes Brian was not unlike Robert Stewart: strength was linked in his mind with more and better technology and technological progress. It was unpleasant, if not actually threatening, to him to think of risks that might be consequences of these "strengths." Alice's emphasis, like Lenore Stewart's, was almost the opposite. But despite associations of depression and even masochism —and the loss of the "marching band" emotion—Brian had gradually entered into an examination of what constitutes risk, strength, and vulnerability in the nuclear age. Moreover, he was willing to share with Alice "the political component" of responsibility within the family, which included talking with their children about the nuclear issue. Together they "broke silence," although it is likely that if it had been Brian alone calling the shots the issue would have been far less salient in their family. Although there were still negative associations attached to doing so, the fact that Brian took these steps made it easier, I believe, for Jared to become an activist in his later teens than would ever be likely for the Stewart boys, even if they became persuaded of their mother's position. (It may have been easier, too, for Jared to pick up on what was essentially a cue from his mother —talking to her children about the nuclear issue was, she said, "a conduit to activity"—because she projected competence and strength.)

THE IMAGE OF THE CHILD

The new strength that parents can find when the nuclear issue is "unlocked" for them has the potential to help their children as well. Before we turn to this subject, however, let us look at the ways in which the image of the child is used in the peace movement in an attempt to mobilize the same kind of breakthrough that occurred for the individuals described above. When children and their future have been a prominent factor in "unlocking" the nuclear issue for an individual, the step into activism may involve children, the parental role, or the image of the child. Perhaps the most notable instance of this inspiration has been Helen Caldicott's impassioned campaigning against nuclear weapons and the arms race. She has spoken as a pediatrician, appealing to her audience as parents and protectors of their children's future.

The mobilizing value of the parental role and the image of the child guided the strategies Glenn Hawkes and other members of Parents and Teachers for Social Responsibility (PTSR) pursued. This was the significance of the infant undershirt that Hawkes carried in his back pocket.

PTSR's pamphlet *What About the Children?* appealed to readers in their role as parents. Moreover, while they were producing this pamphlet members of PTSR were exerting pressure on the local school board of Moretown, Vermont; the Vermont Department of Education; and the Vermont Civil Defense office. How, they inquired, did these bodies entrusted with the care of children during the school day plan to protect children in the event of nuclear war? School administrators replied that they had no plan and came to the decision that none was feasible. Clearly, this strategy, which spoke to officials in their role *in loco parentis,* had at its core the image of the child. But advising parents on how to respond to children about the nuclear issue, or involving children in antinuclear activism, was not part of the group's agenda. "A lot of people look to us to tell them what to do with their children," Hawkes said. "We basically back off. We say other groups are working on this."

Another group, Parents and Friends for Children's Survival (PFCS), based in New York City, was inspired by both the image of the child and the parental role, but pursued a different strategy. PFCS, which was founded late in 1981, sought ways to support family involvement in antinuclear activism and to encourage the visibility of family issues in the peace movement. The group led a children's contingent in the June 12 rally in 1982 and coordinated activities for families associated with the rally. Subsequently PFCS sponsored, among other events, a town meeting, the subject of which was the effect of the nuclear threat on young people; an essay contest among New York City schoolchildren; and family "peace actions" at the annual Christmas-tree lighting at Rockefeller Center. In addition, PFCS members, working in conjunction with the New York Public Interest Research Group, wrote five curricula for public school students in grades kindergarten through high school. By the summer of 1986 about seven thousand of these had been distributed. An activity book for young children produced by the group, "Peacemeal," has sold ten thousand copies. PFCS emphasizes attention to children's special needs when they participate in a public demonstration; for example, a special "children's park" was arranged at the June 12 demonstration, and a special bus was hired in August 1983 to take to Washington families who wished to participate in the large rally of progressive groups commemorating Martin Luther King's "I Have a Dream" speech.

Activists who make children central to their efforts are trying at least implicitly to answer one or more of the following questions: How can I help children deal with the nuclear issue? How can children participate in antinuclear activism? How can the image of the child be used to mobilize opinion? The authors of *Watermelons Not War* set themselves the task of answering the first question, and Helen Caldicott's efforts to rouse audiences around the image of the child and the parental role addressed the third. The members of PFCS, most of whom were political activists, addressed all three, but the second in particular, as have activist organizations for young people with a strong adult presence, such as the student–teacher organization STOP.

The first question is most pertinent to this book, but it is best not to consider it without some attention to the other two, since many activists tend to blur together all three "questions" and their "answers." Thus, PFCS members wanted to find a way of involving their children as sensibly and comfortably as possible in their own political activities, but they were not averse to making children "visible"—not necessarily the same goal.

"The whole rationale for setting up Parents and Friends for Children's Survival," said Carl Stein, one of the founders of the group, "was that there were a lot of adults who wanted to be involved in the peace movement but hesitated, because the issues were unacceptable because of what they did to children."

Then he added, taking a somewhat different tack, "Having children and families very visible was a very important tactic, but having done it, we thought it was very important to do it responsibly in relation to children."

Similarly complex motivation is suggested by the words of the Reverend James Antal, one of the founders of STOP. Antal, who was chaplain of the Northfield Mount Hermon School at the time STOP was founded, saw the empowerment of young people as the key function of the organization. "I try to create a safe enough atmo-sphere, and then say, How can you make your opinion make a differ-ence," he said. "What this does is teach young people they don't have to be secretary of state to make a difference." At another point he said, "I want to create conditions so that kids will speak with authority by affiliating themselves with a national organization." But he was well aware of the dangers of unloading the nuclear issue on young people. "On the one hand, they believe they are powerless, and on the other they are told 'This is really your issue.' I've heard this said to them again and again, and I would curse the day I said that to a kid."

Yet I could sense the temptation when he said that he be-lieved that children "saw through to simplicity," and that "as a result of their lack of historical investment they can cast aside the givens."

The experience of a filmmaker, Barbara Zahm, is another ex-ample of a complexly motivated "answer." In 1982 Zahm made a short film, *Bombs Will Make the Rainbow Break,* which shows a young people's peace march; children working on peace posters; interviews with children about their fears of nuclear war and hopes for peace; and footage showing members of the Children's Campaign for Nuclear Disarmament reading aloud children's letters to Presi-dent Reagan outside the fence surrounding the White House on their second visit, in May 1982. The film also includes a lyrical slow-motion sequence of children playing out of doors—the visual lyri-cism of which is counterpointed by the sound of bombs exploding on the sound track.

I asked Zahm what led her to make the film, and she began by saying, "It has to do with when I first had children, and the ambiva-lence I had about having a child because of the world I was bringing children into. It was, as far as I could tell, such a terrifying place that I felt guilty having children. That has always bothered me. It angered me incredibly. I have felt guilty toward my children, giving them existence—which I think is an incredible paradox. And I lived with that paradox because I wanted children. It's a very complicated thing that I don't think people have had to feel in any other period of history."

More specifically, activities involving young people around the time of the June 12 rally in 1982 inspired her. "I began to notice there was going to be a Children's Walk for Life the week before June 12. I realized a number of things. I realized my children had to —I could not deny the truth to them. So, rather than deny the truth and say, 'Yeah, isn't it a shame,' I had to show them that I was actively involved in trying to do something. They needed that out of me. I needed that out of me. And then what better way than to give a film? It could fulfill my needs as a parent, which is to try to help disarmament, which is what I need personally and as a parent. It used my husband and my skills and talents and resources, and it used the symbol of children and their voice."

Had she thought consciously when she set out to make the film about the use of the image of the child as the innocent teller of truth—a symbol that has been very much part of our literary, and by extension political, heritage?

"I think," she replied, "when I first thought of it, it was that 'kids can speak the purest' kind of thing. They had a purity in their voice that was true for everybody, but maybe the layers of sophistication and denial conceal it. We'd find the simplest and purest voices, that's what we were looking for, that clean voice, so they would symbolize everyone's voice but in the purest form."

Thus Zahm embarked on the film with two far from identical purposes both more or less present in her mind. She wanted to help children give public voice to their anxieties, to help them "break silence," as she herself was breaking silence. At the same time she hoped their "clean voice" would reach others; that is, she wanted to mobilize public opinion.

The Peace Book and the play adapted from it, *The Peace Child,* are among the best examples of the use of the image of the child in the peace movement.[3] *The Peace Book* was written by Bernard Benson, a scientist–inventor whose career has been involved as much with the pursuit of victory in war as the pursuit of peace. Born in 1922 of a British father and a French mother, Benson was raised in England and showed early signs of inventive genius, being awarded his first patent at the age of fourteen for an automatic scoring device for dart games. He now has more than one hundred patents to his name, mostly in the field of computer technology. While still in his teens, he joined the RAF at the outset of World War II, and was one of the developers of the first missile guidance systems. "I put intelligence into the torpedo," he told me. After the war he moved to the United States, where, in the course of fifteen years, he made a large fortune in the computer industry and fathered seven children. (In recent years a second marriage has added three more to his family.)

In the years immediately after the war Benson persuaded himself that he had no tie to the military. "I washed my hands of the military after the war and prided myself on working for medicine," he said. But he saw more and more clearly that his inventions could be the servants of many masters. His concern about the arms race and the way in which his work was implicated in it contributed to an ethical and spiritual crisis that led him to abandon science in 1959. In the early Sixties he moved to France and bought a small château near the village of Montignac in the Dordogne. A quest for a new kind of truth had begun—except that in a sense it was not new to him at all. "I was always very sensitive to human suffering," he said. "When I was in my teens I used to spend my weekends at an orphanage. I was always involved with people who needed service." His quest took him on several trips to India, where he met a number of the Buddhist lamas who had escaped from Tibet after the Chinese invasion in 1950. Benson became a Tibetan Buddhist, supported a number of lamas, and in time moved a group to the Dordogne, donating to them tracts of his land. Their prayer flags—green, yellow, red, and white—were an exotic presence as I drove down the country road that leads along the crest of a hill to Benson's château.

To many Benson's conversion—if conversion it was, and not a surfacing of what had always been latent in him—might seem hard to reconcile with his scientific self. Benson does not see it that way. "Buddhists," he said, "appeal to scientists because they don't ask you to believe something unless you've found it out for yourself." And from another point of view he is still as concerned with "how things work" as any scientist, although the area of his concern has shifted. "It's very simple," he said, using a favorite phrase and telescoping in retrospect a process that took some years. "When I gave up science, I asked myself what's the most positive thing I can do with the rest of my life. And I realized you can't tell who's winning if you don't know the rules of the game. I knew I couldn't figure them out alone and I soon realized that there is only one culture that is so steeped in the understanding of the human mind—the Tibetan."

In line with his beliefs, it is in the untrammeled ego that Benson sees the driving force behind the arms race.

During the time that he spent in India Benson became friends with a Canadian diplomat, James George. George visited Benson in the Dordogne in 1979 and, as Benson tells it, told him, "For God's sake, write a peace book, we are in a prewar period." George's suggestion inspired Benson to write *The Peace Book*, a fable about a little boy who brings an end to the arms race through his intercession with the leaders of the superpowers. The story uses the time-honored, Alice-in-Wonderland, emperor-and-his-clothes device of the innocent who alone can see the truth in a world gone mad. For instance, the boy hero asks the president of one of the superpowers the meaning of the abbreviation T.L.D. He has heard his father, a scientist, say to his colleagues that if the country can get its T.L.D. up from 115, where it now is, to 125, "we will be safe." The little boy is told that T.L.D. means "Tolerable Level of Destruction."

"Whatever is that?" asked the little boy.

"It means that if only 115 million of us are killed we're still all right."

"We're all right! What about the 115 million?"

Benson's *Peace Book* is informed not only by his Buddhist outlook but also by a thoroughly Western understanding of the importance of modern communications and of the concepts of empowerment and political voice:

> . . . issues have great power for good or for evil and the scientists had created vast communication networks, so that ideas, good and evil, could in a flash spread around the world. Now the peoples of the world could *hear* and make themselves heard.[4]

The little boy who is the hero of the fable is as savvy as his creator about the power of "communication networks." He says to his friend, a little girl, about the arms race: "We must simply tell the whole world what is going on. Nobody wants to die. Together the people will make them stop when they understand."

"But how?" she asked.

"Just walk into a television studio and do it. Simple!" he answered. "I'm going to do it!"

When he walks into the television studio and the cameras are trained on him, he cries out, "I don't want to die! I want to live! All the children want to live! The big people want to live!"

This fictional child, portrayed as no more than a stick figure in Benson's illustrations, conveys the same message that Hannah Rabin and her colleagues told the press outside the gates of the White House when they were refused admittance, the same message conveyed by *Changing the Silence* and Barbara Zahm's film, *Bombs Will Make the Rainbow Break*.

Benson feels that there is little difference between his own vision and that of a child. "I've never really grown up," he said. "I'm really more comfortable with kids in many ways. I have no consciousness of time or age." Of his book he said, "I think I sat down and looked at the arms race as a child would look at it and just set down what I saw."

We have seen that although there is a way in which the "raw vision" of some young people about the nuclear issue resembles the moral directness with which the hero of Benson's fable views the arms race, at a very early age a process of socialization begins that means that children gradually cease (if they ever were) to be those innocent "tellers of truth" adult critics of the society want them to be. Nevertheless, in a sense Benson is right—he does see with the vision of a child, the "child" in himself, one closely connected with spirituality and with the capacity of inventive genius to keep seeing things fresh, including the ability to see that the emperor, although in this case bearing arms, is naked.

Soon after the publication of *The Peace Book,* a British playwright and film maker, David Woollcombe, who radiates a rare mixture of conviction and joyousness, adapted the book into a play for young people with music by the composer, David Gordon.

In the play the friendship between the little boy and the little girl, which is incidental in the book, becomes much more important. The boy, Bobby, is an American, the girl, Katya, Russian. They meet while their parents attend an embassy party in Washington. As in *The Peace Book,* their initial strategy for halting the arms race is to appear on television proclaiming their fears for the future. Media attention wins Bobby an audience with the president—something more than it has ever won young activists in real life. But in the end it is not Bobby's knowledgeable lecturing about the dangers of the arms race that persuades the president or subsequently the Soviet premier, nor his innocent's ability to show up their thinking, but a suggestion that Russian and American children live in each other's society for a year as guarantees of peace . . . an exchange program of the young that envisions children as hostages guaranteeing their own future . . .

The play is a tract with the child cast as a "teller of truth," the "clean voice," but it is made possible from the point of view of performance by lovely songs that can be sung by large choruses, giving many children other than the principals a chance to participate. (At the premiere in this country at the John F. Kennedy Center for the Performing Arts in Washington, which I attended, the chorus consisted of several hundred children from forty-five different countries, all apparently having a very good time.)

The Peace Child was performed for the first time in 1981 at the Royal Albert Hall in London. Since then thousands of children have participated in more than 260 performances in the United

States. Abroad, the play has been performed in Canada, France, Switzerland, and the Soviet Union as well as in England. In the summer of 1985 one of Woollcombe's dreams came true when a joint Soviet–American production, involving seventeen American and twenty-four Soviet children, was staged at the Children's Musical Theater in Moscow—not quite the "exchange" of children the play envisions, but a step in that direction. *The Peace Child* was also featured on a live "Space Bridge" satellite television program linking Moscow and Minneapolis early in December 1985 and rebroadcast in New York on Christmas Day, 1985.

How can children be helped to deal with the nuclear issue? How can they participate in antinuclear activism? How can the image of the child be used to mobilize opinion? *The Peace Child* is a multiple "answer" to the "questions" activists face when they involve the image of the child—and children—in their work. In the introduction to the script of the play Woollcombe is explicit about his intentions to raise adult as well as child consciousness: "We work with children to remind adults of their earlier innocent conviction about Life's potential; and we work with adults to guide children, to enlighten them about the dangers facing our planet, and collaborate with them in the search for solutions."[5]

The Peace Child uses the child not only didactically, to "teach" about the dangers of the arms race, but, in a less explicit and more affective way, to remind adults of what is precious and not expendable in their lives and therefore implicitly of sanity, responsibility, and vulnerability.

At the same time, the adult teacher or director who uses the study guide that accompanies the play is supposed to "enlighten" the child about the arms race (in fact, very little enlightment may take place: the study guide is sketchy and certainly not essential to staging the play). I believe that a message about empowerment is far more important than any "enlightenment." The underlying concept of the play is the idea that the child can make himself or herself heard and therefore discover that he or she has a voice. In one sense that voice is a political voice. In another sense—the sense that is central to Benson's original inspiration—it is a moral and spiritual voice, which we believe is "clean" when it comes from children.

Before one scoffs at *The Peace Child* (and it is easy to scoff at tracts, even when the cause is good), it is worth remembering the importance of *Uncle Tom's Cabin* and other books that have helped change consciousness. Minds are not made up by facts alone.

"LEAVING IT UP TO THE CHILDREN"

On the other hand, *The Peace Child* does suggest a problem in the relationship of adult to child with respect to the nuclear issue. An adult sense of helplessness—feeling like a child—can lead to a kind of abdication or role reversal, conveying to the child the message "This issue is up to you to solve."[6] Such a message was expressed explicitly by Benson: "You the children of the earth must with courage and wisdom undo what we have done. . . . But we have left a legacy of confused minds. . . . You must not listen to our *minds* . . . but to our *hearts.*"[7]

"It's up to you" is a message that has the potential to make children feel even more pessimistic, helpless, and abandoned than a number already do. As Sibylle Escalona put it, "To address oneself to children in such a way that you say that they're the ones who are going to cope is a cop-out. It assigns a heavy burden to someone who, because of his place in the scheme of things, can't assume it. In this culture children need to feel that adults will care for them and protect them."

Glenn Hawkes was outspoken about the problem: "We've had enough movies of children from Westchester and Newton talking about eyeballs falling out," he said. "There is a way in which we're using children in a nonconstructive dialogue. The single most important thing any adult can do is to be involved in trying to solve the problem—but not necessarily by involving children and not necessarily by talking about it except to answer their questions. As adults we need a definition of ourselves as creators. We need the image of our stewardship role." A role, be it said, that the helplessness and powerlessness associated with the nuclear issue make very difficult to achieve.

Context—what adults supply in the way of support, or what they fail to supply—is important in determining whether the political use of the image of the child is empowering or the opposite. Without support the child is made into the mouthpiece and the icon, but the adult has left by the back door.

Empowerment is the lesson *The Peace Child* sets out to teach, and many children have felt that participating in the play was an empowering experience; but this may be more the result of participation itself, with all the adult and peer attention it entails, than a result of the message of the play. Certainly this message is a double one: on the one hand it promises resoundingly that young people can have a political voice, but, on the other, it does nothing to demonstrate that adults are doing very much to care for and protect children—and this, at least implicitly, is far from empowering. (In fact, in suggesting that children become hostages for their own future, the play implies that the burden of care and protection has fallen on them.)

Barbara Zahm felt that empowerment was the result for the young people whom she filmed for *Bombs Will Make the Rainbow Break*. Hannah Rabin concurred that the CCND members whom Zahm filmed felt "heard"—and accurately so. "Barbara Zahm did a wonderful job of coloring the film with our emotions," she said. On the other hand, the success of the film in helping those who *view* it feel that they can make themselves heard depends, I believe, on factors beyond the film itself. I was far from comfortable on one occasion when several teenage activists showed it to a largely Hispanic fifth grade in East Harlem—a group in which several children, their teacher told me, had thought until she told them otherwise that a "nuclear plant" was a botanical item. After showing the film the teenagers gave a necessarily rapid run-down on the nature of nuclear weapons and the arms race—just the bad news, and no indication of how anyone, kids or—particularly—adults, was acting to change bad to better. Then the period was over, the teenagers departed, and the fifth graders were left to go back to spelling and fractions—and whatever they might feel. My hunch was that unless their teacher could supply a great deal of information, interpretation, and support it would be impossible for them to feel much of anything, and certainly not the empowerment the film intends to inspire. The nonfeeling route of the survival artist seemed to me their most likely reaction to the experience.

HOW YOUNG PEOPLE REACT TO THE USE OF THE IMAGE OF THE CHILD

The use of the image of the child to rally and inspire adult opinion becomes particularly complex for young people who are involved with adults in activist groups.

Roxanna Tynan, a young activist, reflected on the relationship in the spring of 1982 between young people in a New York group called Future Generations and adult activists, many of whom were members of a group called Performing Artists for Nuclear Disarmament.

"I felt adults wanted to use kids in the movement as tear-

jerkers," she said. "I'm not against the mothers who campaign outside nuclear power plants; if it works, do it, but I don't want to be
part of it."

Her own commitment to activism complicated her position:
"I felt a little manipulated but I let myself be. We were not needed
[at meetings of PAND] to talk about money. We were there for the
tear-jerker purpose."

Tynan resisted being seen as an "innocent victim" and defined
her own outlook and strategy rather pragmatically. "I realized I was
a bit sick of adults' saying, You poor kids, you won't have a future.
Of course, I agree that it's terrible if humanity is annihilated, but
humanity being destroyed is too big for me to think about. I'm in
this because I think money needs to be redirected and I believe in
educating on this and other issues. I don't think there's one big
solution. I think things are solved in little ways."

She did not subscribe to the romanticized vision of the innocent child, the Benson vision. "I don't believe," she said, "that 'children like to create rather than destroy.' This is part of the tear-jerker
aspect of the movement—the 'walking in green fields' kind of thing."
But, in line with her commitment to activism, she once again added
a caveat: "Not that I object if it gets a heartfelt response."

Eventually, however, the desire for less adult involvement
contributed to her decision to help found Kids' Outreach, an organization of high-school activists that was intended to perform a function she saw as appropriate—"kids in the movement are there to
educate other kids"—rather than "to educate adults or show adults
how big the issue is."

Hannah Rabin had somewhat similar memories. "I remember
being at one conference in Finland where I suddenly just felt
swamped, because there were all these adults who were working on
various peace issues and issues of children and war and at one point
they all surrounded me and said, 'Why don't you come to Northern
Ireland and organize the kids? Why don't you start a campaign for
the kids in Iran?' Stuff like that. That's crazy."

But she felt that she herself had been well aware of the power
of the image of the child—the "fresh, naïve, beautiful" emotions of
the young and their power to persuade. While working in STOP (too
old, as a high-school student, to be part of CCND any longer) she
became aware that "there were some adults who were beginning to
use kids in this way. They were using emotional kid leverage, something politicians have always loved. There were adults in STOP who
would say, 'We've got to find more eloquent kid speakers,' and I

would feel, 'My God, what is going on? The point of this organization is that everyone should say what he feels.' " At the same time, Hannah and her friends tried to make the most of the image they projected for their own ends: "We took an almost pragmatically crass view of our image, particularly in relation to the media. We would go into interviews reminding each other, 'Remember, we use them more than they use us!' in order not to fall into the trap—the image—that was invariably laid for us."

But, in thinking back to her experiences in STOP, Hannah did not feel that the use of the image of the child was as important an issue as the struggle of the youthful members for an equal role in an essentially adult-directed organization. "The adult–kid role was something we dealt with just endlessly." But as an experienced organizer, Rabin took a long view of such difficulties: "It's hard to know whether it was individuals who would be taking over anyway or whether it was an adult–kid kind of thing. There are always problems of power in any organization."

Although Rabin felt that she had been able to act effectively in STOP, she contrasted her experience with her earlier involvement with the Children's Campaign for Nuclear Disarmament. "Coming from CCND," she said, "we were fueled by emotion. We felt we had to have a right to speak out because it was a question of our life or our death. CCND was the real expression of my anger and fear."

She felt that the adult organizers of STOP, despite their interest in the inspirational quality of young people, played down the kind of emotion that keeps an activist going in favor of building an organization. "A lot of times, I felt they didn't have tolerance for the emotions of the kids. The organization was what was important to them. They wouldn't allow emotion to fuel the group." Yet, with her usual long view, Rabin noted that organizations cannot be built to endure on emotion alone, and she went on to say, "The important thing to remember is that there is a place for adults and place for kids in the peace movement. No one can excuse himself. We're all involved. We're all going to die. It's the entire planet."

In helping young people to find this place it seems to me least effective to use them as an icon and most effective to encourage their own efforts or to give them a role as apprentices and interns in what are clearly defined as adult efforts.

RESPONSIBILITY AND VULNERABILITY

The use of the image of the child in the peace movement offers insight into the psychological struggle we all face in attempting, as Roger Wilkins put it, to "wrestle with the nuclear issue right now, in our own time." This is a struggle between an effort to find a new model of strength, one that begins with the recognition of a degree of vulnerability never confronted in earlier generations, and the tendency to be overcome by a sense of helplessness, not only in relation to the nuclear vision but in relation to the dwarfing scale of modern institutions. The child is a potent symbol for our struggle, conjuring up for us images of both responsibility and vulnerability.

We have seen how the image of the child has been used in the peace movement in an effort to mobilize the same connectedness that brought about new awareness for Glenn Hawkes and Ellie Deegan. Connectedness inspires a sense of responsibility in relation to future generations. The image of the child as it has been used by Helen Caldicott or Parents and Teachers for Social Responsibility calls upon adults to bring to mind and heart their role as stewards in relation to the next generation and their duty to act wisely in that capacity. Moreover, the image of the child has been important to us in relation to our struggle with the nuclear issue because it is associated with intense feeling—feeling that can break through the abstract, technicist, game-playing cast of mind implicated in the perpetuation of the arms race, a cast of mind that wants to believe that accidents don't happen and one that tends to disregard the dangers of the unforeseeable ways people act in crises. This intensity of feeling asserts what has been called "the reality of qualities," that "fullness of human reality" which a quantifying, "objective," analytic approach cannot adequately comprehend.[8] This is what the lyric passage of children playing out of doors in the film *Bombs Will Make the Rainbow Break* and the songs in *The Peace Child* seek to bring to mind. The qualities the image of the child asserts have to do with love, joy, hope, and nurturing; but once one lets these into consciousness, others can enter too and one can begin to perceive the reality of "the deep, destructive impulses of the human psyche, to which a purely technical reason is as oblivious as it is to the sources of genuine creativeness."[9] Only by vivid consciousness of the reality of both the dark and the light in our nature—the sound of the bombs on the sound track as well as children playing in *Bombs Will Make the Rainbow Break*—will we be able to control the destructive possibilities of the technology we have created.

However, the image of the child is easily debased and reduced to a sentimental image of innocence. When this happens it risks projecting an image of helplessness rather than one of responsibility —and a sense of helplessness is the other pole of our struggle with the nuclear issue. Moreover, the power of the sentimentalized child to trigger awareness is much attenuated, since sentimentality is associated with the diminution of emotions. Used for political purposes, a sentimental image conveys a grossly oversimplified message that power has no allure and that the "deep, destructive impulses" have no reality. This is the weakness of *The Peace Book* and *The Peace Child;* their vision is one of millennial improvement in human nature, with the implication that the dark "impulses" can be overcome once and for all. This same message is conveyed by the weakest part of the peace movement.

In its sentimentalized version, the image of the child becomes part of what the physicist Freeman Dyson has called the "world of victims." At the beginning of his excellent book *Weapons and Hope,* Dyson states that he lives in two worlds, "the world of the warriors" and the "world of the victims." He notes that "the world of the warriors is the world I see when I go to Washington or to California to consult with military people about their technical problems." It is male-dominated and includes many who are not in the military: "expert negotiators at the United States Arms Control and Disarmament Agency, and professors of International Affairs at the universities of Princeton and Oxford. It includes doves as well as hawks, scholars as well as generals." The warriors have a distinctive intellectual style: "Their style is deliberately cool, attempting to exclude overt emotion and rhetoric from their discussions, emphasizing technical accuracy and objectivity, concentrating attention on questions of detail which can be reduced to quantitative calculation." [10] The warriors, in other words, are masters of the "purely technical reason" which is "as oblivious of our destructive potential as of our creative."

The world of victims, on the other hand, is "the world I see when I listen to my wife's tales of childhood in wartime Germany, when we take our children to visit the concentration camp museum at Dachau, when we go to the theater and see Brecht's *Mother Courage. . . .* when we sit with a crowd of strangers in church and hear them pray for peace, or when I dream my private dreams of Armageddon." Unlike the world of warriors, the world of victims is not a male world. "It is, on the contrary, woman-and-child-dominated. It is, like the Kingdom of Heaven, difficult to enter unless you come with a child's imagination. It is a world of youth rather than age. It pays more attention to poets than to mathematicians." [11]

In the last two sentences Dyson himself succumbs to sentimentality and detracts from his insights. Many women would attest that the world of victims does not necessarily have to do with youth or poets but has a great deal to do with an awareness of vulnerability —which is not only a sense of how easily one can become a victim but a sense of care and carefulness and a longing for the greatest good for the greatest number. They would say that it is a world only too easy to enter, requiring neither a key to the kingdom of heaven nor a child's imagination.

What Dyson refers to as the world of warriors and the world of victims are close to what I have called the "realism of strength" and the "realism of vulnerability." Both "worlds" or "realisms" will always exist, and both are necessary, but the tremendous destructiveness of our technology means that it behooves the warriors— and they are not just soldiers and politicians—to make part of their consciousness a greater sense of care and carefulness, more concern for the greatest good for the greatest number, more of the realism of vulnerability, than they have in the past. The use of the image of the child in the peace movement is an effort to persuade them.

Will they be persuaded? On good days I think they are being so persuaded, bit by bit. On bad days I think never. But if they are, it is by individuals like the O'Briens whose sense of responsibility has been aroused—who have found a model of strength that does not depend on silence—and not by a sentimental image of the child that speaks of helplessness and the world of victims.

IN IT TOGETHER

Mary O'Brien's expression is spare, intense. With a wide, thin mouth, her face looks like the faces of pioneer women in faded nineteenth-century photographs. But there is nothing faded about her. In profile, her nose is sloping, pointed. Her cheeks have the nearly chapped ruddiness of someone who is out of doors a lot. Tall and thin, she wears her long dark hair in a single braid that reaches halfway down her back. Her fingers are long but a bit stubby at the ends. When I first met Mary—outside the O'Brien home on the outskirts of Eugene, Oregon—her hands were covered with dirt: she had been gardening. Later I learned that she has a doctorate in botany.

An ardent feminist and an activist on behalf of the environment and against nuclear weapons, Mary is a fighter, a mover and shaker, someone, one senses, who hardly suffers fools at all, let alone gladly. Both Mary and Bob O'Brien—known as O'B in the family—did draft counseling during the Vietnam war and, more recently, have been active in the antinuclear movement. In addition, Mary works for a leading pesticide reform group, the Northwest Coalition for Alternatives to Pesticides (NCAP). (Member groups of the coalition were the first in the nation to succeed in halting the spraying of herbicides such as Agent Orange on federal timber lands.) To add to her already full work load, at the time I first met her in the spring of 1984, Mary was county coordinator for Margie Hendriksen's Senate race against Mark Hatfield.

People like Mary don't come out of nowhere. Her father, a Presbyterian minister, was a conscientious objector during World War II. Bob's father, a Quaker, likewise opposed the war. "His proudest moment," Mary told me, "was when he helped relocate five thousand Japanese from internment camps to colleges during World War II."

I first met Mary on one of those spring evenings when long hours of light allow children to play out of doors after supper and parents to catch up with yard work. Her elder son Josh, aged eleven, and his brother, Zeke, nine, were playing with a neighbor on the scrap of front yard in front of the O'Briens' red frame house. Bob, Mary's husband, tall, kind-eyed, redheaded, and red-bearded, came to greet me. He called Mary from the yard in the back of the house.

We went in. A large Japanese paper fish swung from the rafters of the porch—and a number of plastic bags were clothespinned to a line. (They had been washed and were to be used again.) The living room was small and simple. Mary, Josh, and Zeke sat on a couch covered with a crocheted blanket. Bob and I sat on straight chairs. Looking at the family assembled, I took in that Josh had his mother's dark hair and Zeke red hair like his father. Josh had the seriousness of many first-borns, and Zeke, one of the most spectacular grins I have ever seen.

At first the boys did most of the talking. I asked about the chapter of the Children's Campaign for Nuclear Disarmament Josh had started in Eugene.

"We started about two years ago, and our main activity has been one big march and a rally downtown for two hundred and fifty or three hundred people in the mall," Josh said. "And we've handed out literature and we've had two bake sales and speeches at Erb Memorial Union and I've been at lots of rallies and I have a skit."

I asked how he had heard of CCND. Zeke, who had been bursting to put in a word, said, "We heard of it because when my grandma died my grandpa married someone whose child lived in Vermont and she knew Hannah."

His older brother brushed aside this explanation.

"There's this thing called Letter Lobby in Eugene," Josh said. "They send out a sheet of paper with printing on both sides with about ten different issues each month to write letters about—you know, pretty liberal ideas—and we saw one that said send letters to Children's Campaign for Nuclear Disarmament because, you know, that big thing in New York [the June 12 rally of 1982], well, they were going to read them there. So I sent some letters and they wrote me back."

I asked how many kids were involved in the Eugene chapter of CCND.

Josh said eighty or ninety at its peak.

"But nine out of ten don't really do much," said Zeke. "Like we sent out a letter saying if any of you guys, any of you people, want to help, but we didn't get enough people so we're not going to have a second parade. A lot of people don't really want to do anything. They sign up on a sheet and they don't have responsibility."

"But there are four or five people who are really good at working," Josh said. "We haven't done much for a year now, unless we want to run the parade—that's what we did last year."

I asked about the parade.

"We did a walk around the mall," Josh said, "about eight blocks. We filed around and came to the center, there's a big courtyard there. And we got some sound equipment and lots of people did speeches but one person did a dance."

I asked what they thought they had learned from their work in CCND.

"Lots of people want to be in the movement," Josh said, "but they don't want to do very much organizing."

After I had talked with the boys a while longer, Zeke asked his father if he could make brownies, sensing that my visit had the makings of a party (parties are more fun than interviews). It turned out that Zeke and Bob were the family's cooks for the week.

"We divide all the jobs in the house," Mary explained, "and each week we all draw three of them."

"We don't always eat cheese sandwiches when Zeke and I cook," Josh assured me.

"Josh does real good things like enchiladas," said Zeke admiringly. "Sometimes I do blintzes. I've been doing egg in the hole since I was five. You know, where you cut a hole in the bread and put an egg in."

Zeke and Bob went into the kitchen to prepare the brownies. Mary and Josh and I went on talking. Mary told me about her career as an activist. I asked her if she ever had qualms about involving her children so closely.

"I suppose the question always comes up, are you making your kids too serious," she said.

"Lots of people think you're spoiling their young life," Josh put in. "But if you don't they won't have a grown-up life."

"Josh was out with me last weekend," Mary said. "We were putting up signs for the Margie Hendriksen campaign."

"I put up thirty signs in three hours," Josh said.

"When we got back," Mary said, "Josh bounded out of the car and went to play with a five-year-old neighbor. When I see that I don't worry."

"It's one thing if kids were saying they didn't want to do it," Josh said.

My questioning made Mary think of her own upbringing.

"My parents influenced me a great deal along religious lines," she said. "I'm not religious, but I carried another message from them, a sense of responsibility and a sense that you don't just have to be acted upon. Josh may grow up to disagree with me and I tell him he may, but I hope I pass on this same sense of responsibility, even if the issues are different."

Here was the word Zeke had used—responsibility; it had stood out as a five-dollar word in his nine-year-old usage, and now I knew why. Here, too, in what Mary said, was a very American and contemporary message about a parent's recognition of a child's right to grow into his own person, to disagree and pick his issues, but coupled with the hope that basic values would be transmitted—in this case a conviction about the importance of action and responsibility beyond the narrow circle of private life.

Mary made a distinction between her parents' religious outlook and her own, but a few minutes later, when we were talking about *The Day After,* the distinction seemed a slim one. "The saddest moment was when the missiles went off," she said. "I think you have to connect with the saddest moment for yourself; like for me it would be if Josh learned the missiles had gone off and we had failed. Then you come back from that feeling and get active. And in the meantime you have to be happy because otherwise the holocaust has already got you, if they've taken away your day, every day. That's sort of the way I feel about death anyway. I mean there's never been anyone who hasn't died, but the message is to live a hundred years in each day. That's why I haven't been afraid to tell the boys everything.

"When I was becoming a botanist," she continued, "and I learned how fast the rain forests and lots of plant species were disappearing, I thought, How could I stand it? And I thought that if the last thing they've left—they, whoever they are, the forces of extinction—is dandelions and grass, then I'll protect the dandelions. In the face of the very worst thing you can do something."

Mary thought of herself as a nonreligious person, but it was hard to believe that anything but an essentially spiritual source could nourish her conviction about the preciousness of life, a preciousness made all the greater by the inevitability of death. It was hard to believe, too, that the same source did not nourish her conviction that even in extreme situations one does not have to take a passive position.

"Kids are so concrete," she went on, "that kind of message works for them: here's what you can do; you can walk with me and deliver a pamphlet and we may change somebody's mind today. If the support is there, if you've got more than despair, kids can handle anything."

Not that Mary was saying that what she asked of her children was easy.

"Zeke is much more interested in approval than Josh," she said, "but he came home early in the winter and said, 'I disagreed with my teacher today.' Someone had asked what a Purple Heart was and the teacher had said it was a medal you got for being brave. And Zeke had said that it was something you got for doing awful things, that is, killing. But it had been so stressful that he kept his head under the blanket when he told me."

The brownies were in the oven by now. Bob and Zeke rejoined us. Bob sat on the couch and Josh curled up between him and Mary. Mary cuddled him.

We went on talking, and our conversation was like few others I had ever had in a family with children as young as Zeke and Josh.

It was as if the O'Briens' program of shared housework applied to the intellectual and political arena as well. I found myself talking with four people at once; but, unlike a visitor's experience in many families, when children try to divert their parents from the visitor or the visitor from the parents, struggling in a not so subtle contest for equal time and attention, Josh and Zeke were welcome in the conversation and confident in participating. At the same time, they were not cast in a role of "little adults." Their parents had not surrendered their authority, and often they were informally instructing them, filling them in.

We talked about Mary's work for NCAP.

"It's the best pesticide newsletter in the country—" Bob said.

"Because of Mary," Zeke added.

"The federal timber agencies may be forced to close down spraying everywhere in the country because of information that came out of an office the size of this room . . ." Bob went on.

". . . bigger than this room," said Zeke.

Mary talked about Carol Van Strum, another Oregon pesticide activist, who had written a book on the forestry spraying, *A Bitter Fog.*

Why, Josh asked, had Carol first wanted to call her book *A Trout in the Milk?* It comes from a line by Henry David Thoreau, Mary told him. "Sometimes circumstantial evidence is very high, like finding a trout in the milk. If you find trout in the milk then you really know it's not pure milk." (In the case of the spraying of the timber lands, the "trout" had been the disproportionately large number of women who miscarried and whose babies had birth defects.)

Zeke looked puzzled. Bob explained that a long time ago people had sometimes cheated by putting water in milk.

"Do they still put water in milk?" Zeke asked.

His father said no.

"Half and half?" asked Zeke, not one to give up easily.

A few minutes later we talked about Greenham Common. One of us had heard that the soldiers on the base had been forbidden to make eye contact with the women protestors. Why? both boys asked at once. Eye contact is very powerful, Bob explained. "If a boss is going to fire a guy he may look away."

"It's like I read in *Time* magazine," Zeke said, "if you smile at people, they smile back. I tried it. I smiled at the bus driver. It worked."

With a smile like that, I thought, even a bus driver . . .

The brownies were done. Bob made cocoa to accompany

them. Zeke set the kitchen table with a cloth. It was clear that he really meant this to be a party. He went out into the garden, dark by now, and came back with a handful of rhododendron blossoms. He set each blossom in a small, low glass and set the glasses among the candles.

"Thanks a lot, Zeke," said his brother warmly—a remark that said more about the O'Briens than hours of talk.

We sat down. Zeke wanted me to have a special surprise mug for my cocoa. I had to drink quite a bit of cocoa before I found out what the surprise was—Kermit the Frog staring up at me from the bottom of the cup. We were all having a fine time; it felt like more of a party than I had been to in a while. I complimented Zeke on the brownies and on the rhododendrons in their little cups. He told me that while hiking with his parents and Josh he had been to a place where "you can see rhododendrons like a sea."

While we went on talking Josh remembered that he had promised to make enchiladas for a fiesta in school the following day. He mixed the dough for the tortillas and started to make them one at a time, putting a smallish ball of dough in a cast-iron press, closing the press, and then standing on it while continuing to talk to us. Then all at once the mood changed. Zeke got silly. He and Josh began to get on each other's nerves. Bob stood up and put an arm around Zeke, warmly but firmly. Time for bed. Zeke kissed him but then backed away and raised his arm for an instant to deliver a mock blow that stopped in mid-air, suggesting what one might feel after an evening with an ebullient younger brother who was not above trying for the limelight. Mary went off with Zeke. Josh was tired too. Bob said he would finish the tortillas. Then in the morning they would finish the enchiladas together.

I said goodbye and drove back to the center of Eugene in the dark. Everything we had said rushed through my head, including these words of Mary's: "I certainly couldn't say we're a model family. We scream and yell and fight, but we're there for each other."

And Josh entering in: "I bet you there are less than a hundred model families in the world."

Mary and Bob presented to their children a model of strength about environmental and nuclear issues capable of recognizing the historically unprecedented degree of vulnerability for life on earth that we now live with. It was the very opposite of a model built on silence. It brought together knowing and feeling and insisted that the two could not be separated. Their political activism was the expression of basic beliefs that shaped other aspects of their lives, not only their politics. Their conviction about the value of life itself ("the message is to live a hundred years in each day") had a moral and spiritual intensity. This same intensity characterized their conviction about the individual's ability to act on his own behalf, not to be a victim. ("In the face of the very worst thing you can do something.") They offered their boys faith in life and a hopeful view of human beings based in large measure on the vision of the possibility of responsible action even in extreme situations. This meant that they could be open about their concerns: awareness was possible, since there was always something you could do. You were never totally helpless.

Their convictions meant that they offered their children something bolder, tougher, and stronger than protection through silence or the quasitherapeutic response of "We feel the way you do," or "Mommy and Daddy are working on it and everything will be all right." They were not at all sure that everything was going to be all right, and their concerns extended as much to environmental issues as to the arms race. But they were sure that it was possible to fight for what you believed and they were sure the fight was worth it.

What was it like for Josh and Zeke to live with such a model?

There is no question that their parents' concern with the issue made the boys worry in a sharp and "close to the surface" way. Some time after my visit with the family I read a composition Josh had written when he was ten:

> Some nights when I go to bed I stay awake because I am thinking that a nuclear war could happen any time. Right now a bomb could be dropping or people could be getting in an argument that would set off a war. In a couple of minutes thousands and millions of people could be dead. The whole human race could go. Even greater numbers of plants and animals would die.
>
> It all started by people wanting to stop Germany from conquering Europe and killing Jewish people. Once we had figured out the A-bomb the Russians wanted one, too. After we had dropped it on Japan, they thought we might use it on them, too. And once the Russians had one, we wanted to be ahead and vice versa. Now we've got an arms race.
>
> The trouble is, why do we want enough killing power to kill the world seven times over? Why do we even want enough to kill the whole world *once?* Even if we never have a nuclear war, there's a massive amount of money being poured into it. That same

money could have been spent on medical care for all the people in the whole world. It could be spent on educating people and feeding all the starving people in the world. It could be spent on maintenance of wildlife preserves. The world would have a better standard of living if we didn't have an arms race. People wouldn't have to WORRY so much. . . .

At the end of his essay, Josh wrote:

If I could talk to Reagan and the lawmakers, I would say, "Stop scaring everybody in the world that they could die any moment. There is nothing in the world that should be solved by having a nuclear war. Remember, the Russians are human beings. In Russia there's probably a little kid about my age who lies awake in bed some nights thinking there could be a bomb dropping any minute. DON'T KILL THAT LITTLE KID.

Mary and Bob's teaching is clear, as is its impact. But nothing about Josh or Zeke suggested that living with a considerable degree of awareness and concern was not tolerable. Both were remarkably ebullient and productive. Mary put her finger on a characteristic quality of energy and joy when she remembered that Josh had "bounded" out of the car to play after he returned with her from a long day of posting political campaign signs. (On my second visit to the family Josh "bounded" out of bed to play the cello for me—at seven A.M.)

What were key factors in maintaining this combination of awareness and even anxiety with a very positive and hopeful approach to life?

Antinuclear activists would reply that it was Mary and Bob's activism itself that was the key. They would say that activism on the part of parents helps children feel less helpless and more optimistic, and they might fondly tell a now apocryphal story. A teacher asked her class of young children about their concerns about the threat of nuclear war. Every child was worried with the exception of one, who said he was not worried "because his father went to meetings."

So far there is not enough research evidence to prove conclusively the role that parental activism does or does not play in children's attitudes, but the little that does exist supports activists' contentions—up to a point. The study of California children referred to earlier is one of the few in which parents as well as their children responded to a questionnaire. Susan Eileen Light, the author of this study, found that the activism of parents was positively correlated with children's sense of empowerment: "Parents who are more active in anti-nuclear causes have children who are more likely to feel that they and their parents can, have, and will do something about the nuclear threat."[12] This (not surprising) finding suggests that some degree of action on the part of parents is a good antidote to the sense of powerlessness that leaves young people little option but the strategy of the survival artist. It is worth noting, moreover, that the activism of Light's respondents did not involve extreme positions or big commitments of time and energy. These were parents who for the most part might write a few letters and sign a few petitions. Yet their modest actions made a considerable difference to how their children felt.

It is also worth noting, however, that parental activism did not increase the chances of communication between the generations about the issue. (In this sense, as in others, the O'Briens are an unusual family.) This lack of communication, even in families where parents had taken some steps toward activism, suggests how anxiety-laden the issue is, as well as its distance and abstractness in relation to daily life. Nevertheless, children "picked up" enough about what their parents were doing to be influenced by it—proof, as often in family life, of the power of doing as opposed to saying.

The relationship of parental activism to the concerns and the optimism of children, in contrast with their sense of empowerment, was much less clear in Light's findings—and did not confirm the simple, upbeat message that the story about the boy whose father went to meetings tries to convey. Light found a slight, but not statistically significant tendency for children to be more concerned the more their fathers were activists, which is consonant with the findings of research indicating that the political messages of fathers have more weight in the family than those of mothers. The same tendency was true with respect to optimism but only in the case of boys. (There is much more to be learned about the different political responses of girls and boys.) I see the relative independence of concern and optimism from parental activism in Light's data as confirmation that "big world" issues have a direct impact on young people independent of their parents' "filtering." But at the same time her findings suggest that parents are very important models and inspirations for "handling" that big world.

The fact that parental activism may not bear decisively on a child's concern, optimism, or pessimism may be thought of from another point of view as well. Our aim should not be to rear a child who isn't concerned but one who is hopeful (not necessarily the same thing as optimistic), for whom a sense of risk and vulnerability in relation to the nuclear and other world issues is not blocked out; one who can tolerate "staying worried" sufficiently to act in his own and his fellows' real interests. Josh and Zeke (and many other children, such as those pinpointed by the Canadian study referred to earlier) suggest that this is possible and that a sense of empowerment is key.

What can the O'Briens tell us about this sense?

The same convictions that shaped their political life informed their family life. If life mattered, then family life mattered in all its details—questions answered, plastic bags washed and clothespinned to the line, brownies baked, rhododendrons, Kermit the Frog. All four O'Briens were intensely committed to each other, and this meant that they sacrificed so that each could pursue his or her own interests—and sacrificed so that they could be together. I sensed that the strength of their commitment was a large factor in making the anxiety of working on difficult issues tolerable. Clearly and strongly Mary and Bob conveyed to their sons the message "We are in this together." In it together meant many things: sharing housework; the choice of each other's company; the inclusion of children in adult interests and activities; and finally the decision not to shield them with silence from the issues of the day.

But to a degree unusual in many families they accompanied commitment with the encouragement of a sense of competence, support for risk-taking, and the determination that each family member should have a voice within the family. (It was Mary's "speaking up" that had led to the sharing of housework.)

These "encouragements" were, in fact, considerable demands and might seem excessive or inappropriate to some, but they were made on the assumption that children can make a real contribution in every area of family life—be it cooking dinner, doing laundry, or talking about world issues. However, meeting a demand involves a risk, although sometimes so small that it might hardly be perceived as one—the bungled enchilada, the white shirt stained red in the wash, the angry or disappointed parent or sibling, and, in the case of the discussion of public issues, being shown up as "no more than a child." But taking a risk contains the possibility of success if the risk does not outstrip the child's capacities, and success so gained adds to a sense of competence and growing mastery, a sense that is basic to empowerment.

Too many demands and too much risk that is inappropriate

and without support may be too stressful, but quite a lot—with sufficient support—is strengthening. In this respect it is important to note that the demands Mary and Bob made did not involve an abdication of their own role as parents. They were not only loving but also, as far as possible, clear in the boundaries they set. The support they gave meant that the demands they made and the risks involved in meeting them were not too onerous but, rather, played a positive role in building a sense of self-esteem and competence in their sons.

Yet Mary and Bob's style was quite different from the norm in earlier generations; they were authoritative but much less authoritarian than most families in the past. In this they were very much themselves, and at the same time acted in line with profound changes that are shaping American family life. Many factors are contributing to these changes, among them changes in the nature of work, in women's roles, and the sheer rapidity of change itself. The shift in the "balance of powers" among institutions is a factor, too— although not evident with the O'Briens—making it harder for a parent to feel in command, even in his own family. All of these changes —and in many families the effects of divorce—have meant shifts in the "political alignments" of the family. These shifts at their best involve a more "participatory" style and a greater democracy within the family, and often greater assertiveness for girls and women; at their worst they cast children in the role of "little adults" and in burdening them inappropriately have the potential to make them feel less in control rather than more.

It is not easy to arrive at a more "participatory," democratic style and still be authoritative as a parent—acting as comforter, guide, and disciplinarian. But bringing together the authoritative and the democratic is a foundation for a sense of empowerment outside the family as well as within it. It is particularly valuable as an antidote to those aspects of the society that tend to make the individual feel dwarfed and out of control.

The way Mary and Bob raised their boys can be compared with characteristics that have been used to describe the rearing of the so-called "invulnerable child." This concept, which is something of a misnomer, was formulated to describe children who despite sometimes severe adversity within their family—a physically ill or psychotic parent, for instance—continue to thrive, and more than thrive. The term is in no way meant to suggest a superhuman immunity to anxiety, but rather the ability to live productively despite it. Characteristics of the "invulnerable child" have been found to include a confident and trusting relationship with at least one parent; knowledge about and a critical understanding of the problems in his family; and a competent, flexible approach to the world calling sometimes for "defensive" and sometimes for "offensive" coping skills. These strengths make it possible for the invulnerable child to rise to the challenge of even a very difficult situation and find a way to master it. There is risk involved in doing so but he can meet the challenge. One might say that the invulnerable child finds a way of being more than just a "survival artist" in his own—very difficult—situation.

The parent or other care-giver on whom he can rely is apt to be "not less protective, but less anxious than average parents and more likely to leave matters to the child himself even to the extent of taxing his immaturity." [13] They are less possessive and more likely to foster autonomy, but this "fostering of autonomy is based on a realistic appreciation of what the child can do when extended and in no way constitutes an excuse to shed parental responsibility." His flexible coping skills, the autonomy he has been given, and his capacity to take risks mean that the "invulnerable" is apt to be something of a nonconformist and creative in his approaches to problems— "and there should be evidence to indicate that authoritarian parents are less prone to generate invulnerability." A characteristic that is emphatically not associated with invulnerability is overprotection.

Clearly, the characteristics of the "invulnerable child" could be said to be much the same as those one might use to describe a person who feels empowered; that is, someone who looks on the world with a sufficient degree of basic trust and hopefulness, who has relevant knowledge and a critical understanding of his situation, who feels that he is not helpless, and who, because he does not feel helpless, can tolerate a considerable degree of anxiety.

The concept of the "invulnerable" child provides us with a metaphor, if not a model, for a way to raise our children (and ourselves) in a world that includes the "psychotic parent" of nuclear weapons and the arms race. (Suggesting this analogy does not, of course, imply that a child's fears of "big world" issues, including the fear of nuclear war, put him in the intensely taxing situation he would be in if a parent were psychotic, severely ill physically, or dying. Clearly this is not so.) It holds out a new model of strength, a new model of "invulnerability" in a world from which the old model of invulnerability has disappeared. It speaks of strength that does not depend on silence and argues that children can respond creatively and with resilience to even the most difficult situations. And it suggests that although some of their ability to do so reflects their innate psychological and physical endowment, much of it can be fostered by those who love and care for them.

Clearly, as a psychological concept, the "invulnerable" child is not necessarily associated with political activism, although it speaks of a person who in the most basic and best sense is active on his own behalf. But by extension it can be seen as a foundation or a stance in relation to the world and one that can be a guide and inspiration for parents as they seek new ways to protect children in a world where an earlier illusion of protection is no longer possible. It can appeal to the growing number of parents who are concerned about the impact of big-world issues on their children—a group that is far larger than the relatively small number who have the time, interest, or energy to be politically active, let alone as intensely as the O'Briens.

If I seem to heap yet another burden on the backs of already overburdened parents and on children already pressured toward "pseudoadulthood," I plead that what I suggest is liberating as well as demanding. Bob O'Brien had an opportunity to enjoy his children more fully than many men traditionally have had. Mary had time to pursue interests and assert her convictions in a way that in the past has been possible only for the most privileged women. Josh and Zeke thought about the "big world," and often were concerned about its fate and their own, but they had enormous fun too. Zeke went to every football game at the University of Oregon in the autumn of 1984—Bob staked him to the first and Zeke and his friends collected enough bottles and cans littering the stadium after the game to pay for the next and the next.

And, after all, we are talking about power, not just the management of anxiety—parents' power to help children and the power of children to help themselves. Ultimately, when this power and the competence and capacity for responsibility from which it springs are extended beyond the home, we are talking about the power of individuals to make a contribution to resolving the issues of the day.

But I also plead that parents need support. The shift in the "balance of power" among institutions, and the increasingly global nature of the world we live in, is changing the nature of the relationship between the individual and the "big world," and the family and the "big world." The fact that the individual can feel dwarfed, and attempt to fight a feeling of helplessness with the strategy of the "survival artist," is a potential threat to democratic process. Paradoxical as it may sound, one of the best defenses against this danger lies within the intimate, small world of family life, where individual parents can model a message about response and responsibility, about taking risks and having a voice. This message, communicated within the family, has become more important rather than less; it is closely connected with the preservation of freedom. But it is a hard message for parents to convey if they feel alone and beset, economically or emotionally, as many do. Often they need support in many areas of their lives, and their sense of being supported or having access to support is important to their ability to give their children a sense of empowerment. To express their convictions about "big world" issues—breaking silence—most parents need some support that supplements their own resources. This may take the form of membership in some kind of political group, the more local the better. If they are religious it may be the support of their church. This is what Patrice Centore wanted and deserved. Or it may be the support of other parents—which was what the authors of *Watermelons Not War* gave each other and eventually encouraged in their community. For some, the support of their own parents can be important. Perhaps, above all, parents need the support of schools, especially when it comes to communicating relevant knowledge and critical understanding about current issues to children. The O'Briens were in a position to provide their children with a great deal of knowledge and understanding about issues in their community and the world. This is not possible for most parents, but they can demand that these be provided by schools and the media.

KNOWING AND FEELING:
NUCLEAR-AGE EDUCATION

SEARCHING FOR NEW "MODES OF THINKING"

Late in 1982 a small group of Milwaukee citizens began meeting with members of the city's Board of School Directors. It was time, they urged, that peace studies became part of the school curriculum. In April 1983, as a result of these conversations, the Board of School Directors passed a resolution mandating that peace studies be included in the curriculum at every level of the city's schools, kindergarten through high school.

The next step was the appointment of a task force drawn from the community members to set guidelines for developing a peace-studies curriculum. The composition of the task force reflected the gamut of political opinion—as was only wise, given the heated nature of the hearings preceding the vote on the resolution. The chairmen of the task force were Rose Daitsman, a professor of engineering and a member of the local chapter of Educators for Responsibility—a group concerned with educating young people for the nuclear age—and John Kwapisz, an attorney known to the community for his conservative views, "almost to the right of peace through strength," as one member of the task force put it. By January 1984 the task force had completed its work, and by May of that year the Board of School Directors had accepted the proposed guidelines. Teachers were now assigned to develop the curriculum itself, which was seen as essentially part of the social-studies program. Their work was completed by the fall of 1984. In the spring of 1985 the new curriculum began to be taught in the Milwaukee public schools.

Thus within one of the most conservative institutions, the schools, one community began to break silence with its young people about issues of peace and war in the nuclear age. Breaking silence about the nuclear issue in the schools is a political act, and one that most educators have approached cautiously, if at all, as a glimpse at coverage of the nuclear issue in high-school textbooks over the last several decades suggests.[1] Hiroshima and Nagasaki have been mentioned in American history textbooks for high school and junior high ever since the late Forties, usually on the last page of the chapter covering World War II. However, most texts mention the dropping of the bomb without or almost without the information or analysis that would give a young person a hint of the magnitude of the events alluded to. (And most find the arms race too political a subject to allude to at all.)

Typical is this bland report from a 1959 textbook: "Then in August, 1945, an American flier dropped an atomic bomb on Hiroshima, a Japanese city. Three days later a second atomic bomb was dropped on Nagasaki. Both cities suffered terrible destruction."[2]

No photograph of Hiroshima, no effort to explain what made the atomic bomb different from any previous weapon, no discussion of President Truman's decision to drop the bomb. Such a statement is not simply the result of the compression necessary in preparing a comprehensive text for a youthful audience (the same book devotes several pages to a description of the Cold War). It has far more to do with the necessity perceived by the authors of textbooks—and often more importantly by their publishers—to produce what Frances Fitzgerald has called "essentially nationalistic histories . . . written not to explore but to instruct—to tell children what their elders want them to know about their country. This information is not necessarily what anyone considers the truth of things. Like time capsules, the texts contain the truths selected for posterity."[3]

The time-capsule truths of the Fifties—the fear of communism, the image of the United States as "the greatest nation in the world and the embodiment of democracy, freedom, and technological progress," could not be reconciled with an image of annihilation or with the moral questions raised by nuclear weapons. The solution was not to leave them out entirely—to make them a complete nonsubject—but for the most part to associate the bomb with prowess and progress. If some mention of its annihilating power was included along with the moral issues this power raises, it was done in such a general or oblique way that the reader, especially a young reader lacking sufficient background, would have no informed way to think about what was alluded to.

An example of the "prowess" approach, from a text directed at less able students, is a brief paragraph on the development of the bomb which the editors boxed off from the main body of the text under the heading "The Men Who Made the A-Bomb." After several sentences to the effect that by 1939 it was known that it was feasible to make the bomb, and a sentence saying that certain of the scientists who worked on the bomb had fled Nazi Germany, the text reads:

> They [the scientists] feared that Hitler might learn the secret and build an atomic bomb in Germany to use against other nations. Albert Einstein, the most famous German scientist in the United States, warned President Franklin Roosevelt of this danger.
>
> Einstein was right. Hitler did try to develop an atomic bomb. However, the best German scientists were gone, and Hitler failed. But the United States did not fail. On July 16, 1945, our nation successfully tested the world's first atomic bomb. Much of this American success was due to those scientists who left Germany and Italy to come to our free nation.[4]

Casting the development of the bomb as just another American success story—with the traditional American tale of welcome to immigrants as a subplot—effectively diverts attention from the destructiveness of the weapon or from the moral issues inherent in such destructiveness.

An example of the oblique way in which the power of the weapon is described can be found in a textbook published in the early Fifties. The advent of the atomic age is described thus:

> On August 7, 1945, an American plane flew over Hiroshima and dropped an atomic bomb. This was a new kind of explosive, so powerful that one bomb could almost destroy a city. In a blinding flash of light, accompanied by a shattering explosion, Hiroshima was nearly wiped out.[5]

But a few pages later comes the next unit, entitled "The United States Today Faces a Great Challenge"—one of those catchall phrases that allow an editor to be upbeat and to organize material at the same time. However, all is not as rosy as the title suggests. One challenge (that is to say, unsolved problem, for the unsolved problems of the society are the downbeat way of describing the subject matter of this unit) turns out to be atomic energy. "Atomic Energy Raises Many Questions" a subhead says, and the passage that follows reads:

> When the United States used atomic bombs to bring the war with Japan to a quick end, few people realized the importance of the new discovery. Soon, however, men and women began to learn

about the new force. They found that atomic energy could be used for good as well as for evil. The question was how could the world make sure that atomic energy would be used only to help people.[6]

Evil? Where did that come from? Presumably it is linked with the sentence in the earlier unit that said, "This was a new kind of explosive, so powerful that one bomb could almost destroy a city." But the connection is not made, let alone expanded upon.

The authors go on to describe the founding of the Atomic Energy Commission in 1946 and to portray the development of peaceful uses for atomic energy. The first disagreements with the Soviets over nuclear weapons are then noted, and the United States is portrayed as entirely reasonable and the Soviet Union as unreasonable. The section on atomic energy ends with these pious generalities:

> The question of atomic energy is still a number one problem [N.B. a problem now, not a challenge]. The American people are well aware of the need for success in controlling this tremendous force. All share the task of finding an answer to this and other questions. How well we accept this responsibility may determine the future of our nation and of the world.[7]

Future of our nation? Future of the world? What is the student to make of these statements, especially if the word "evil," so old-fashioned in its absoluteness, still echoes in his mind? His most likely conclusion is that this is a subject that makes adults very anxious but one they don't really want to talk about or help him understand. What is his teacher to make of these statements? A quite likely conclusion, although probably made unconsciously, is that he can evade doing anything about them at all because they are general enough to slip by without eliciting much in the way of questions from students.

It would, of course, be incorrect to imply that texts such as those quoted were the sum total of what students learned about the atomic age over a thirty-five-year period. Individual science, English, and social-studies teachers taught their students about the splitting and harnessing of the atom or assigned books such as John Hersey's *Hiroshima* and Nevil Shute's *On the Beach*. But they did so against the background of the standard set by the textbooks, which reflected what the mainstream of the society was willing to tell—or not tell—its children about the bomb. Yet, as Frances Fitzgerald has noted, in textbooks the truth is from time to time rewritten, and in the twentieth century this happens at shorter and shorter intervals. Over the last twenty years social-studies texts have had to take account of the civil-rights movement, environmental problems, the Vietnam war— all stories hard to tell with the idea in mind "that the United States was a pure, high-minded nation and a model of virtue among sinners"[8]—an idea Fitzgerald finds present in the textbooks of the Fifties and traces back through American history to the Protestant notion of an elect people.

Much more slowly and tentatively, what was said in at least a few textbooks about Hiroshima began to change too. A relatively sophisticated text published in 1971 included this sentence: "Many persons have wondered whether it was really necessary to drop a first and then even a second atomic bomb on Japan. Certainly the decision to use this weapon was among the major tragedies of history."[9]

A text published in 1979 is at least as marked a contrast with accounts of the Fifties:

> On August 6, a lone Air Corps bomber flew over the industrial city of Hiroshima and dropped a single atomic bomb. . . . Truman and his advisors never doubted that the atomic bomb should be used. In their minds, that was the whole point of making the weapon. And by bringing the war to an end, the use of the bomb may well have prevented a million American casualties. Yet a later generation would question the decision to use the bomb. Some scientists who worked on the bomb had recommended that the first one be exploded far from a populated area in the presence of Japanese observers to demonstrate the bomb's power. Whatever the wisdom of the final decision, the use of the bomb not only ended World War II but ushered in the Atomic Age.[10]

Compared with the tidbits of narrative in earlier textbooks, or passing mentions of evil and generalized allusions to threats to the future, this is a far fuller statement. It is much more difficult for a teacher to skate over such material and, in fact, the teacher's edition of this text includes a suggestion that he or she hold a classroom debate about the decision to drop the bomb. It suggests a changing public consciousness and consequently a modification in the truth that the society selects for its children—a changing consciousness that was reflected a few years later in the Milwaukee Board of School Directors' vote to make peace studies part of the curriculum for the city's children.

*   *   *

"Someday," Dara Peterson said, "there will be a course for all the things that people don't want to talk about." As a result of gradual changes in consciousness small groups of people, mostly teachers but in some cases physicians or other professionals making presentations in the schools, have been working in the last several years to make "someday" now.

We have indirectly witnessed their efforts in this book through the essays of students or their letters to President Reagan, all assigned or encouraged as homework or class projects. All of these letters, essays, and the teaching that accompanied them were considered "nuclear-age education" or "peace education" by the teachers who assigned them.

The relationship of nuclear-age education to the more general term "peace education" can be understood in terms of short- and long-term goals: "Education faces a dual task: a short-term one of marshaling all available forces to turn the present situation around [the escalation of the arms race], and a long-range, permanent task of forming those structures of consciousness and of society that alone can make possible a just and sustainable peace."[11] Peace education, the "long range," is more concerned with promoting the acceptance of social justice and nonviolent resolution of conflict not only as ideals but as practical necessities in an interdependent world. In a less clearly definable but in the long run important sense it also promotes the imagining of a peaceful world—a sort of counterimage to the socialization for violence provided by much of the culture. Nuclear-age education, the "short range," provides information about nuclear weapons and the arms race and tries to equip the student to think about the complex issues they raise.

This chapter for the most part discusses nuclear-age education, but the two are not entirely separable. A teacher may pursue both goals within the same course, feeling that one cannot be thought of without the other. In the case of a curriculum for a school or school district, such as that developed in Milwaukee, the emphasis may vary depending on the age of the student. A peace-education component emphasizing the importance of resolving interpersonal conflicts peacefully is used with younger children without any specific reference to the nuclear issue, whereas junior-high students may begin to learn about nuclear weapons and the arms race.

The group most prominently identified with the advocacy of

nuclear-age education in the schools is Educators for Social Responsibility. ESR was founded by Roberta Snow, a masterful teacher and teacher of teachers. She is a dark-haired, dark-eyed woman in her later thirties with a manner that mixes informality, charismatic intensity as a public speaker, and an engaging ability to question and doubt herself. Snow started ESR in the spring of 1981—"I started small with two friends; I sent out the newsletter from my living room." The organization that fit in her living room in 1981 had 105 chapters in thirty-five states and eight thousand members by the summer of 1985. It had published six curricula which in all had sold nearly ten thousand copies. Through workshops for teachers conducted by the national organization, and through the efforts of local chapters, ESR has reached many thousands of teachers.

Despite its success, ESR has had something of an identity struggle. Is it an advocacy organization educating its membership of teachers? Or is its purpose the education of young people? In the latter case, given the prohibition of specific political views in the classroom, there is no way it can also have a role as an advocacy group. At its inception it was much more nearly an advocacy group, and as it has evolved it is, at the national level at least, much more nearly an educational group.

But for all its considerable reach, ESR certainly does not define the extent of nuclear-age teaching. Every major antinuclear organization, SANE, Physicians for Social Responsibility, the Union of Concerned Scientists, to name only a few of the most established, as well as organizations for which the nuclear issue is one item on an agenda, such as the United Nations and numerous churches—prepares materials that are available to schools. At the same time, a variety of recent policy decisions by educational organizations favors nuclear-age education. In 1982 the National Association of Independent Schools made it a priority. Within the public schools at the local level such education is beginning to be suggested or required. School boards in San Francisco, Baltimore, and Los Angeles, as well as Milwaukee, have passed resolutions calling for nuclear-age education. At the state level Oregon passed a bill (later vetoed) calling for the preparation of peace-education materials to be made available to local schools; California legislated a recently completed statewide study of the question. Perhaps the best proof of the increasingly mainstream nature of interest in the subject was a vote in 1984 by the National Congress of Parents and Teachers (the national PTA organization) at their annual convention in favor of the preparation of nuclear-age curricular materials. This was followed at the 1985 annual meeting by a second resolution in favor of the education of parents.

To a degree, nuclear-age education is a response to a "felt need" on the part of students. Roberta Snow's experience is instructive in this respect. Before she started ESR, Snow was involved in the development of curriculum materials for an organization called the Facing History and Ourselves National Foundation. Federally funded in the mid-Seventies to develop curricula and train teachers for the teaching of controversial issues, the foundation began by formulating a curriculum that examined issues associated with genocide in the twentieth century. This curriculum, first taught in 1977, has been revised and validated as a national model by the United States Department of Education. During the school year of 1984–1985 it was adopted in full in two hundred and fifty schools in Canada and the United States and less completely in many more schools. More than twelve thousand teachers have an ongoing association with the program. It has been particularly sought after by school systems in communities where there is considerable ethnic or racial conflict. The curriculum and the teaching approach help the student to think critically about issues that are usually kept a secret in history texts and in the classroom—"the things people don't want to think about" —that is, the eruption of unmatched destructiveness and violence in the twentieth century. Moreover, the curriculum encourages students to "apply the lessons of history to themselves and the future." [12] In this respect it fosters ethical scrutiny of the public as well as the private sphere in a way that is exceptional in the classroom.

Genocide itself is not the only subject of the curriculum; among others, the role of propaganda and the image of the enemy are discussed. The social responsibility of the citizen is also a prominent theme of the course. In its content and in the teaching techniques the content calls for, the Facing History and Ourselves curriculum is a precursor of nuclear-age education.

In classrooms where the curriculum was being taught early in the Eighties, Snow heard the subject of nuclear weapons come up again and again, although they were not mentioned in the materials that were part of the course. "The last chapter of the curriculum," she said, "was 'Facing Today and Tomorrow.' We didn't mention nuclear weapons, but the kids started talking about them. Of course, that was a logical step for them: okay, there's the Holocaust, but there's this. But I pretty much ignored what they said. I'd let them talk, but I knew nothing about it. Then I got involved in a letter-

writing project to the Soviet Union, truthfully for financial reasons—
someone was going to pay my salary. We wanted to offer kids some
projects to be part of, some way of being active. But as I got involved,
I realized the depth of their fear of the stereotyped Soviet Union.
Kids would just talk about nuclear war and dying and their brothers
dying. Everywhere I went—rich, poor, it didn't matter, seventh
grade, ninth grade—everywhere there was such an outpouring of
fear and pain, I was blown away. I couldn't understand where they
got it from—how they knew about it. At that time there was nothing
on TV, no articles. I barely knew about nuclear weapons. And they
asked alot of questions I couldn't answer. We stopped the letter-
writing project because I panicked, and we started working on materials for raising these issues in the classroom."

The design as well as the subject matter of the Facing History
and Ourselves curriculum created an intellectual and emotional setting in which the silence that usually prevails between the generations about the nuclear issue could be broken. And Snow was able
to "hear" what the students were asking.

In time she revived the letter-writing project, but kids had
more questions. "Is there anything we can do?" they asked. Their
questions hammered at Snow's defenses. "Being a hopeful person, I
said, 'Of course, there's things you can do. Learn more about it.' Then
I started thinking, is there anything we can do? I finally let that in."

It was at this point that she started ESR.

The impulse for the local chapter in Paradise, California, was
a similar response to young people. Jim Umenhofer, one of the
founders of the Paradise chapter, was running a group home for
hard-to-place foster children with his wife, Gloria, and two friends in
1981. One of the children in their care told him that he was very
scared of nuclear war. At first Jim tried to downplay his fears. "Come
on, I told him," Jim recalled, "you sleep all right at night." But the
child told him, "No, we're all scared." The nuclear issue had been on
Jim's mind for some time: "I remember thinking when the Vietnam
war was winding down, well, now we can get to coping with the
nuclear thing." But it was this conversation with a child that galva-
nized him. He and Gloria had read about ESR and they sent away for
information.

However, nuclear-age education is not only a response to
young people. To a far greater extent it is an assertion by adults—at
least some adults—of what they believe young people need to know
for their own and the world's survival. This is the significance of the
acceptance of a peace-studies unit by a school system such as Mil-

waukee's. Despite resistance to thinking about the issue, an increasingly large segment of the public is moving toward entering the debate about nuclear weapons, and this shift, as already suggested, is beginning to be reflected in the schools. As a rule, what adults want children to learn in school is what they themselves are willing to recognize publicly as important to the society. What the public is beginning to want for young people with respect to the nuclear issue is no more than what they are beginning to want for themselves— the information and the critical ability to participate in decisions that they feel have not been solved by those in power in the society.[13] A small but significant body of people do not want to go on being "survival artists"; nor do they want their children educated as "survival artists."

What does nuclear-age education consist of? The best way to begin to answer this question is to point to the unprecedented situation in which the possibility of manmade annihilation puts the teacher (as well as everybody else).

Although everybody hates nuclear weapons they cannot be uninvented. From a teacher's point of view this means there are no easy answers, indeed, scarcely any answers; the teacher is thus deprived of the authority based on being the one "who has the answers" that is assumed to go with his or her role.

In this respect Roberta Snow contrasted the nuclear issue with other complex issues. "If you think about teaching about Central America right now, it's very complex. There are different perspectives and different people feel different things about it; there's a report that says this and counterreports that say that. But there is still some system to fit it into—you can fit it into the fact that this country is a democracy and people should choose. You can talk about options. You can say, 'If we got out of El Salvador and Nicaragua, the people would decide, and the Soviet Union wouldn't be there either, and so it would be okay.' There's an 'if.' But with nuclear weapons I've never heard anybody say 'If we did this and this and this, it would be fine.' There's always, 'Well, we'll always have them, the third world will have them, there's Qaddafi . . .' There's never a completion. So that it's very hard to enter into it, because there is no sense that you can ever solve it; it's not a solvable issue. And the way we teach is solvable issues—but here we are, we've come up with the biggest one that is not solvable, there's no answer to it. Scientists and politicians and everybody agree that it will never be

safe, we will always live in nuclear dread, period. I think the acceptance of that is so difficult and so painful that we really don't want to
let it in on some level.

"So what we're really saying is that there's this new category:
'even though.' Even though it will never be safe, we still need to
enter into the debate. We still need to find ways to solve the situation
as a crisis."

Nuclear weapons raise the specter of man's capacity for un-
bounded evil toward his fellow man, just as the Nazi holocaust and
the other genocides of the twentieth century do; little in the prog-
ress-minded, entirely secular culture of the public school enables a
teacher to handle such an issue. (In this sense, for all its difficulties,
the issue is easier to teach within a school with a religious orientation, because it is acceptable to take an explicit moral stand in relation to a public issue.) At the same time, as I have said, just to raise
the issue of nuclear weapons is a political act. The teacher is limited
in the position he or she can take for fear of eliciting accusations of
bias or indoctrination.

Finally, for most teachers the imparting of knowledge is a
hopeful act, but in the case of nuclear weapons and the arms race
knowledge is easily associated in a quite opposite way with helplessness and hopelessness. In this regard Robert Jay Lifton has written:

> We are accustomed to teaching as a form of transmitting and possi-
> bly recasting knowledge. And in the service of that we form various
> narratives and interpretations of that information. But we have no
> experience teaching a narrative of potential extinction of ourselves
> as teachers and students, of our universities and schools, of our
> libraries and laboratories." [14]

Given the overwhelming difficulty of such a narrative and its
political overtones, the easiest approach is to keep silent, not to tell
it at all, or as scantily as possible. As discussed earlier, there is considerable social pressure to do just this, pressure which the schools
are particularly sensitive to. Now, however, as a number of teachers
break silence, they must, given the difficulties of the issue, find a new
stance in relation to the subject matter and to the student. Tony
Wagner, the former executive director of ESR, has described the
search for this new position in terms of a search for those "new
modes of thinking which Einstein implied we had to find when he
said that 'The splitting of the atom has changed everything save our
modes of thinking.'

"We don't even have a language to describe what we're trying to do," Wagner continued. "We need a language that describes a kind of thinking that is both tough-minded and moral, tough-minded and open-hearted. Peace education sounds mushy and softhearted and something only liberals can be interested in. Conflict resolution sounds much too technical and limited and value-free."

Nuclear-age education is still trying to define itself, searching for a mode of thinking that is equal to the times. On occasion it has been simplistic and propagandistic but at its best it brings together elements that meet the criteria of tough-mindedness and open-heartedness: one element is an attempt to provide students with information about the destructiveness of nuclear weapons, the arms race and its historical setting; another is the development of critical thinking; a third is the fostering of a capacity for empathy; a fourth is the encouragement of an active, participatory style of learning that builds a sense of empowerment. It is very much to the point that three out of four of these elements concern the "how," not the "what," of teaching; the complexity of the content and its emotional and political payload necessitate a search for innovative approaches to teaching.

IMAGES OF ANNIHILATION

The young people who worked at the newspaper *New Youth Connections* had asked for a factual presentation about nuclear weapons and the arms race to accompany Maya Gillingham's *Changing the Silence* workshop. Ernest Drucker, a psychologist, and Tom Roderick, a teacher, were invited to make this presentation. After an introduction conducted by Maya and Jody, Drucker began his presentation by flipping on a slide projector and clicking the cartridge forward to a slide of the first explosion of an atomic bomb in the New Mexico desert near Alamogordo on July 16, 1945. While the picture was on the screen Drucker spoke first about his own memories; when he was growing up in the fifties, he said, you saw pictures of atom bombs and hydrogen bombs and mushroom clouds, but what these weapons were and what they did was never really discussed. In contrast, he felt that the group had invited him to tell them what was known about them; he implied that he wanted to help make their youth different from his own with respect to nuclear knowledge. He quoted Einstein's "modes of thinking" remark and went on to point out that the "everything" that has changed is the power available from the unleashing of the atom. He explained Einstein's formula, $E = MC^2$, and then came back to the slide on the screen. "What is the unit of destruction we're talking about?" he asked, then clicked the first slide out and clicked the next one into view—a diagrammatic presentation of the effects of the explosion of an atomic bomb—the blast, thermal effects, radiation. As he described these, he clicked on slides that in one way or another had to do with Hiroshima—the devastated city itself, the shadow cast by a person on stone during the explosion, a woman's back with the plaid pattern of her kimono seared on her flesh—and then more and more excruciating images of the victims themselves.

"One of the reasons I care," he concluded, "is that this means death, not just my death, but the death of all the generations hereafter. It can take away the future, and that's something we never had to think about before. People have had to survive terrible things. Half of Europe died in the plague. But this is something different."

Drucker's presentation was drawn from materials put together by the physicians' antinuclear organization, Physicians for Social Responsibility. Similar presentations draw on materials disseminated by a dozen or more activist organizations or by educational groups, or put together by individual teachers out of their own researches. At the core of the great majority of these presentations is information about the weapons and their development and images on slides or on film of the mushroom cloud and the fireball and the victims of the Hiroshima and Nagasaki bombings.

Lifton has written that Hiroshima is "our text," in the sense that it brought into the world "an image of extinguishing ourselves as a species by our own hand, and with our own technology." [15] Ever since the Fifties antinuclear activists have made this text their own, bringing information about and images of Hiroshima and Nagasaki to their audiences. They insist that however terrifying, or, in the case of images of victims, however unbearable, this information, these images must become part of our consciousness if they are not already. They are an essential part of our history, and it is at its own peril that a generation fails in remembering and "digesting" experience of the previous generation when such experience is a key to survival. This belief is the most basic premise of nuclear-age education.

However, conveying such anxiety-creating material, with its message of the possibility of futurelessness, raises many pedagogical questions—and deeply personal questions for teachers. Does it frighten more than it instructs? Does it contribute to feelings of helplessness that students may already have? Do they have any course other than to numb themselves self-protectively—rather than developing the active concern for the issue which the presenters of the material seek? Does such material encourage "survival artists" more than "activists?" Once again, the context of presentation, the "how" of teaching, is important.

Two interrelated factors are critical: the opportunities afforded for students to process the feelings that the content arouses, and their empowerment to think about the issues raised. When students are not given an opportunity to express what they feel and to reflect on those feelings, they are in effect left alone, "abandoned" with their feelings, and this in miniature repeats the abandonment they may feel—unconsciously if not consciously—in relation to adult failure to curb the arms race. They are not "heard," and not being heard will contribute to feelings that they have no voice, that is, to feelings of powerlessness and voicelessness they may have, not only in relation to "big world" issues, but to adults in general. Cynicism, apathy, anger and, above all, a sense of helplessness can be the result. Moreover, when students are not given enough information or a sufficient analytical approach for thinking about the issues raised by nuclear weapons and the arms race, they are put in a position where they cannot help but feel even more powerless than they may already have felt.

Presentations by activists, as well as more traditionally conceived teaching, can fail to provide opportunities for processing feeling or a foundation for thinking about issues. In reaction to the public silence that always tends to envelop the nuclear issue, and out of anger at the upward spiral of the arms race, many activists—teachers, writers, film makers—have in recent years assaulted their audience with images and information pertaining to annihilation.[16] Nearly overwhelmed themselves by the horror of a "narrative of potential extinction," they more or less abandon attempts at providing context or analysis and give the audience nothing but grisly facts, grisly images, in order to increase political and emotional impact. Their aim is to arouse concern and raise consciousness. (Often, too, the justification for skimpy or absent context is the need for brief presentations.) But when nothing mediates the message of images and information there is a risk that the audience, "freaked out," will take refuge in the protective self-numbing the presenter would most like to change. At the same time, deprived of sufficient historical or moral context (should Truman have decided to drop the bomb? What were his alternatives? What would have been the consequences of not dropping it?), the audience is given little to enable it to think about what is presented, although thought, as well as emotion, is presumably what those presenting the images wish to elicit. Without sufficient context, images and information take on the quality of propaganda, although this would be a dirty word to most of the purveyors of such information to young people. (Again, I am not advocating the whitewashing of bad news. The bad news of the narrative of potential extinction is what people need to know; but they cannot know it in an actively concerned way if they feel assaulted and if they are not given information and strategies for analyzing the issues raised.)

One particular presentation to fifth- and sixth-graders about environmental issues, as well as issues of war and peace, is an example of these deficiencies.

One winter morning I accompanied Martie Harris, a peace activist, on a visit to an elementary school in a tiny Connecticut town that still had a country air to it. A red-brick building housed the school. Next door was an old shed, once a barn; in the yard to the other side of the school was a canoe upturned on sawhorses for the winter. Within, the building was sunny. The walls of the high-ceilinged rooms were painted a cheerful yellow. We entered the sixth-grade classroom. The small class was friendly and well-mannered. Each had a tiny Santa sitting on the corner of his or her desk. We waited for the fifth grade to join us.

A large collage made by the students of the "natural and man-made wonders of the world" decorated the bulletin board. A French château, the inside of a space vehicle, and a refrigerator were among the man-made wonders; a profusion of flowers and animals among the natural. A computer stood in the corner of the room. Above the blackboard, just below the ceiling, ran a frieze of the alphabet—big *A*, little *a*, and so on—in a cursive style. Beside the blackboard was a sign entitled "Our Rules," reading:

1. Walk.
2. Don't interrupt when someone is talking.
3. Do keep the volume down.
4. Do let people work.
5. Keep your hands and feet to yourself.

The fifth grade arrived and took their places. Martie Harris began her presentation. "We're going to talk about the future," she said, "the kind of future you'd like to have and the things that make it hard to get there." She asked the class what might be the obstacles to reaching the future they wanted.

"Nuclear war," volunteered a plump girl in a blue turtleneck.

"Pollution," others said, and "garbage."

"Very dangerous chemicals, that we're not even sure what to do with," Martie added. Despite the "wonderful things" that come from our technology, she said, "we don't even know all the harmful things that come from it. Our minds and our technology are getting away from us and we have to learn to take care of this." Martie then presented a slide show that began with a bumper-to-bumper scene on a highway, a NO GAS sign at a gas station, views of a public dump featuring mountains of plastic containers, and higher mountains of crushed cars. The next image was of flowers decorating a veteran's grave, a smog pall over an urban landscape, and a cake-mix display. Then an obese man carrying a surf board, books on how to lose weight, a policeman grappling with a black man, a soldier silhouetted with a bayonet, battle scenes, then missiles, sleek and ominous, then missiles taking off; finally, the globe seen from space and shots of children of different races. Throughout, the sound track chanted, "It's a closed system," occasionally interrupted with remarks such as "Don't be old-fashioned, people should be able to do anything they want," and "We keep building garbage cans while hungry people die."

When the slide show was over, Harris asked the group what they thought it meant. "How the world's gotten worse," said the plump girl in the blue turtleneck. Harris asked whether anyone knew what a "closed system" meant. Another girl proposed that it meant "We don't have choices," suggesting that what she had taken in was a message of powerlessness. Harris explained that a closed system meant that we can't live without our planet. Then she asked them how they would like to see the future. "No wars," said a small blond boy. "No people fighting against each other," said another small blond boy. Harris turned the discussion to the subject of violence. "What do kids do when they get angry?" she asked. "They hit," came an answer. "What do grownups do when they get angry?" "They holler." Harris said a few words about resolving conflict without fighting. Then she went on, "What do our governments do when they get mad?" "They figure out ways of hurting each other," a girl said. Harris asked if anyone had seen *The Day After,* which had been shown several weeks earlier. Most had, some had not. The fifth-grade teacher who had accompanied his students said that he had felt "confused" by the *Nightline* panel discussion following the program. One child said she had seen "just the ad they had for the movie and it got me scared." Harris told the class about the nuclear fears she had had as a child, which had been made very concrete for her by the dog tag she had been made to wear around her neck.

"My uncle was in Vietnam," a girl said, "and he told me it was terrible."

Once again the plump girl in the blue turtleneck spoke. "We're building bombs to kill the whole planet," she said.

Harris asked what alternative we had. "You don't make any more bombs, we won't"; "We have such good bombs we don't need many"; "We should talk it out," the answers came. But how do Americans feel about the Russians? Harris asked. "They're threatening us"; "They're doing terrible things"; "We're doing the same thing they're doing and they can't understand," various children volunteered.

At this point time was getting short. Harris suggested that the way the class could help the situation was to exchange artwork with students in the Soviet Union and to try to find Soviet pen pals. Then she added, "You can do a better job in lots of ways than adults, because you don't have the fears adults do."

She ended the presentation with another slide show that opened with a view of the planet shown from space. The sound track proclaimed that, seen from space, the planet has no political boundaries ("no frames, no boundaries" was the precise phrase used). There followed a capsule sketch of the development of weapons, leading up to pictures of the explosion of the atomic bomb. After this came pictures of maps showing national boundaries, with the soundtrack's caution that fifty thousand nuclear weapons defended these boundaries. The final shot was again the globe seen from space, with the reiteration that seen from space the boundaries are "not really there at all."

A few seconds after the slide show ended the bell rang.

For their homework after Harris's presentation the sixth-grade teacher asked her class to write compositions describing their vision of what they wanted for the future. It was from this group of essays that the selections in an earlier section, "A Sense of Power-lessness," were chosen. Although certain members of the class wrote happy visions of private contentment in a consumer paradise, a number portrayed science-fiction visions with a survivalist and escapist feeling to them, suggesting an implicit feeling of helplessness and powerlessness. I have wondered if Harris's presentation did not reinforce these feelings.

In any case, there was almost nothing in her presentation—in the slide shows in particular—to counteract any feelings of despair or pessimism she aroused. Nor did she make any attempt to help her audience process their feelings. Moreover, in my view she did not help them think productively about the issues raised. The first slide show demonstrated, as the girl in the blue turtleneck very accurately put it, "that things had gotten worse," but it provided a minimum of facts or analysis that might begin to help young people lay the groundwork for a critical understanding of either the environmental or nuclear situation. In the second slide show, the "analysis," such as it was (the remark that national boundaries "were not really there at all"), was seriously misleading—granted, in the interest of promoting a global viewpoint. Moreover, in suggesting that students could do a better job than adults of breaking through the impasse with the Soviets "in lots of ways," Harris laid a large burden on their shoulders, implying her own underlying sense of helplessness and a consequent tendency to reverse roles with them.

I believe that brief presentations such as Harris's (or the one-day workshop format that has been a frequent approach in many schools in the last few years) make it almost impossible for students to process what they feel, especially if the material is presented in simplistic or propagandistic fashion. The difficulties of such brief presentations, even when care is taken and sensitivity exercised, were suggested by the *Changing the Silence* workshop at *New Youth Connections.*

Fortunately, on that particular occasion, the way in which Maya and her colleagues conceived of their workshop provided a context for the expression of feelings—or at least some of the feelings—that were generated by Drucker's presentation and by the other issues that arose. But feelings were not aired easily and were not always explored. It will be recalled that the first remark following Drucker's presentation was "Why does anyone care?" This may have been evidence of an effort on the part of the speaker to protect himself against the images and information with which he had just been confronted, as well as of a rejection of Drucker's attempt to convince his audience of the importance of an issue that this young man did not see as his own. Whatever the young speaker intended, others responded to him in terms of why *they* cared, not in terms of what he felt.

It is pertinent, too, that only at the end of the workshop was one of the most heartfelt remarks made: "I've been here for a while, and no one seems to be very realistic. God gave us one more chance and we blew it. We have snowballed to this point. All the talk, all the singing, it's very beautiful and we can have it in our family, but we're not going to get it any other way. It's got to the point where I just live day by day, and if I can go to college and become a journalist. . . ."

There was no time within the three-hour format of the workshop to address the deep pessimism of these remarks and the sense of futurelessness they conveyed. Nor was there time to question their assumption of political impotence. It is worth noting that many presentations to young people are as brief, or briefer than, those at *New Youth Connection* and the Connecticut elementary school; nor are they structured in such a way that frank feelings and opinions can emerge.

Brief or assaulting presentations are, however, not the only way in which feelings are short-circuited. Another way is the teacher's limiting of the presentation to what one might call an "objective mode." This is particularly tempting, since it insulates the teacher from his or her own emotions—that is, from the possibility of feeling helpless or guilty in relation to his or her students. Moreover, it is a mode only too easy to fall into, since it is an aspect of the positivist, technicist outlook that is the preferred modern approach to reality —an approach that in itself facilitates the development of nuclear weapons and the arms race.

When Hannah Rabin was a high-school student at Phillips Academy in Andover, Massachusetts, *The War Game,* a BBC film about nuclear war, was a required part of an American history course. But it was shown without any accompanying discussion. "The auditorium emptied out at the end of the film, pretty much," Hannah recalled, "but there was still a group of kids sitting there crying."

I asked Hannah about the lack of discussion.

"I think it was very wrong," she replied, "because the only way for each individual to deal with the film was to forget about it; that's the only thing anybody could expect. The doors should have been shut, a teacher or a student should have stood up and said, "Let's hear some responses to this. Let's talk about it.""

One may speculate that as long as Hannah's teacher could pretend that nuclear war was "like any other subject," he could feel quite justified in merely arranging for a showing of the film and not planning "special arrangements" for a discussion. Thus he could maintain the objective mode that helped him keep distanced from his students' feelings—and his own. He could try to have it both ways: he could break silence and yet maintain his own silence and that of the students.

Frequent discussions, frequent writing assignments, and creative work such as Maya's *Changing the Silence* are good ways for teachers to elicit student feelings. Keeping a journal is another useful device. Roberta Snow commented: "When you're talking about genocidal issues, the way we are, kids really need that support, they need the comfort of having something that they can write in, and also something where they can begin to record some of the things that don't come out in class."

Journals can be used not only for the expression of feelings but to foster critical understanding. Snow continued, "Another way we use journals is for kids to think about not only what they're learning but how they're learning. They become very sophisticated, not just with the process, but about how they get their information, what the newpapers are that they're reading, what the TV shows are that they're watching, how they are presented—really looking at what propaganda is."

This brings us to the second element of nuclear-age education: the ability to think critically, as important as a chance to process feelings if students are to handle what they learn about the nuclear issue.

CRITICAL THINKING

The principal of the South Eugene High School in Eugene, Oregon, usually plays Santa Claus at the Christmas assembly, but he was away from the school on the day of the assembly in December 1984, so Bob Veeck played the part. Veeck is a tall man in his forties, a shade overweight, just enough so that he confessed a bit of embarrassment as he pulled on the pants of a Santa Claus costume during a global-studies class he co-taught. The students had spent the period role-playing Soviets and Americans in a debate that was the culmination of a unit on Soviet–American relations. Veeck's colleague was asking the class for their opinions and feelings as a result of the debate. "The Soviets must stop saying they will try to take over the world," a young man said, as Veeck thrust his arms into the sleeves of a red tunic trimmed with white. "We should ignore problems inside Soviet society," a young woman said. "We'll never agree on internal things." "We both have to agree more on nuclear disarmament," another young man said as Veeck buckled a belt over the tunic. "A summit should not just be a media event," said another, a moment before Veeck left the room, carrying Santa's pack and tossing the class handfuls of candies from it.

A few minutes later, now bearded, he entered the gym. The whole school was assembled, its good mood made even better by the musical-chairs contest with which the assembly opened. Veeck tossed candy to the crowd, then took his place on a chair to listen to Christmas wishes. Candidates were pulled out of the crowd by their friends and forced to sit on Veeck's knee. One six-footer said he "wanted to date all the girls on the rally squad." He was applauded. A girl wished that students would be allowed to eat food in the halls. Then another tall fellow was pulled out of the crowd and shoved onto Veeck's lap. His wish was for peace on earth.

After the assembly Veeck was back in class, minus costume, teaching a semester-long elective on the arms race. This was one of the first meetings of the class, and the students—a group of some twenty young men and women, mostly juniors and seniors but including a few freshmen and sophomores—took seats at desks arranged in a rough oval. Veeck handed out a photocopied sheet. On one side was a detailed description of two Soviet missiles, the SS-17 and the SS-19. On the other side was a description of the SS-18. For the time being Veeck said nothing about the sheet and turned to the day's homework.

For that day the group had read a Soviet pamphlet entitled *Whence the Threat to Peace?* Veeck asked, "If you remember today's reading, the Soviet Union wants—what?" His blue-gray eyes engaged them sharply, almost sternly. He did not look at all like Santa Claus.

"Peace," many voices responded.

"How many of you, when you read this, said, I didn't know this, they really sound like friendly people, why don't we make peace with them?"

There were a few murmured yesses.

"How many of you thought you were reading a pack of lies, that the Soviets are out to deceive us?"

A few more affirmative murmurs.

"How many of you didn't know what you were reading?" He paused, and then, unable to resist the school-teacherly perennial—though delivered rhetorically, with an edge of humor—asked, "How many of you didn't do the reading?"

A few smirks.

"Now, I am not going to tell you," Veeck went on, "whether *Whence the Threat to Peace?* is the truth or a partial truth or a partial lie or a lie, because I don't know. My personal hope—when the author says the Russians would like to have détente, cooperation, and peaceful coexistence—my personal reaction is Yeah, let's have détente, let's be friends, let's go fishing. But I'm afraid there's a slight chance this wonderful book may be disinformation."

He paused, put down the pamphlet, and picked up a journal from the desk in front of him. "What I'm going to read you now comes from *Orbis* magazine, a journal of international affairs," he said. Reading from the journal, Veeck presented a summary of key points of Soviet military strategy as described in *Soviet Military Strategy* by Marshal V. D. Sokolovskiy. "The date of the book was 1962," Veeck said. "For whom was it written? It was written for the Russian general staff. This book is used, has been used, was used in the Soviet military as depicting Soviet strategic doctrine. What are its points? World War III must be based on the offensive capability of the Soviet Union. That's the first heading. And under this heading these are the major points. All set?"

He looked up. Pencils were poised over notebook pages.

"Nuclear missiles are the most important weapon any country may have. The enemy must be destroyed. Now who is the enemy in this case?"

"Us," voices replied.

"Now you might be tempted to say, Mr. Veeck, aren't you giving us a John Birch, conservative interpretation of Soviet strategy. But no, I am not. I'm giving you what the Soviets say, and what makes this difficult is that the Soviets have official books and they have other official books. They have *Whence the Threat to Peace?* and they have *Soviet Military Strategy.*" Veeck held up a copy of *Whence the Threat to Peace?* and of the *Orbis* article. "Is this true, or is this true?" he asked, giving first one and then the other a little shake. "Ronald Reagan would say that *Military Strategy* is true. Walter Mondale would be more likely to say *Whence the Threat to Peace?* is true. How are we to know? That's a lot of what this class is about. The easy part in this class is the sheet I gave you today. Are there SS-17 missiles? Yes, there are. What do they do? What do they carry? I can tell you that. It's pretty well known. The only lie on this paper might be the CEP, the "circular error probable," and we'll study that next week. But I can't tell you how the Soviets intend to use the SS-17, that I don't know. *Whence the Threat to Peace?* says they don't intend to use it, and the information I'm giving you from *Soviet Military Strategy* says they do intend to use it. You have to be what a democracy assumes that you are; in our system we assume that you are intelligent, that if they have data the American people are capable of analyzing that data and coming to the truth."

Veeck paused and then went back to the text he was summarizing. "Let me continue. Another major point under offensive capability is that the Soviet Union will rely on massive nuclear strikes. Maximum force is to be applied from the beginning. Finally, what is the strategic aim of World War III? The strategic aim of World War III, according to Sokolovskiy, is to thoroughly destroy the enemy. Do you have any questions about this first part of *Soviet Military Strategy?*"

A young woman asked when *Soviet Military Strategy* was written.

"1962," Veeck said.

"Is it still used?" she asked.

"Still used and still taught," he told her. I wondered whether she was simply daydreaming or whether anxiety associated with the subject matter had made it hard for her to take in what Veeck had said earlier.

A boy now asked, "Wasn't 1962 kind of around the time the Soviet Union was gaining most of its new power? They didn't have many warheads before that, did they?"

"Thank you," Veeck said, picking up on what the student had implied rather than said. "I appreciate your comments. That should be your first reaction—doubt—because it's rather grim, isn't it?"

He turned now to a discussion of the Soviet strategy of defense, which led to a long digression on the ABM treaty and the difficulty of antimissile defense. At last Veeck steered the discussion back to the direction he wished to take.

"If you had to decide which theory is more correct, the theory expressed in *Soviet Military Strategy* or *Whence the Threat to Peace?,* how would you go about it? What would you use to prove or disprove your hypothesis that the Russians are coming?"

"Past action," suggested one member of the class, a boy.

"That's good, but it's not the answer I wanted."

A girl suggested, "Instinct."

"I'm asking you not to base your judgment on instincts; instincts can be wrong," Veeck retorted. "We've been out of the jungle a long time."

"Their interest in arms control," a boy said.

"Okay," Veeck said, "that's an answer, their willingness to negotiate, but it's still not quite the one I wanted. Come on, thinking caps on, I know it's Friday, sixth period. All kinds of excitement tonight, parties, the Lambs, the 49ers, but a little brain strain never hurt anyone. I feel like a dentist about to pull a tooth."

People grinned a little sheepishly and shuffled their feet under their desks, made particularly uncomfortable by my presence and that of another visitor. Veeck was laying it on a little thick, perhaps out of frustration with himself as much as with them: he had not found a way to lead the group to ask the questions he wanted them to ask. He surveyed the room, then gave up. "How many of you want me to call on Ken and get me off your backs?"

Ken was a college student, a former student of Veeck's; he too was visiting the class today. He did in fact have the answer Veeck was looking for; he suggested the truth of the two strategies could be inferred from a study of Soviet weapons. Which strategy was supported by the weapons the Soviets were building?

Veeck asked the group to study the sheet he had handed out at the beginning of the class, turning their attention first to the SS-17 and the SS-19. He started reading aloud from the sheet, commenting as he went along: " 'These rockets were developed in competition with each other as replacement for the SS-11s.' Underline that. Now when the Russians had only SS-11s we were pretty safe. Probably the SS-11 was most dangerous to the crews who tried to load the fuel on to it. They blew up quite often. 'The SS-17 is a two-stage rocket using storable liquid propellant.' That means it's primitive. That's the reason it's so big. 'It's the first Soviet rocket in service'—now underline this—'to use the cold-launch technique.' We talked about this yesterday. The purpose of the cold launch is what?"

"Save the silo," the answer came.

"So that you can bring another missile in and fire again," Veeck said, and then went on, reaching the point he had been aiming for all along: "Now is there anything in Soviet strategy—look back at your notes very quickly—that calls for having a cold launch?"

A girl had the answer: "Maintain the capability to fight a nuclear war."

Confirming what she had said, Veeck added, "If the Soviet did not mean that, if they were just joking about having the capability to fight a nuclear war, then why are they building cold-launch rockets?"

He paused and looked around the room. Then he went on: "Does the U.S. have any cold-launch weapons? The answer is no. All of ours use a hot launch. What are we assuming when we make only hot-launch missiles?"

"It's only going to happen once," a girl said.

"And we are probably going to fire them as a second strike," Veeck continued. "So—are you all with me on this—we are making all our missiles hot-launch missiles, the assumption being that we will use the missile and the things behind the weapon once. Now, I would want to ask the Russians, If you are really interested in peace as you say you are, why are you building cold-launch weapons? You say you are for détente, cooperation, and peaceful coexistence— wonderful, comrade, then why do you want cold-launch weapons?"

Then the bell rang—but Veeck had accomplished a great part of what he wanted to for the day.

Bob Veeck was not just dispensing information to his students, although information was a necessary part of what he was giving them. He encouraged his students to think critically about what they learned. He did not allow them to rest with easy assumptions or ready conclusions. He pushed them to "complicate" their thinking—to use a word favored by Roberta Snow to describe an essential task of nuclear-age education. He prodded them to test their hypotheses in the light of the data they had at their disposal. Although he did not provide much opportunity to process feelings and did not see that as part of his role, he provided an analytical context often missing in brief or very emotional presentations.

The influence of Veeck's course on his students' thinking and feelings had not been formally evaluated at the time I visited his class, but he believed that the course not only equipped students to think about the nuclear issue but to a degree reassured them. "They don't necessarily feel empowered personally, but they feel mankind has the power not to use nuclear weapons by the end of the course," he said. "They're less afraid when they leave the class; they fear a first strike less because they understand the triad."

His impressions of student reactions to a similar course he had given the previous year were much the same. "While they see that the Soviet threat is there and has to be acknowledged," he said, "it is by no means as great as they thought before, and the knowledge brings a certain amount of security. As a matter of fact, they see the U.S. as destabilizing the world with the cruise missile and the B-1 bomber. They are much less hawkish at the end of the course. It's not just kids from well-to-do homes who feel this way, but all kids. I find concern with the problem, and with what the U.S. is doing, but also a relaxation of tension on their part. Their concern is mostly projected into the future. But they do want the problem addressed.

"And they do worry about the machinery. They don't want a set of computers to make the decision to launch, and therefore they don't want us to go to launch on warning. They honestly don't think sane leaders would launch.

"The other thing that bothered them was the possibility of nuclear winter. In one class, twenty-eight out of thirty-three students [in a two-day simulation in which the class played the president's role in an escalating conflict with the Soviets] chose not to launch in response to a Soviet first strike. Their basic reason for not striking was first that they would regard it as murder and revenge, and, second, that they did not want to risk setting off a nuclear winter. They would absorb the blow. An equal number of boys and girls felt this way, although at the beginning of the course the boys were much more hawkish than the girls. But I will admit," Veeck concluded, "that the hawks who were left were boys."

Thinking critically in the way Veeck encouraged has always been an ingredient of good teaching, not only of teaching about the nuclear issue. However, in recent years it has received a new emphasis at the high-school level. This is particularly true in the social studies, in part as a response to the complex and fast-changing nature of contemporary society—viewed nationally or internationally. Helping young people learn to make good decisions rather than telling them what is right has seemed to many educators a vital strategy, and indeed the only one possible in our times. However, it is still rare to find it applied at the high-school level to current political issues such as Soviet–American relations and nuclear weapons—yet this is what nuclear-age education at its best tries to do.

The need for critical thinking raises many problems in terms of teacher as well as student preparation, the nuclear issue aside. Many teachers do not have Bob Veeck's background or skills, and many groups of students are not as well prepared as those at South Eugene High School.

Herb Mack, an educator who is co-director of the Inquiry Demonstration Project, a program in a number of New York City high schools aimed at developing critical thinking in students, commented about these problems in relation to his program: "Although we're very much interested in process, our strong feeling has been that you can't think in a vacuum. It requires facts, and it requires a considerable amount of research in order to support whatever opinion you come to. So we're really dealing with helping students to do a lot of research and helping them come to some informed opinions. That's not an easy situation in many of the places we're working. There's a lack of information, there's a lack of background. We're not just talking about kids who haven't thought often about the issues we're interested in. We're talking about kids who don't read the newspapers except for the sports page and the horoscope and maybe Ann Landers. We're talking about kids who don't read very frequently—things that we want them to read; they read other things. What we're really facing is, how do we get them, a massive number of students who are not concerned at their core with the issues we're concerned about, to actually consider those issues and to consider them in some depth." [17]

Teachers who themselves may have had no training in the teaching of controversial issues, who may fear involvement in such teaching, and who in any case already feel overburdened often find it all they can do to "cover the material," let alone to cover it in a way that would make possible critical thinking and questioning on the part of students. Far from being simply a matter of mandating a program in a particular school system and developing curricula (not that these are simple matters), nuclear-age education calls for intensive education and support of teachers themselves. Herb Mack commented: "What we try to do is work with individual teachers in each of their classrooms, and we tend to try to develop groups of teachers within each school where we're working. We try to have teachers work with each other in developing materials. And we recognize that teachers are at different points, and that although you'd like someone to be doing a particular thing now, it may be a year or two until he or she is doing that, and there's no way to force it, there's no way to mandate it. This is very difficult when you're working closely with a board of education where the tradition is to mandate."

If the "particular thing" is the ability to encourage inquiry and critical thinking, "now" may be a good way off for many teachers; for them, conveying the content of nuclear-age education, despite its complexity and anxiety-laden nature, may be easier than giving students tools to begin to handle the issues the content raises.

THE NEED FOR EMPATHY

Although critical thinking based on sufficient information is necessary when thinking about nuclear weapons and the arms race, it can be the tool of the technicist—the person who takes no ethical stand at all, who says values are somebody else's problem—or, put another way, of the person whose values are narrowly utilitarian. Cultivating a technicist viewpoint is antithetical to the aim of nuclear-age education. Beyond the purveying of information—the achievement of a kind of "nuclear literacy"—and the encouragement of critical thinking, nuclear-age education takes an ethical stand against war in an era when war on any scale has become overwhelmingly destructive. This stand may be implicit or explicit, depending on the teacher. It was quite explicitly the motive behind Ernest Drucker's presentation at *New Youth Connections*. It was hardly evident in Bob Veeck's teaching. (In fact, Veeck dissociated himself from any peace-activist position: "I was one of the founders of ESR in Eugene," he told me, "but I withdrew because it was too unilateralist. I am not a unilateralist. I believe in a strong, sensible foreign policy." He added "A number of people think I'm giving them an easy way out, that a course in European history or international relations would be more valuable. They can't conceive of a course like mine being anything but a litany against nuclear weapons." No litany, his nuclear-weapons course nevertheless implies that war has become too serious to be left to the experts, and this in itself is an ethical message.)

There is another ethical element to nuclear-age education as well, and one that is related to its antiwar stance. Nuclear-age education encourages empathetic understanding of the point of view of others, even when those others are longstanding enemies such as the Soviets. At first glance empathy may seem a matter of the emotions, but it has ethical implications. It encourages the recognition of the other as being as valuable as you, as being as "real" as you, however different. If the other is as "real" as you are, your understanding of his needs and interests will be more extensive and subtly developed than it would be if you saw him as less "real" and possessing less value than you—if, for instance, you were master and he were slave. If he is as real to you as yourself and, as a result, your appreciation of his needs and interests is highly developed, this understanding will influence the way in which you understand his interests, interpret justice in relation to him and, more broadly, approach the settlement of conflicts between you: it will not be as easy for you to see him as an enemy. In its concern with empathy, nuclear-age education is very much a part of the wider area of peace education, the cornerstones of which are the encouragement of a sense of justice for all and the exploration of nonviolent approaches to the resolution of conflict.

The encouragement of empathy, for all its tentativeness and apparent amorphousness, is politically the most daring aspect of nuclear-age education and over the long term the most potent. This is so because empathy undermines the ability of the leadership of a nation to organize people around the vision of an enemy, the vision of "them against us" and "us against them."

Speaking of the importance of encouraging empathetic understanding, as well as the difficulty of doing so, Roberta Snow said, "If students are learning about Yalta we make sure that they understand and try to believe the Russian point of view or the British point of view. If they're studying Truman's decision to drop the bomb, it's not only Truman they must understand, but points of view all around the world. When we have space weapons as an issue, and a guest is invited to speak in support of them, we try to open up a way for students to really believe that they might work. So that when students come to their own judgment, they're not just leaping to it and saying, 'Well, that's just the way I feel about it,' but they really have considered carefully many different opinions. While we all might agree about that, we also know how difficult it is, even for adults, to really let in another view; how hard it is to help people understand that the truth is very complex."

If discussing the point of view of a variety of speakers is one way of encouraging empathy as well as critical understanding, the design of the curriculum can be another. This was the approach Veeck used in a course he gave on Soviet–American relations and the nuclear threat (the year before I attended his classes). He began the course with a summary of American foreign policy since World War II, and followed this with one unit on American interests, another on threats to these interests—"students quickly conclude that the threat is not communism per se"—and a final unit on military strategies. Then he turned around and taught units on exactly the same topics, but from the Soviet point of view. He found the unit on Soviet interests "the hardest thing to teach—we're ethnocentric enough to believe that they don't have interests." But gradually students began to see things from the Soviet point of view, and this understanding expanded further when they came to studying the unit on threats. "This is where it gets funny," Veeck said. "Students say, 'Hey, I've got problems. I've got the U.S.; I've got troubles with the Warsaw Pact; I've got third-world troubles.' That's a break-through," he concluded. So far in the course, Veeck had not raised the topic of nuclear weapons, although, he said, students frequently asked, "When are we getting to the nukes?" Only when the class had clearly seen issues from the Soviet point of view did he teach a unit on nuclear weapons, beginning with the identification of relevant terms and then going on to a detailed examination of both arsenals. Only then did he use more emotional material, showing *The Last Epidemic,* a film sponsored by Physicians for Social Responsibility, and a videotape of President Reagan's "evil empire" speech to the evangelicals. And only then did he turn to a discussion of what to do about the arms race, including an examination of concepts such as the freeze, and build-down. "By now," he noted, "students have iden-tified survival as the number-one interest for both nations, so you have a basis for discussion. In a nuclear age, how do you pursue a strategy that will assure survival? Most students see that more weap-ons don't equal more security. They also come away with the ability to see that all conflicts are not East–West conflicts."

AN ACTIVE ROLE

An active or participatory role for the student—the fourth element of nuclear-age education—is the key to the development of two interrelated qualities, a sense of empowerment and a sense of responsibility. Each is as essential to learning as it is to citizenship—and essential in combating the feeling of helplessness that is the most usual response to the nuclear issue.

Education helps empower, but it can do so to a far greater degree if the student is treated as in some measure responsible for his own education; that is, as an active participant rather than a passive vessel into which the teacher pours facts and interpretations.

A democracy, particularly in a complex technological society, needs a sufficient number of citizens—far more than a relatively small elite who are in positions of power—who not only have the critical skills to analyze the complex problems of society but have learned to see themselves as actively participating in the democracy —that is, to see themselves as taking responsibility. But they are unlikely to be able to sustain feelings of responsibility unless they feel to some degree empowered. As noted earlier, many factors influence a sense of empowerment, most notably socioeconomic positions, but also, I suggested earlier, the style of family life. To these might be added the style of schooling they have experienced.

Knowledge and critical understanding are in themselves factors, although access to them is to some extent associated with socioeconomic position. Yet knowledge can better empower when the learner has a sense of himself as someone who can act on the basis of what he learns. (Throughout this century, but most particularly in the last twenty-five years, educators have struggled to help minority students with the intertwined issues of learning that empowers and empowering them so that they can act on the basis of what they learn.) As well as race, class, and socioeconomic position, temperament and gender influence a sense of empowerment and therefore of responsibility. These questions are made even more complex when what is learned is intrinsically anxiety-creating, as the nuclear issue is.

There has been much confusion among nuclear-age educators about how to go about realizing an active or participatory stance, and even about what it should mean. Simplistically put, does "active" imply "activism"? The American ideal of freedom makes it unacceptable to inculcate a particular political viewpoint in the classroom— that is, to educate antinuclear activists while educating about the nuclear issue. But many of the teachers most drawn to nuclear-age education are activists who feel a constant pull to cross the boundary between what is permissible in the classroom and what is their right as private citizens outside the classroom. If they cross this boundary they open themselves to criticism, especially from political conservatives, and at the same time, not incidentally, they narrow the base of their appeal. Tony Wagner cautioned ESR members:

> Obviously if we are strongly identified as just another "peace group," our ability to organize in schools will be seriously compromised. How do we respond to this challenge, while maintaining our convictions and clarity about our goals? Outside the classroom, ESR members may support efforts to bring about bilateral arms control, as the only way to ensure the survival of the planet, and be involved as citizens in community discussions and decision-making about the best means for achieving it. As professionals in schools, however, our first commitment is to inform students about the issues related to the arms race in ways that will encourage them to decide for themselves what is right. While many of us cannot and do not wish to hide our point of view, our goal in the classroom is *not* to get

students to think as we do or to become freeze activists. Our goal as educators is to encourage students to think critically about the crucial issues of our time, and to act on their convictions.[18]

A teacher and a member of ESR defined the boundary he had set for himself—and, incidentally, what he saw as the goal of nuclear-age education: "I don't think I have the right to tell students how to vote, but I think I do have the right to make them well enough acquainted with the way things are now so that they can make sound decisions." Yet at another point he said, "I and other people are interested in helping create a new consciousness, a radically different way of looking at things. We are acting on the optimistic assumption that we'll have enough time to do it and that every increment helps."

However admirable the goal, anyone who makes it his own draws a fine line when one operates in an institution as conservative as the school. One of the country's most thoughtful peace educators, Sister Loretta Carey, R.D.C., director of the Fordham National Catholic Education Association Center, commented about the dangers of crossing this fine line. She was talking about Roman Catholic schools, but the same could be said about public schools.

"Service projects have pretty regularly been part of Roman Catholic education," Sister Loretta commented, "but now writing your congressman or boycotting your supermarket and talking about it in the classroom is fine. But having students do this is too coercive unless parents are involved. In some communities we've had parents who are activists, and then I think activities like this are appropriate. But there are ways teachers coerce children, and we all know that. The criteria for an activity should be educational, because that's what we're in business to do."

The issue of participation is further complicated because it is not always clearly resolved whether it means a participatory mode within the classroom; action in a community with which the child has firsthand acquaintance or one that is easily accessible to him; or action that reaches toward the "big world" in which the source of concern lies. (It can, of course, mean any one or any combination of these.)

There are strong pulls on many teachers and students to favor participation or action that reaches toward the "big world." This approach is encouraged as much by television as by an activist stance on the part of teachers. In making "big world" issues vivid to the child, television exerts pressure on teachers as well as students to see participation in terms of the biggest forum possible—a letter to President Reagan about nuclear weapons, or, turning to another issue, a campaign to raise money for Ethiopia. Unquestionably, such an approach can have amazing results: schoolchildren have raised hundreds of thousands of dollars for famine victims in Ethiopia, and CCND collected more than eight thousand letters to President Reagan about the threat of nuclear war. (There may be less tangible but just as significant results from efforts like these involving the development of a global sense of concern in young people.)

However, there are potential drawbacks to this approach, especially for elementary-school children: it risks making the child feel even more powerless in relation to world issues than he is likely to feel already. His efforts are very unlikely to be reinforced with concrete results—chances are President Reagan is not going to answer his letter. Worse, he may be vulnerable as television brings him news of a setback to his cause—cruise and Pershing missiles deployed in Europe, famine-relief supplies rotting on a dock in Africa. Although television has brought the "big world" into his psyche as it brings it into his living room, the way this big world works is still obscure to him. There is little chance that he has the information to begin to understand the politics that result in the deployment of Euromissiles or grain rotting on docks. To some degree these politics can, of course, be explained, but if he is young they will be hard for him to grasp (they are hard enough for adults to grasp), and, moreover, if he is young he will be inclined to want quick and tangible results.[19]

A participatory mode within the classroom and, if appropriate, in the community of the school or a community known to the student is more apt to encourage a sense of responsibility and empowerment, since the student, particularly the elementary-school child, can thus have a fuller understanding of what he is trying to change or influence and is more apt to receive reinforcement. Any sense of empowerment gained will contribute to an inner foundation that in the long run will help him in other and wider arenas.

To see this participatory mode at work in the child's own world let us look at a fourth-grade classroom—although, strictly speaking, to do so leads us into "peace education" rather than "nuclear-age education." During the school year of 1982–1983 James Tobin's fourth-graders at P.S. 41 in New York invented a culture. This project was the core of their social-studies curriculum for the year, and it was intellectually a very demanding one. Early in the year, for instance, Tobin hid food in the classroom and the Simbalay tribe, as the group called themselves, had to find it. But once they found it, how would they eat it? They had no implements or tools. And how should they divide it among themselves? How should they organize themselves to make decisions?

When they had spent considerable time thinking about food, and then about dress, they began to think about shelter—and one day this led to war.

Tobin had taken the class to Inwood Hill Park on the northern tip of Manhattan. The goal of the trip was the construction of houses or shelters out of whatever branches, rocks, and other material they could scrounge. The tribe divided into teams, and, characteristic of children this age, boys and girls preferred not to work together. There were two all-boy teams and two all-girl teams. In the course of the day, war broke out between the two teams of boys. The incident that provoked the war was the attempt of Art, a boy from one team, to pull a stick out of the ground near the shelter the other boy's team was building. Eddie, the leader of the "defending" team, "bonked" Art with a horse chestnut, which were plentiful on the ground at that season. Art returned to his team and marshaled them for battle. They armed themselves with horse chestnuts and with the sticks they had been using as building materials. A battle ensued— until Tobin intervened. But Tobin was not content simply to stop the fighting. Back at school he called a meeting of the Simbalays to discuss what had happened and how conflict might have been avoided.

I entered Room 430 at P.S. 41 just as the Simbalays were settling down for their meeting. They sat on the floor in a large circle. Many were in "tribal" costume; feathers were stuck in headbands, lengths of cloth were wound around legs or arms. One girl wore electric-blue gloves; a boy wore a furry rug around his shoulders, and another, a plastic crocodile suspended on a leather thong. Tobin, a tall, energetic, engaging man, stood at the front of the room. How had the war begun? he inquired.

One of the "defenders" said, "Art came over. He started pulling up a root, a stick, and Eddie started throwing chestnuts."

Others volunteered their memories, talking excitedly and interrupting each other.

At last Tobin said, "Hold it a minute. Lisa is asking a question."

"I was just asking why they didn't try to settle it," Lisa said.

"Because we were too busy fighting," said a defender. "We didn't have enough time. People were throwing these sticks at everything."

Art for the first time spoke for himself. "I thought the vine that was stuck in the ground was a stick. So I thought of pulling it. Then Eddie started throwing chestnuts at me and then I went back to get my people."

Now Tobin asked Eddie for his version. "Art was pulling on the vine to get it out, and I was throwing chestnuts at him to get him out of here."

"Why?" Tobin asked.

"Because it's our land, and we don't want him taking any of our stuff."

"Yeah, it's our land," said another of the defenders.

"I mean it's our property," added Eddie. "If we find a stick, it's ours."

A girl suggested that Art could have said he didn't know the stick was on the property of the defenders.

One of the defenders brushed aside this suggestion. "Well, he should know. He shouldn't have gone on our land in the first place, our part of the land. He should have looked on his own place for his —the whole hill is our land. We have the whole hill."

A girl countered, "Well, you were saying that it was your land. But when the Indians were using the land, they didn't think of it as 'their land.' They thought it was the gods' land, and they just used the land. But they didn't own it."

"Well, you see, the whole hill was our land," one of the defenders said. "We were the first people to find it."

"The Indians got there before you," said a boy, reiterating the argument of a moment earlier.

"It was our land," insisted another of the defenders.

"To use it, you had to build a shelter," said a member of Art's team. "But that doesn't mean just because you plan to build a shelter that you own that property."

Now Eddie took the floor. "Well, you see, the Indians weren't there anymore. And we know it was theirs first. But Mr. Tobin said we could build a shelter someplace, so we built it there. And we didn't say, 'Oh, we're going to live there, and we're going to call up the furniture people and tell the furniture people, "Bring my television." ' We didn't say that. We were really just using the land for the whole day. No one else could build on our land that day. No one else could take any of our property. If we claimed the land it's ours."

Now Tobin refocused the discussion, which threatened to bog down, and went around the room asking each member of the tribe for suggestions about how the conflict could have been avoided.

"I want to tell Art there were plenty of sticks around," a boy said, "and he could—I mean, he's just like—I feel that Art is making up this whole thing and he thinks it's funny and he wants to start a war."

A girl said, "Well, I think if they both wanted that stick very badly, if they got it out of the ground, they could see how long it was, and if it was long enough they could break it in half."

A boy said, "I think he should have—if he's having that much trouble finding a stick, then I think they should just get the stuff that they already have with their land, and go away and find another spot where there is stuff that they need."

A girl said, "I think one way to solve the problem before it starts into a really big fight is to—you know, if this is a really good stick and they both need it and they both want it a lot, then maybe they should bury it or something, and neither of them have it."

A boy said, "I think that if they both needed that stick, then they must have needed a stick real bad. So what I think that they should have done was he should have took his stick, and they should have both built their house together."

Yet another boy said, "I think they should have given the stick to some other family so neither of them got it. Instead of saying, 'This is my stick, this is my stick,' they should have both said, Let's think of a suggestion, like, maybe, 'Well, this stick is too small to divide.' Then they could have thought of something else, like maybe giving it to another family."

Another boy's suggestions were based on favorite decision-making techniques of childhood. "Well, they could have just whipped the stick out of the ground and thrown it, and whoever— they could have thrown the stick and run and see who can get it, or something—like shoot for it."

By now, everyone who wished had had a chance to speak. The discussion had been hard on Art, and at times he had edged his way outside the circle, once almost reaching the classroom door.

"Art," Tobin said, "could you come back here until the bell rings? Because I think we're talking to you—and Eddie."

Eddie meanwhile had become restive, and at several points had risen and, until Tobin told him to stop, had engaged in a mock duel that replayed his role in the horse-chestnut war, with embellishments. Although Art had provoked the war, Eddie, at least, had been more than ready for it.

Tobin asked Art if any of the suggestions appealed to him, but he stuck to his position.

"Well, you see," he said, "Eddie's team, they weren't using the stick for anything. And, you see, I was coming there, and that was the first stick I saw, because I was looking for it—"

By now, a few of the girls and most of the boys, absorbed in the discussion, had pressed in closer and closer to Tobin. But many of the girls and a handful of the boys sat more or less where the original circle had been, separated physically and, it seemed, in spirit from the discussion, as if it had little meaning for them.

Tobin asked the group to reform the circle. Then he called on one of the girls who had been sitting without speaking on the fringe of the group. "Kelly, what do you think about all this?" he asked.

After some hesitation, Kelly said, "Like if they were fighting all the time and not getting ready for winter and not making shelters, then in the winter they would die anyway."

Kelly introduced a new theme of vulnerability, one very much connected with feminine concerns with care and taking care, rather than with protecting territory and asserting strength.

Tobin reinforced what she said. "That's a good point," he said. "If you were really out in the woods there, you would die if winter came—in fact, it's going to get very cold this weekend. So really it's very important to build a shelter. That was really what everybody was doing, but two groups stopped doing it. I hear some of us saying that the reason was that Art grabbed the stick, but I sense that maybe something was happening before that. What was happening?"

He pressed Eddie's team to recall what they had been doing. They had been collecting wood, they said, and building their shelter. They had pulled branches off a dead tree and added it to their construction. They had included a piece of burlap. When Art came up, they had yelled, "Get out of here! Get out of here!"

There was something Tobin was digging for, but in the end he had to supply it himself. "I guess what I noticed," he said, "and nobody's brought it up—is that you also, your group, were collecting weapons." Eddie's group had been stockpiling horse chestnuts, missiles that were only too handy when Art "invaded" their territory.

"Why were you collecting weapons?" Tobin asked.

"Because we knew that there was going to be a war," came the reply. "We could tell it in our minds, that—you see, everybody was going to Nadia's land, and then Doris's land [Nadia and Doris were the leaders of the girls' teams], so we knew that someone was going to come into our land and take something. So we took the chestnuts."

"Did any of the other groups collect weapons?" Tobin asked.

It turned out that Art's group had begun collecting horse chestnuts, too, once they had seen Eddie's group was doing so.

Now Art felt the need to plead his case. "See," he said, "I just came over there, and I thought it was a piece of thick vine. I started pulling. You was right they were watching me try to pull it, and I was trying to pull it. And then Eddie started throwing the chestnuts."

"Did he start throwing the chestnuts right away?"

"Yup," Art said.

Tobin was not sure this was so, and a member of Eddie's group disagreed with Art's assertion.

"When he told you he didn't want you around there, what did you do?" Tobin asked.

"I was just standing there like this," said Art, posing, "and he was throwing chestnuts."

"Why did you just stay there?" Tobin asked.

"Because I was pulling the thing. I wanted a big stick."

Now Tobin chose volunteers from the group to take Art and Eddie's parts. The object was to see if there might have been another way to solve the conflict over Art's invasion, short of war. A girl took Art's part, but she and her antagonist, a boy, could not solve the problem.

"What are you feeling now?" Tobin asked after they had struggled with it. "Is it hard to solve this problem? Maybe it's not so easy." He chose another pair, both girls this time.

"Well, I would say," said the girl impersonating Art, " 'Can I have this stick, and then I'll get off your land and won't come back.' "

"There are plenty of sticks around," said her opposite number, impersonating Eddie. "Aren't there any in your shelter?"

Their tone was civil, but they didn't find a solution.

Tobin asked for suggestions from the group.

"Look how much land there is," suggested another girl to the girl playing Art. "We use the sticks around our land. You should have built your shelter in a place where there are a lot of good sticks, so you don't have to go into other people's shelter."

The real-life Eddie still favored his original approach. "What you can say," he said, "is 'Get out of our land or I'm going to give you a chestnut right in the eye.' "

"Let's take Eddie's suggestion," Tobin said, "and see where that leads us. I think we know where it led us. It's like a snowball. When a snowball goes down a hill, it keeps collecting more snow, until eventually you have something that's very, very dangerous. And

I think the same is true here. I believe the snowball started off with you guys collecting weapons, because if you hadn't had weapons maybe you would have had to think of a different way to solve the problem. My question, I think, is: As soon as you start building weapons, what is it that you start to do?"

"We were starting to act like a nuclear plant," a boy volunteered, his terms confused but his meaning apparent.

"Why do you say that?"

"Well, the reason why we started collecting weapons," volunteered a boy from Eddie's group, "is we saw Art and other people going into the girls' shelters and taking all these sticks. We knew they were going to come to our house and take sticks, so we started collecting nuts."

"You saw there was a threat."

"Yes."

"And you thought that the only way to meet that threat was with weapons."

"To threat back."

"Now, please, everybody," said Tobin, raising his voice to catch the attention of those who were growing restive, "this is very important, I think. Eddie and his group started collecting weapons because they wanted to do what? What did they want to protect?"

"Their land."

"Their land—and their shelter," Tobin said. "But what eventually happened?"

"Like Art's group took away their tools. Like, they took away their things to make their shelter."

"So what happened to their shelter?" Tobin asked.

"It was never made."

At that moment the bell rang.

The bell kept Tobin from making all the connections between "big world" issues and the experience of the Simbalays that he might have liked to, but I do not doubt that his fourth-graders' discussion of their horse-chestnut war was a more effective form of participatory learning—and ultimately more empowering—than writing letters to President Reagan, as they had the week before. The Simbalays analyzed their own experience. Precisely because direct experience was involved there was an informed and concrete vividness to their thinking—and thinking vividly about direct experience is an important foundation for taking responsibility. This vividness helped the

Simbalays reflect with considerable sophistication on what had happened to them, although, as nine-year-olds, negotiating and critical thinking of the kind Tobin sought did not come easily to them.

Although Tobin had difficulty involving the girls in the discussion, a far larger proportion of the class voiced their views than ever would have if he had simply ended the horse-chestnut war and not discussed it, or ended it with disciplinary measures and a school-teacherly homily. His efforts encouraged competence in articulating convictions particularly important for girls. He worked to make everyone feel that he or she would be heard—that is, had a voice. Moreover, by avoiding homilies and conventional disciplinary measures (once he had cut short the war) and calling for a full discussion of the event, he invested the Simbalays with responsibility for understanding what had happened, and through this understanding helped them take responsibility for the event itself. To make this possible he let go a little of a teacher's authority—at least in a traditional sense —or changed somewhat the terms on which he had authority, assuming a role that was closer to that of facilitator and coach. (The way in which Tobin modified authority can be compared with the style of family life the O'Briens attempted.) "I almost saw myself in two different roles at the same time," Tobin said. "I saw myself in an authority role and in the role of the person who was going to change that." This shift within Tobin himself was a vital part of empowering his students to reflect actively on their experience. His faith in their intellectual and ethical capacities was an important element of the stance he took. Yet in no way did he abandon them; he was a strong presence in the classroom.

Tobin's "anthropological" approach to his fourth grade's social-studies course, with the many opportunities it afforded for active learning, was motivated to a considerable degree by his desire to empower students. "I guess I'm responding to a parochial-school education," he told me, "in which I never had choices. I want to give my students a chance to change things and challenge me, and that's hard because I'm a pretty powerful authority.

"What I hope is that when they grow up they can change things by looking around and starting the process; that's what I never knew. I really grew up believing that the way it is is the way it's going to be. I grew up with the Vietnam war, but I didn't try to change things, I just tried to avoid the draft. But I was radicalized by the war."

Tobin thought carefully about laying foundations for a sense of empowerment in relation to big-world issues and issues closer to the student's own experience. "Before the congressional elections [in the fall of 1982] we talked about nuclear disarmament," he said. "We talked about what a bomb is. Most of them didn't have any idea. I told them they could write letters to anyone they wanted, to Reagan, to Brezhnev, to themselves. But generally I try not to do much of this. I want them to learn to change things around them first. My idea is that kids are more afraid of their parents and teachers than they are of nuclear war. I don't think they're going to change things if they can't change their parents and their teachers."

By changing teachers and parents Tobin did not mean the surrender of adult authority, but he did mean that if learning is made active young people will have a voice and through that voice influence the adults around them. "In changing them," he concluded about his students, "I was changed."

Let us take another look at an active mode of learning at work in a classroom where students a few years older than the Simbalays discussed an aspect of the nuclear issue.

Sam Brian, an outspoken man in his thirties, teaches a year-long course in American government and, concurrently, a course in current events as well. His students are eighth-graders at the Bank Street School in New York. Brian has strong feelings about the importance of current events in the education of children. "It's one of the most sorely neglected pieces of curriculum today," he commented. "If allowed in at all, it's done at the discretion of the teacher and as a frill. Its absence in a child's life is one of the most undermining parts of education today. Without it students can't bring the insights from the past to bear on the present, or vice versa." Brian noted that many teachers are intimidated by teaching current events, quailing at the thought of having to become "experts." But, Brian insists, being an expert is not necessary; he himself eschews the role of expert—which, in fact, is antithetical to what he is trying to achieve.

Every week, for his current-events course, his students clip a newspaper or news-magazine article and write a précis of the article and then their own comments. With their articles, summaries, and comments they gather with Brian in a large circle. "The rules of the road are simple," said Brian, describing what happens next. "The teacher can kind of stay out of it. You're not there to give your opinion. You are there to help them *form* opinions. And you are there to help them with communicating with each other. They need lots of help with this. I stop them constantly to make them clarify for one another. You are leading a group inquiry in which you are a partner as well as a leader."

He noted that not only teachers but also students bring fears and inhibitions to such a discussion: "They don't want to look dumb. You have to create a climate where ignorance is the ticket of admission. What's difficult is creating this climate, and, prior to that, getting yourself to the point where you wade in and say, Dammit, I've got to be able to handle these things." (But too much ignorance adds to inhibition, especially about technical terms; Brian is careful to teach the vocabulary that will enable students to understand the articles they have clipped. When I visited his classroom the following words were listed on the blackboard with a big SAVE beside them: vulnerable, deter, deploy, disarm, mutual, unilateral, negotiate, bargaining chip, MAD.)

By Christmas Brian's eighth-graders have learned enough about current events—and in their American government course enough about the way our government works—so that they can bring each to bear on the other in a mock senate that continues for the rest of the year. Although such simulations are a standard device for teaching civics and debating certain issues, the thoroughness with which this particular example is carried out is notable. Moreover, it was a student who proposed the senate. "One of the kids said," Brian recounted, " 'Instead of debating the priorities of our national budget, why don't we be Congress?' That was such a striking notion that I thought, well, gee, why don't we?

"The way it works," he explained, "is that each student becomes a senator and represents a state. They don't mimic a particular senator; they just research their state. They try to promote its interests, as well as promoting the national interest. They become members of a party, and they learn to unite to do a job. They also serve on a committee. We have five standing committees in our classroom each year and committee hearings take up most of our senate time.

"We all watch the State of the Union address and they write bills in response to the president. They debate, they lobby, and finally, toward the spring, there are climactic roll calls, and the year winds up, much as the congressional year winds up, with many bills untouched and others that have been resolved."

Brian's role during many of the senate proceedings is very much that of a coach, with some of the qualities of a referee. He reminds students of the senate procedures if they forget, sometimes he encourages the more retiring to be more outspoken, occasionally he helps them take a breather from the strain of role-playing. He is a strong presence, just as Tobin was with his fourth-graders, and he is the ultimate authority, but to a very great degree he empowers his students to proceed on their own.

Several years ago the mock senate considered a bill recommending the funding of one hundred MX missiles. One day the Defense committee heard the testimony of "Brent Scowcroft," played by a boy with considerable poise and style. The chairman called the committee to order.

"Is there anything you would like to say before we start questioning you?" student A asked "Scrowcroft."

"I was planning to state my opinions before you questioned me," Scowcroft replied smoothly, then hesitated a bit. "All right, well, I'll begin, okay?" he went on. "As you know, I'm here to give you a better perspective on the MX missile, and it's a great concept, you know. First, I'll tell you its advantages, and I'll leave someone else to talk about its disadvantages. I'd like to say that first of all the MX missile is more accurate than the present Minuteman III missiles which are presently deployed. Second, they have more destructive power than the Minuteman III. And the Russians regard the MX missile as a threat, due to its accuracy and destructive power as compared to the Minuteman. Also it's a deterrent against a Soviet first strike and it can be used as a bargaining chip in arms-reduction negotiations. Okay, all right," Scowcroft paused. "Now I am open to questions from anyone."

"I understand that you believe, from what I've read, that the MX is vulnerable to attack," came the first comment from student B. "So if they felt, if they were afraid of the power of this, and I think since it is very accurate it suggests it might be used for a first-strike weapon, what would keep them from attacking us?"

Another student, C, had a comment before Scowcroft could reply: "A commission said that the MX is too big to be mobile, and the Soviets might penetrate even superhardened silos."

Scowcroft was forced to reply rather lamely, "Are you sure of that?"

"That's what it says right here," said C, her index finger on an open page of *Newsweek* magazine.

Scowcroft had by now got his wind back. Referring to student B's remark about the vulnerability of the proposed MX basing system, he said, "Might penetrate. Note the word 'might.' "

"Okay," student C said. "But it also said that there's no practical way to make the MX invulnerable if the Russians were to strike first."

Now another member of the Defense Committee, student D, spoke up. "Why couldn't you harden these silos and leave the Minuteman in them? I mean why would these silos be good enough for the MX but not for the Minuteman?"

Yet another member of the committee, E, joined in. "Did you or did you not say the MX would not be vulnerable to Soviet attack?"

Under this barrage Scowcroft was beginning to be flustered. "I may have said that previously. I can't remember everything that I have said. But I'm saying now, and this is final, they are not vulnerable to Soviet attack."

"Are you sure that's final?" E asked.

Scowcroft looked frustrated, played with a ballpoint pen.

C, responding to his frustration, asked, "How can we question you?"

At this point Scowcroft slipped out of his role. "How can you?" he asked. "Well, I'm a nice guy."

Everyone laughed and the class relaxed a bit. A few minutes later Brian urged them to resume their roles. E said, "I want to know what would be any advantage if by the time the MX is put into use it was not effective, since it would be outdated by then?"

Scowcroft had recovered his aplomb and replied smoothly, "I'm not going to answer that question right now. I can get back to you about that" [a phrase Brian had taught the class for getting out of a tight spot]. At this point he seized the initiative and himself became the questioner. "But I'll ask you personally what you would do in that situation."

"I don't know," said E, "but I certainly wouldn't go along with the MX."

"Why is that?" Scowcroft asked.

"Because by the time it was put into use, it wouldn't be effective any more and I see no purpose for spending $16.6 billion on it."

Scowcroft asked, "Do you see any alternative?"

"I can get back to you on that," E said, making everyone laugh.

Now a student who had not yet been heard from entered the discussion. G addressed Scowcroft, saying, "Okay, you say this is a bargaining chip. Isn't it a bit of a waste to spend billions of dollars on just a way to negotiate with the Russians? I don't think that's really worth it, if all you're going to do is build it, then negotiate with them, and then dismantle it. I mean is that what you're saying you'd do if you used it as a bargaining chip?"

"That's exactly what I'm saying," Scowcroft replied.

"Doesn't that seem like a waste to you?" G asked.

"What would you pay for your safety? What is the price of your safety?" Scowcroft asked.

Now the chairman of the committee commented, "I think we're in a poker game where the stakes are too high, and we don't have a good hand."

"What do you want to do, fold?" B asked.

Laughter.

"At the moment," the chairman said, "I think it would be better if we waited for the next round."

Once again Scowcroft felt close to overwhelmed by his role. "I can't say that the MX is ever going to go anywhere," he said. "I'm just hoping that it will, and that's my view. It's not my vote that counts here. It's all of these people and others. So don't leave it in my hands."

Now the chairman found a metaphor to express the feelings of many in the group. "My son, a few years back—I think at two, or one and a half—I bought him a little Atari video computer system. His friend next door, two months later, got an Intellevision, and my son's little Atari was outdated. We spent twice as much as we spent on the Atari which was a thousand maybe, including cartridges. We spent maybe three times more buying a new system. And if we keep on going more and more, we're wasting our money. And I think that's what the government is doing now."

A moment later Scowcroft excused himself, saying he had another engagement, and the committee called another witness.

Sufficient preparation and information made Brian's eighth-graders feel that they were empowered to discuss the subject of the MX, and the mock senate gave them the forum in which to do so. The most striking characteristic of the hearing was the intense engagement of the students, a marked contrast with the more usual classroom, where so often the teacher does most of the talking and students supply answers or simply wait—bored, sullen, or truculent—for it all to be over. The excitement of Brian's students was the best testimony one could have for the value of active learning.

Role-playing is not the only technique that helps students participate actively in their own learning; learning to interview speakers or drawing up and administering a survey of other students, parents, or community members are other valuable approaches. Brian said of role-playing (but much the same could be said of other approaches), "I think it's an effective technique to promote critical thinking, and I think it's also important in promoting the expression of diverse opinion in the classroom. It's an antidote to apathy, to passive thinking, to parroting, and to derivative thinking. I've found that kids in role-playing situations will be led to positions which they never thought they'd maintain, positions which perhaps are counter to their parents' opinion and perhaps counter to their friends' opinions, but nonetheless they've reached them themselves through reason and through being in a role where they are forced to be on the line. Role-playing allows children to explore unpopular points of view without exposing themselves to undue personal criticism." He then recalled a debate over the deployment of Euromissiles. "I found in one context that nobody was willing to join the debate on the 'To Deploy' side. But when I told the class that they were able to join the debate team and espouse any point of view and it needn't be their own, we had a lively debate. When we used the secret ballot to see what people thought before and after the debate, lo and behold there were eight, then nine souls who said deployment of the Euromissiles would be an important step for the United States to take. But before the debate, you could not find a hand raised even to say 'I want to be on the To Deploy team.' "

There are advantages to these approaches for teachers as well as students: when the subject matter is controversial, they allow the teacher to handle controversy without courting an accusation of bias.

PRAGMATISM AND IDEALS

Jim Tobin created a forum in which a large proportion of his fourth-graders could practice citizenship—as fourth-graders and as Simbalays. He helped them find a voice—even the girls most inclined to tune out—and in finding a voice to take a step toward a feeling of empowerment. He helped them think critically about what had happened, even those who had been only too eager to act without reflecting. Their steps toward empowerment could also be thought of as steps toward responsibility, responsibility that he further encouraged by giving them the "room" to act, as he let go a little of his authority.

Sam Brian created a forum in which his eighth-graders could be citizens in much the same way. He coached them as citizens, giving them practice in forming an opinion, making it heard, and fighting for their beliefs (practice which Tobin had also provided in a way suitable to fourth-graders).

Practice is the key word; in this regard Tony Wagner, former executive director of Educators for Social Responsibility, has commented, "Students must have the experience of putting their ideals into practice. That's the only way you learn pragmatism. The only way to learn to struggle is to struggle."

Pragmatism is a word that sounds like a sellout to many idealists, including idealists of the peace movement. But in the sense that Wagner meant it—or that Brian's eighth-graders or Tobin's fourth-graders were learning to exercise it—it is not a sellout. It need not connote a narrow concern with technique or an abandonment of ends for means. Rather, it speaks of a tough-minded ability to hold on to ideals in an arena bigger than the private world which many Americans have come to believe is the only place one can have an ideal—"All the talk, all the singing, it's very beautiful and we can have it in our family, but we're not going to have it any other way," as the young man at *New Youth Connections* put it.

Many of us are uneasily aware that public involvement is not what it should be to make democracy work or to solve our society's problems.[20] Sometimes we think of the failure of involvement in terms of the failure to vote, sometimes in terms of the society's propensity for violence, sometimes in terms of very small phenomena—the hand (our own) that tosses the beer can and the fast-food wrappings out the car window. We are less likely to think of it in terms of the privatization of our values or the inadequacy of an ethic that finds it sufficient to say that "the right to swing your fist stops at the tip of my nose." Nor are we likely to think of it in terms of the creeping sense of powerlessness that is insidiously associated with the scale of our institutions and technology. Yet these may be the most critical factors in the decline of our public life, a decline which has serious consequences for us as a society: "It is the deterioration of public life, together with the privatization and trivialization of moral ideas, that prevents a collaborative assault on the environmental and military difficulties confronting modern nations."[21]

Teaching such as Brian's, Tobin's, and Veeck's combats a privatization of values and a "deterioration of public life." It helps students develop the skills, the competence—and the courage—to step out into the public arena and stay there until they get what they want, or a piece of what they want.[22] They learn that it is not easy to fight for what they believe—"Scowcroft" gave way a couple of times under the pressure, or nearly so—but that it can be done.

THE CULTURE OF THE SCHOOL

The need for such teaching leads one to ask what are the prospects of nuclear-age education. It is too soon to tell, but one can foresee that although modest amounts of new information about nuclear weapons and the arms race may be added to the curriculum, the acceptance of nuclear-age education as a process along the lines I have described will not come at all easily. The reasons for this lie in two general areas: the so-called "culture of the schools," and the political nature of nuclear-age education itself.

The "culture of the school" does little to foster teachers such as Sam Brian, Bob Veeck, or Jim Tobin, and much to discourage them. "Schools," Roberta Snow said, "are such powerless places." In general teachers have very little control over the way they spend time, locked in as they are to covering a prescribed amount of material in a prescribed number of weeks (and they have not, in most cases, had a chance to participate in prescribing the material or the time spent on it, or, in many cases, the approach to teaching it). The lockstep of the school curriculum and the school year encourages a routinized approach, antithetical to the kind of inquiry that is at the core of nuclear-age education. The same pressures, plus the difficulties of handling a large group of children, a fair number of whom may be behavior problems, encourage teachers to see the maintenance of authority and control—or rather a certain conception of authority and control—as the first order of the day. But, as suggested earlier, this concept of authority and control is incompatible with inquiring, active learning. Active learning calls for the teacher to be "first among equals," often to join in the inquiry as a kind of facilitator or coach, and to eschew pat answers. It demands a certain autonomy for the student (but not a lack of discipline), or, put another way, a recognition of him as a thinking and feeling person. But it is only too easy for a teacher to treat his students as he himself has been treated within the system of the school, that is, as a relatively powerless individual with few "constitutional rights."[23]

The pressures for a quick cure for some of the ills of American

education further threaten the chances for inquiry and active learning. Quick cure is only too often thought of in terms of "tightening
things up"—tighter adherence to specific curriculum guidelines and
tighter classroom control—precisely the kind of "tightness" that will
make the inquiry process and the students' active involvement seem
more of a risk to the teacher, faced with ever greater pressure to
"cover the material."

Yet there is a ray of hope: recent critiques of the schools
advocate changes that are very much in line with nuclear age education at its best. One of these critiques, *High School: A Report on
Secondary Education in America,* speaks specifically to the problem
of citizen education. The author, Ernest L. Boyer, a former United
States Commissioner of Education and currently the president of the
Carnegie Foundation for the Advancement of Teaching, points out
the serious decline among students in knowledge of the structure of
government and of the political process:

> Between 1969 and 1976, scores for seventeen-year-olds on knowl-
> edge about the government dropped from 64.4 percent to 53.9
> percent. In 1976, only 31 percent of thirteen-year-olds and 53 per-
> cent of seventeen-year-olds tested knew that each state has two
> United States senators. Forty-two percent of the thirteen-year-olds
> knew it was not illegal to start a new political party. One out of
> every seven seventeen-year-olds thought the President does not
> always have to obey the law.[24]

Boyer comments on the risk of such "civic illiteracy":

> Unless we find better ways to educate ourselves as citizens, we run
> the risk of drifting unwittingly into a new kind of Dark Age—a time
> when, increasingly, specialists will control knowledge and the
> decision-making process. In this confusion, citizens would make
> critical decisions, not on the basis of what they know, but on the
> basis of blind belief in one or another set of professed experts.[25]

In response to the threat of such a situation, the report pro-
poses that a one-year course in American government be made a
required part of a core curriculum to be followed by all high-school
students. As an example of the kind of work such a course might
include, Boyer mentions that "Each student might take one con-
tested issue now before Congress, a state legislature or community
governmental body, reporting in depth on the history of the issue,

points of conflict, and plausible resolutions"[26]—very much what Brian's eighth-graders were doing. (Such an assignment is one way in which a student could choose to examine an arms-race issue, in effect designing his own nuclear-age education.)

Another critique, *The Paideia Proposal,* summarizes the thinking of a distinguished group of educators on an approach to the ills of American education. The author, Mortimer J. Adler, suggests that there are three modes of teaching and learning and that only by restoring the balance of these modes can American education be significantly improved. First, the student must acquire "organized knowledge," that is, the standard stuff of school imparted in the standard didactic fashion, but far more fully and intensely than the "inadequate and fragmentary" body of knowledge that most students now carry out of high school. The second mode concerns the acquisition of skills; "reading, writing, speaking, listening, observing, measuring, estimating and calculating" are the skills the author singles out. In their fostering the teacher assumes the role of coach:

> Since what is learned here is skill in performance, not knowledge of facts and formulas, the mode of teaching cannot be didactic. It cannot consist in the teacher telling, demonstrating, or lecturing. Instead it must be akin to the coaching that is done to impart athletic skills.[27]

The Paideia Proposal then goes a step further, specifying the need for a third mode of learning—"an enlarged understanding of ideas and values," to be achieved by means of "socratic questioning and active participation." Adler suggests that fiction, poetry, drama, history, science, and philosophy are the content on which this questioning is to be based—but not textbooks. Participation in the arts is another path to this understanding. Moreover, Adler specifies that this "enlarged understanding of ideas and values" must be applied to "the ideas underlying our form of government and the institutions of our society." He is intimating with this statement that questions of value—and questioning about values—must be part of education, and that this questioning cannot be restricted to clarification of the individual's private standards for himself. The implication is that questions of value are an essential part of public life and of the life of individuals as citizens.

Widening his view beyond any one mode of learning, Adler urges that the reforms he advocates are essential not only so that individual young people can grow up to earn a living and live a good life, but also to "preserve our free institutions." He notes:

Democratic government and the institutions of a free society are of very recent advent in the world. They are as recent as the enactment of truly universal suffrage and the effort to secure the human and civil rights of the whole population. These are gains made in the twentieth century and not before, made only in a few places on the planet, not everywhere.

What occurred in a few countries for the first time in the twentieth century brought into existence only the initial conditions of a democratic society. It remains to be seen whether these conditions will be preserved and put to good use—whether their promises for the future will be fulfilled.

Both depend in large part on our being able to succeed in improving education in the broadest sense—to produce an educated electorate.[28]

Fine words are far from assuring change in entrenched bureaucratic institutions, but the emphasis of these two blue-ribbon critiques suggests that the direction of concern about American education overlaps substantially with the point of view of those trying to make nuclear-age education a reality. In a certain, very real, sense, nuclear-age education is simply good education, education as it can and should be.

A POLITICAL MESSAGE

In another sense, however, nuclear-age education is clearly not simply good education, although at its best it is indeed that. Because it teaches about nuclear weapons, the arms race, and the threat of war it is very political education. As such it is controversial. What is the real nature of this controversy? Bias is the most frequently heard accusation, and it is true that some teaching is biased, as are some curricular materials.[29] But accusations of bias and talk about the need for "balanced debate" beg the question. Bias in favor of what? Everyone hates nuclear weapons. Everyone wants peace. Just what is a balanced debate about nuclear weapons, grotesquely unbalanced in their destructiveness as they are?

We can find the beginnings of an answer in the opinions of Dr. Charles Larsen, with whom I lunched one day in Paradise, California.

Dr. Larsen is in his later fifties; he is a Mormon, a dentist, and a member of the school board in Paradise. His manner is unassuming and understated, but conversation gradually reveals his stubborn opinions. After a few minutes of small talk I asked him about the ESR curriculum, "Perspectives," which had recently been presented to the school board for possible adoption in the Paradise schools. "When the group presented us with the material, I thought it was disgusting," Larsen said. "It didn't have one thing positive to say about our nation, the greatest nation in the world." He went on to talk about what to him was the dangerously pacifist nature of the curriculum. "It seemed to me that they were trying to make decisions for the kids that were just unrealistic. I didn't think there was any place for that material in our schools." To echo Frances Fitzgerald, he did not think ESR had produced a sufficiently nationalistic history. "Perspectives" was not the "time capsule" he wanted passed on.

Dr. Larsen's words suggest that the core of the debate over nuclear-age education is not only, or not really, the weapons themselves, but questions of nationalism and patriotism, prowess and progress, of perceptions about what constitutes strength and what constitutes vulnerability. In effect, Dr. Larsen recommended a degree of silence about the dangers of nuclear weapons, because he believed in a certain concept of strength. One aspect of this concept involved military strength, of which a strong nuclear deterrent was for the forseeable future a necessary part. But his words suggested that this concept of strength did not allow for dissent, since the act of questioning itself undermines the emotional loyalty necessary to defend the freedoms Americans prize. Dr. Larsen's position did not necessarily mean that he himself was comfortable with the weapons or comfortable with government policy. In fact, he indicated he was not. When we came out of the restaurant into the California sun, he began to talk about the years of aboveground testing of nuclear devices. "The incidence of leukemia has been high," he said, "in the areas like Utah where they did aboveground testing. The government was not prudent and less than candid."

Larsen's point of view implied that we must continue to think of strength as strength has always been thought of—and conversely to think of vulnerability as vulnerability has traditionally been thought of. In contrast, nuclear-age education implies that in a new era we must continually reexamine what constitutes strength and what constitutes vulnerability, and that this questioning itself is important in protecting ourselves in a time when we can no longer think of invulnerability in classic terms. But an ongoing examination breaks the silence that those who are devoted to a traditional concept of strength want to maintain. In breaking silence, such an ex-

amination in itself provides "balance"—to use a word beloved of
conservatives. It does so because it counteracts the otherwise unbalanced tendency of those controlling the arms race and the portion
of the population that supports them to encourage the silence that
allows them to proceed. It is a genuinely balanced examination that
is itself very political and therefore very controversial, although neither peaceniks nor peace-through-strength-niks like to admit that
this is so. This is all the more true when the setting for such an
examination is the schools. The reason for this has to do with the
mandate of the schools to socialize students as citizens—but not
with the emphasis on a critical examination of issues. The traditional
mandate of the schools has been the socialization of a citizen who is
loyal, patriotic, and—this is key—who unquestioningly accepts the
norms of his society. Patriotism in the broadest sense calls for the
contribution of an individual's strength to his country—his abilities,
his convictions, as well as formal allegiance. A nation will much more
easily elicit the allegiance and the patriotism of its citizens—that is,
enlist their strength—if it appears strong and virtuous to them, or so
it has been believed. It follows, according to this reasoning, that in
order to fulfill their socializing mission the schools—teachers and
textbooks alike—have felt obliged to tell the American story in such
a way that America appears strong and virtuous—and strong and
virtuous according to traditional concepts of these qualities. As suggested earlier, this very often puts teacher and textbook in a very
ambiguous relationship to the truth, or to the search for what may
be true. Frances Fitzgerald has commented on this situation and its
potential for disastrous consequences:

> Throughout history, the managers of states have with remarkable
> consistency defined good citizenship as a rather small degree of
> knowledge of and participation in state affairs. The fury of college
> students in the sixties came in part from their sense that, along with
> government officials, their textbooks and their teachers had con-
> cealed from them the truth about American politics and history.[30]

Some of that fury shaped the educational strategy of Jim
Tobin, who came of age in the Sixties.

The relative silence of teachers and textbooks over the years
about nuclear weapons and the arms race is part of an attempt to
socialize for loyalty. To speak fully of nuclear weapons and the arms
race brings into question the culturally dominant concept of
strength. Moreover, the story of their possession and use at Hiro-

shima and Nagasaki, or information about fighting strategies involving their future use, at least by implication, undermines the portrait of virtue that aims to elicit allegiance. By not teaching about them—or very much about them—the schools have sought to preserve a certain concept of strength and virtue and thus to do their part in socializing a new generation that according to this conception will be strong and unquestioningly lend their strength to their country. A belief in the need for this kind of socialization was implicit in Dr. Larsen's opposition to the ESR curriculum, and in particular in his remark that the curriculum "didn't have one positive thing to say about our nation, the greatest nation on earth."

An individual's school-board vote to reject a nuclear-age education curriculum is one way in which the silence of the schools can be maintained. One might say it marks a point of tangency between individual resistance to thinking about the issue and what John Mack has called "collective resistance."[31]

Nuclear-age education is political not only because it opens the way to questions about strength and virtue in the light of modern weapons technology, but because by the very act of breaking silence it challenges this "collective resistance."

Having said this, it would seem as if genuine inquiry about the nuclear issue had little chance of acceptance in the schools, and it is true that any degree of acceptance has been and will be hard won.

Acceptance did not come easily in Milwaukee, for instance. The task force chosen to draw up guidelines for nuclear-age education in the schools met for upward of sixty hours and subcommittees met for as much as forty hours each, meaning that individuals contributed fully one hundred hours of volunteer time over a period of only a few months. Much of this time was spent in trying to reach agreement among people with passionate differences of opinion. Nancy Lesar, a conservatively inclined member of the task force and at the time president of the Milwaukee City Council PTA, commented about the peace and nuclear-age education advocates on the task force, "I said to my husband every time I came back from a meeting: for supposedly peace-loving people, I've never seen people argue so much."

But the committed antinuclear activists on the task force might have said the same thing about the conservatives.

One important difference was the question of whether nuclear weapons should be mentioned in the lower grades. It was the opinion of the antinuclear activists on the task force that they should be—children already feared the weapons, they claimed, and needed help in handling their fears—but those at the conservative end of the political gamut were absolutely opposed. (In the end they were not mentioned at the elementary level.)[32] There was strong disagreement on many points, right up to the last minute. The conservative co-chairman of the task force, John Kwapisz, refused to sign the task-force report, although he had worked on it all the way. He filed a minority report.

"The whole process was an exercise in democracy," commented Arthur Rumpf, director of social studies for the Milwaukee school system, "and there couldn't have been a better place to do it. You can't talk about democracy and not do it."

An exercise in democracy can be fruitful not only with respect to the "deal" or "product" it achieves, but occasionally in the opportunity for individual learning it makes possible. Nancy Lesar still thinks of herself as a "conservative type of person," adding that at the time she joined the task force "a lot of what I had read or seen on TV [about the peace movement] was what I considered quite a radical point of view." She tended to lump "peace-studies people" and "antinuke people" under this heading. But in the course of working on the task force she came to feel differently. "I haven't changed my point of view," she said, "but I'm not as leery of peace-studies people as I was in the past. I don't lump them together. And I made some friends."

An exercise in democracy may be even harder in a place like Paradise, California. "We just don't pull together here," a longtime resident told me ruefully and, indeed, the town is split several different ways between old and young, liberal and extremely conservative. To some degree old and conservative overlap. Jim Umenhofer, one of the founders of ESR in Paradise, described the older residents as "people who came to southern California, Orange County, in the Thirties and Forties and brought their politics with them. They made it working in aerospace, maintained their politics, and brought them up here when they retired. Their attitude is 'I worked hard all my life, I've fought in one or two wars and I've defended my country, and now my power bills are going up.' "

But not all of the conservatives are older people; many are the parents of school-age children and many are Mormons or members of fundamentalist churches. It was these people in particular whom Jim Powell, a Paradise educator, was thinking of when he said, "I think there's a group in this community that is absolutely immovable. They will oppose any peace education. They'll say this is just what the commies would like. If we lower our defenses the imperialist forces in the Soviet Union will come right in."

The difficulties of winning any kind of acceptance for nuclear-age education in a town like Paradise are somewhat analogous to the difficulties of putting through any kind of sex-education curriculum in the schools. Powell worked for three years with community members—unsuccessfully—trying to reach some kind of consensus on a family-life curriculum, vehemently opposed by conservatives for its sex-education component. "I use all my counseling skills," he said. "I reflect back to them what they've said and I point out to them that they all share a concern for kids. At one meeting they seemed to have reached agreement, but it all began to unpeel in the morning."

Jim Umenhofer was less pessimistic. He felt that acceptance of a nuclear-age curriculum was "several years down the road," and that meanwhile interested teachers could only do "small things" and "keep people informed." But he noted that although "there's lots and lots of people who say we don't want you to scare our children, they're also willing to listen and they want their children to be educated." Meanwhile there was plenty to do, if not directly in the schools, then in the community. Umenhofer was instrumental in proposing that Paradise "pair" with a town in the Soviet Union—a project that was accepted, somewhat surprisingly, by a majority of the town council and led, late in 1985, to a visit to Paradise by members of the staff of the Soviet consulate in San Francisco.

As noted earlier, whatever the difficulties faced by those interested in bringing nuclear-age education to their community, such education could not have come as far as it has if it did not represent a growing redefinition on the part of a number of adults, perhaps a majority, of what young people should know—ultimately for their own protection and for the protection and strength of their country.

This growing redefinition is itself motivated by a debate about concepts of strength, vulnerability, and risk in today's world. What is a strong nation in an interdependent world? What is the strong citizen in a complex technological society? Is he or she the person who does his job and doesn't ask too many questions? Or is he the person who asks the questions that need to be asked and demands answers? If he doesn't ask questions, is he vulnerable to manipulation, or even to tyranny? But—to take Dr. Larsen's point of view—if he is encouraged while young to ask searching questions about American history and current policy, is such questioning compatible with allegiance?

These are difficult and controversial questions and they will continue to be. They are deeply linked not only to feelings of nationalism but to individuals' needs to feel strong and fight off feelings of helplessness—to what a father quoted earlier referred to as the "marching band" emotions. Moreover, the need to feel strong, including the need to feel strong as a nation, finds powerful expression in a faith in technology of which faith in nuclear weapons and other advanced weapons technology is a part. It will continue to be very difficult to question this faith.

Questions about strength and vulnerability, about loyalty and patriotism, are very old questions, which individuals and cultures have struggled with for centuries, but they are being asked today with new urgency—and by unprecedented numbers of people. The questioning is going to go on for years—if we are lucky. The vital thing is that it continue and that it involve young people. There is no simple or single answer, but surely part of what is needed is the education as well as the rearing of young people who have a new concept of strength, a new way of being "invulnerable" in an era of supreme vulnerability.

As Sam Brian put it, "I looked at my eighth-grade class and it suddenly occurred to me they'd all turned fourteen, and that in four Novembers they'd be voting. It was a shock when I realized that, and it helped underscore to me the value of their sifting through the information, sorting their values out, tempering them with debate and other exercises in the classroom, somehow conveying to them that their opinions really count. It's really crucial now; it's not a moment too soon."

NOTES

INTRODUCTION

1. William R. Beardslee, M.D., and John E. Mack, M.D., "Adolescents and the Threat of Nuclear War: The Evolution of a Perspective," *The Yale Journal of Biology and Medicine* 56 (1983): 79–81.

2. On July 15, 1976, twenty-six children ages five to fourteen riding a school bus were kidnapped and buried underground in a truck trailer. Sixteen hours later under the leadership of two of the older boys they managed to escape. Lenore C. Terr has studied the long-term effects of this trauma. See her article, "Psychic Trauma in Children: Observations Following the Chowchilla School Bus Kidnapping," *American Journal of Psychiatry* 138 (1981): 14–19.

3. Jerome Kagan, *The Nature of the Child* (New York: Basic Books, 1984). See particularly chapter 5, "The Emotions."

CHILDREN AND THE NUCLEAR VISION

1. Although Maya Gillingham used improvisational techniques to elicit the content of *Changing the Silence,* she had clear ideas about how to shape it dramatically. She was particularly influenced by several different works. During the previous term Dylan Thomas's *Under Milk Wood* had been produced at the Northfield Mount Hermon School; the play suggested the way in which a group of voices could be orchestrated. Sam Shepard's *Tongues,* in which a drum is a "character," inspired the important use of a drum in *Changing the Silence.* Perhaps most of all, Maya was guided by Ntozake Shange's conception of her play *For Colored Girls Who Have Considered Suicide When the Rainbow Is Enuf* as a "choreopoem" in which music, movement, and voices of the actors come together.

2. Maya's first title for her play was *Hear Us! Voices From a Nuclear Dream.* In the process of working on the piece she arrived at the final title, which has special meaning beyond the obvious one of ending the secrecy and silence that have tended to surround the nuclear issue: in sign language the gesture for "change" and the gesture for "silence," when combined, signify "peace."

3. For a discussion of the significance of the nuclear issue for the generation born between 1940 and 1950, see Michael J. Carey, "Psychological Fallout," *Bulletin of Atomic Scientists* 38, no. 1 (1982): 20–24. See also L. S. Cottrell and E. Eberhart, *American Opinion in the Atomic Age* (Princeton: Princeton University

Press, 1948) and Paul Boyer, *By the Bomb's Early Light* (New York: Pantheon, 1985).

4. Lillian Wald Kay and Irving J. Gitlin, "Atomic Energy or the Atomic Bomb: A Problem in Development of Morale and Opinion," *Journal of Psychological Issues* 29 (1949): 57–84.

5. Michael J. Carey, "The Schools and Civil Defense: The Fifties Revisited," *Teachers College Record* 84, no. 1 (1982): 115–27.

6. Anna Freud and Dorothy Burlingham, *War and Children* (New York: Medical War Books, 1943).

7. Milton Schwebel, "What Do They Think About War?" in *Children and the Threat of Nuclear War,* ed. Child Study Association of America (New York: Duell, Sloan and Pearce, 1964), 25.

8. Sibylle K. Escalona, "Children and the Threat of Nuclear War," in *Behavioral Science and Human Survival,* ed. Milton Schwebel (Palo Alto: Behavioral Science Press, 1965), 205.

9. See Melvin E. Allerhand, "Children's Reaction to Societal Crises: Cold War Crisis," *American Journal of Orthopsychiatry* 35, no. 1 (1965): 124–30. See also J. H. Elder, "A Summary of Research on Reactions of the Children to Nuclear War," ibid., 120–23.

10. Jerome D. Frank, *Sanity and Survival: Psychological Aspects of War and Peace* (New York: Vintage Books, 1967); Robert Jay Lifton, *Death in Life: Survivors of Hiroshima* (New York: Random House, 1967); Robert Jay Lifton, *The Broken Connection: On Death and the Continuity of Life* (New York: Touchstone, 1979); Robert Jay Lifton and Richard Falk, *Indefensible Weapons* (New York: Basic Books, 1982).

11. Jerald G. Bachman and Lloyd Johnston, *Monitoring the Future,* Institute for Social Research, University of Michigan. Yearly volumes, starting 1975.

12. William Beardslee, M.D., and John Mack, M.D., "The Impacts on Children and Adolescents of Nuclear Developments," *Psychosocial Aspects of Nuclear Developments,* American Task Force Report no. 20 (Washington, D.C., 1982), 64–93.

13. Jeffrey B. Gould, M.D., "Exploring Youth's Reaction to the Threat of Nuclear War," in *Growing Up Scared? The Psychological Effect of the Nuclear Threat on Children,* ed. Benina Berger-Gould, Susan Moon, and Judith Van Hoorn (Berkeley: Open Books, 1986).

14. Tytti Solantaus, Matti Rimpela, and Vappu Taipale, "The Threat of War in the Minds of 12–18-Year-Olds in Finland," *The Lancet* 1, no. 8380 (April 7, 1984).

15. P. O. Holmborg and A. Bergstrom, "How Swedish Teenagers Think and Feel Concerning the Nuclear Threat" in *The Impact of the Threat of Nuclear War on Children and Adolescents,* Proceedings of an International Research Symposium, Helsinki-Espoo (1984), 170–80. Copyright International Physicians for the Prevention of Nuclear War, 1985.

16. Eric Chivian, M.D., and Joseph Goodman, "What Soviet Children Are Saying About Nuclear War," IPPNW *Report* (Winter 1984): 10–12. *Report* is the journal of the International Physicians for the Prevention of Nuclear War, Inc., 225 Longwood Avenue, Boston, MA 02115.

17. Chester E. Finn, Jr., and Joseph P. Adelson, "Terrorizing Children," *Commentary* 79, no. 4 (April 1985): 30.

18. Greg Diamond and Jerald G. Bachman, "High School Seniors and Nuclear Threat, 1975–1984: Political and Mental Health Implications of Concern and Despair," *International Journal of Mental Health,* forthcoming.

19. These figures are taken from: The Public Agenda Foundation with The Center for Foreign Policy Development at Brown University, *Voter Options on Nuclear Arms Policy: A Briefing Book for the 1984 Elections* (New York: The Public Agenda Foundation, 1984).

THE QUESTION OF IMPACT

1. Robert Coles, *The Moral Life of Children* (Boston: Atlantic Monthly Press, 1986), 277.

2. Stephen Pope, "The New Vegetarians: Can They Change the World?" *The New Socialist* (July 1985).

3. Diamond and Bachman, "High School Seniors," 15.

4. Coles, *Moral Life of Children,* 275.

5. Escalona, "Children and the Threat of Nuclear War," 203.

6. Diamond and Bachman, "High School Seniors," 15.

7. Scott Haas, personal communication.

8. This anecdote was told to me by Noel Menadier, a teacher and peace activist.

9. See Peter Cooper, "The Development of the Concept of War," *Journal of Peace Research* 2, no. 4 (1965): 3–4. The political socialization bibliography is voluminous. Among the books I have found helpful in writing this section and the following on adolescents are: Richard Dawson and Kenneth Prewitt, *Political Socialization* (Boston: Little, Brown, 1969); David Easton and Jack Dennis, *Children in the Political System* (New York: McGraw-Hill, 1969); Fred I. Greenstein, *Children and Politics* (New Haven: Yale University Press, 1965); Robert D. Hess and Judith W. Torney, *The Development of Political Attitudes in Children* (Chicago: Aldine, 1967); Richard G. Niemi, ed. *The Politics of Future Citizens: New Dimensions in the Political Socialization of Children* (San Francisco: Jossey-Bass, 1974). Articles that have been helpful include Joseph P. Adelson and Robert P. O'Neill, "Growth of Political Ideas in Adolescence: The Sense of Community," *Journal of Personality and Social Psychology* 4, no. 3 (1966): 295–306; Trond Alvik, "The Development of Views on Conflict, War and Peace among School Children," *Journal of Peace Research* 5, no. 2 (1968): 171–95; Jack Dennis and Carol Webster, "Children's Images of the President and of Government in 1962 and 1974," *American Politics Quarterly* 3, no. 4 (1975): 386–405; David Easton and Jack Dennis, "The Child's Acquisition of Regime Norms: Political Efficacy," *American Political Science Review* 61 (1967): 25–38; Gustav Jahoda, "Children's Concepts of Nationality: A Critical Study of Piaget's Stages," *Child Development* 35 (1964): 1081–92; M. Kent Jennings and Richard G. Niemi, "Patterns of Political Learning," *Harvard Educational Review* 38 (1968): 443–67; M. Kent Jennings and Richard G. Niemi, "The Transmission of Political Values from Parent to Child," *American Political Science Review* 62 (1968): 169–84; Lawrence Kohlberg, "Stage and Sequence: The Cognitive–Developmental Approach to Socialization" in *Handbook of Socialization Theory and Research,* ed. David A. Goslin (Chicago: Rand McNally, 1969).

10. Cooper, "Development of the Concept of War," 5–6.

11. Howard J. Tolley, *Children and War: Political Socialization to International Conflict* (New York: Teachers College Press, 1973).

12. Cooper, "Development of the Concept of War," 8.

13. Joseph M. F. Jaspers, John P. Van De Geer, Henri Tajfel, and Nicholas Johnson, "On the Development of National Attitudes in Children," *European Journal of Social Psychology* 2, no. 4 (1972): 347–69. Also, Harry R. Targ, "Children's Developing Orientations to International Politics," *Journal of Peace Research* 7, no. 2 (1970): 79–97.

14. For a discussion of this early adolescent "raw vision" in relation to world events, see Betty Bardige, "Reflective Thinking and Prosocial Awareness: Adolescents Face the Holocaust" (Ph.D. diss., Harvard University Graduate School of Education, 1983).

15. Joseph P. Adelson, "The Political Imagination of the Young Adolescent," *Daedalus* 100, no. 4 (1971): 1013–50.

16. Kagan, *Nature of the Child,* 179.

17. Beardslee and Mack, "Adolescents and the Threat of Nuclear War," 87–88.

18. Susan Goldberg, Suzanne LaCombe, Dvora Levinson, K. Ross Parker, Christopher Ross, and Frank Sommers, "Thinking About the Threat of Nuclear War: Relevance to Mental Health," *American Journal of Orthopsychiatry* 55, no. 4 (October 1985): 503–12.

19. Christopher Lasch, *The Minimal Self: Psychic Survival in Troubled Times* (New York: W. W. Norton & Co., 1984), 16.

20. Ibid., 63.

21. Ibid.

22. Sibylle K. Escalona, "Growing Up with the Threat of Nuclear War: Some Indirect Effects on Personality Development," *American Journal of Orthopsychiatry* 52, no. 4 (October 1982): 600–607.

23. Ernest Becker, *The Denial of Death* (New York: The Free Press, 1973), 23.

24. Escalona, "Growing Up with the Threat of Nuclear War," 605.

25. See Jane E. Pearce, M.D., "Terror/Apathy/Nuclear War," *The American Journal of Social Psychiatry* 3, no. 1 (1983).

26. Scott Haas, "Working Class Kids' Views of War and Peace" (unpublished manuscript).

27. See Marion Joseph Levy, *Modernization and the Structure of Societies: A Setting for International Affairs* (Princeton: Princeton University Press, 1966). Also, Joan Costello and Phyllis La Farge, *Growing Up American: Contemporary Children and Their Society* (Cambridge: Schenkman, 1986).

28. Martin E. P. Seligman, *Helplessness: On Depression, Development and Death* (San Francisco: Freeman, 1975).

29. Lyn Y. Abramson, Martin E. P. Seligman, and John D. Teasdale, "Learned Helplessness in Humans: Critique and Reformulation," *Journal of Abnormal Psychology* 87 (1978): 49–74.

30. Nielsen Television Index, *Report on Television Usage* (Hackensack, New Jersey: A. C. Nielsen Co., November 1983).

31. L. Geddie and G. Hildreth, "Children's Ideas About the War," *Journal of Experimental Education* 13 (1944): 92–97.

32. Tolley, *Children and War,* 98.

33. George Gerbner and Larry Gross, "The Violent Face of Television and Its Lessons," in *Children and the Faces of Television,* ed. Edward L. Palmer and Aimee Dorr (New York: Academic Press, 1980), 150. See also, M. Margaret Conway, Mikel Wyckoff, Eleanor Feldbaum, and David Ahern, "The News Media in Children's

Political Socialization, *Public Opinion Quarterly* 45 (1981): 164–78; Grace Ferrari Levine, "Learned Helplessness and the Evening News," *Journal of Communication* 27, no. 4 (Fall 1977): 100–105; Charles K. Atkins and Walter Gantz, "Television News and Political Socialization," *Public Opinion Quarterly* 42, no. 2 (Summer 1978): 183–98.

34. Gerbner and Gross, "Violent Face of Television," 155.

A PACT OF SILENCE

1. Stephen Zeitlin, "What Do We Tell Mom & Dad?" *Family Therapy Networker* (March–April, 1984): 31–39.

2. Susan Eileen Light, "Empowerment, Hope and Activism in the Nuclear Age: A Study of Children and Parents" (Ph.D diss., The California Institute of Transpersonal Psychology, 1985).

3. Carey, "Psychological Fallout," 20–24.

4. John E. Mack, M.D., "Resistances to Knowing in the Nuclear Age," *Harvard Educational Review* 54, no. 3 (August 1984), 264.

5. See The Public Agenda Foundation, *Voter Options on Nuclear Arms Policy.*

6. See Carol Gilligan, *In a Different Voice* (Cambridge: Harvard University Press, 1982).

7. Although a particular parent may not be as concerned with the issue as his or her child, and despite the fact that the number of adolescents, particularly young adolescents, who react with intense emotion is probably greater than the number of adults who react with similar emotion, adult and youth concern more or less parallel each other. A good indication of this can be found in Holmberg and Bergstrom, "How Swedish Teenagers Think and Feel."

THE INSPIRATION OF THE CHILD

1. Eleanor Deegan, "On Despair, Hope, and Motherhood" in *The Mothers' Book: Shared Experiences,* ed. Ronnie Friedland and Carol Kort (Boston: Houghton Mifflin Co., 1981), 354.

2. Roger Wilkins, op. ed. page, *New York Times,* August 9, 1983.

3. Bernard Benson, *The Peace Book* (New York: Bantam Books, 1982). David Woollcombe, *The Peace Child* (The Peace Child Foundation, P.O. Box 33168, Washington, DC 20033).

4. Benson, *Peace Book,* 21.

5. Woollcombe, *Peace Child,* 6.

6. For many adults the degree of stress in their lives leads to such an abdication or role reversal, the nuclear issue aside. One response to stress is the "shrinking" or "contraction" of the role one plays in relation to others: in this case, if the adult does less, the child is put in the position of having to do more or, to use the psychologist David Elkind's phrase, "hurried" toward a pseudoadulthood. But with respect to concerns about world issues, neither child nor adult is likely to "do more." Unless he or she becomes an activist the child is likely simply to live with silence and a "responsibility vacuum" around the issue.

7. Benson, *Peace Book,* 166.

8. Douglas Sloan, "Toward an Education for a Living World," *Teachers College Record* 84, no. 1 (Fall 1982): 11.

9. Ibid.

10. Freeman Dyson, *Weapons and Hope* (New York: Harper & Row, 1984), 4.

11. Ibid., 5.

12. Light, "Empowerment, Hope and Activism," 253.

13. Anthony E. James, M.D., "The Syndrome of the Psychologically Invulnerable Child," in *The Child in His Family: Children at Psychiatric Risk,* vol. 3 (New York: Wiley, 1974), 529–44.

KNOWING AND FEELING: NUCLEAR-AGE EDUCATION

1. See Dan B. Fleming, "Nuclear War: What Do High School History Textbooks Tell Us?" *Social Education* (December 1983). See also, Lowry Hemphill, "Curriculum Responses to the Threat of Nuclear War," *Harvard Educational Review* 54, no. 3 (August 1984). As well as commenting on the deficiencies of most standard textbooks with respect to the nuclear issue, the Hemphill article offers the best critique so far of nuclear-age curricula.

2. Edna McGuire and Thomas B. Portwood, *Our Free Nation* (New York: Macmillan Co., 1954), 660.

3. Frances Fitzgerald, *America Revised: History Schoolbooks in the Twentieth Century* (Boston: Little, Brown, 1979), 47.

4. Jerome R. Reich and Edward L. Biller, *Building the American Nation* (New York: Harcourt, Brace & World, 1968), 671.

5. Clyde B. Moore, Helen McCracken Carpenter, Laurence G. Paquin, Fred B. Painter, and Gertrude M. Lewis, *Building a Free Nation* (New York: Charles Scribner's Sons, 1952), 512.

6. Ibid., 526.

7. Ibid.

8. Fitzgerald, *America Revised,* 131.

9. Clarence Ver Steeg and Richard Hofstadter, *A People and a Nation* (New York: Harper & Row, 1971), 710.

10. Joseph Dempsey, Herbert J. Bass, George A. Billias, and Emma Jones Lapsansky, *Our American Heritage* (Morristown: Silver Burdett Co., 1979), 687–88.

11. Sloan, "Education for a Living World," 5.

12. Margot Stern Strom, "The Holocaust and Human Behavior," *Curriculum Review* (August 1983): 83–86.

13. A majority of Americans now believe that the issue of nuclear war cannot be left to the experts. Asked whether they agreed or disagreed with the following statement, "The issue of nuclear war is too important to leave only to the President and the experts; citizens must have a say in any decisions that are made," 68 percent of a random national sample agreed (but only 56 percent of those between the ages of forty-six and sixty). Twenty-nine percent disagreed. Growing public confidence in the ability to master information is suggested by another item. Asked whether they agreed or disagreed with the following statement, "The subject

of nuclear weapons is too complex for people like me to think about; that should be left to the President and the experts," 77 percent disagreed. Twenty-one percent agreed, although this figure was 40 percent among those aged sixty-one and over and 34 percent among those earning less than $20,000 a year. See Table 12, "Consensus-level Views About the Role of Citizens," in The Public Agenda Foundation, *Voter Options on Nuclear Arms Policy.*

14. Robert Jay Lifton, "Beyond Nuclear Numbing," *Teacher's College Record* 84, no. 1 (1982): 15.

15. Ibid., 21.

16. The use of film poses particular problems in this respect. A teacher, Robert W. Zuber, has written thoughtfully about these problems. He notes that "For many who teach in this field [educating about nuclear weapons], it is through their use of film and related art forms that the full range of issues and images about nuclear war are brought to direct contact with students' consciousness." He notes, however:

> But films in their various modes are often misused in the curriculum. The conventional wisdom teaches that "the camera never lies." But the pedagogical facts of film usage tend to support a different conclusion. Whether its focus is art or ideology, every film has its own point of view to commend. Film presents to the beholder a battery of concrete images conducive to the promotion of personal feelings and beliefs. In the case of the documentary or political film (such as *War Without Winners*), their creators take on certain of the characteristics of the prophet, specifically the power to develop sensitive issues such as the nuclear arms race, and to foster allegiances to their proposed solutions. This type of film, particularly appropriate for classroom use, undertakes to be both a vehicle for social expression and an artistic attitude of mind. As such, it is inherently more personal and compelling than the typical textual narratives of formal classroom study. As an educational tool, the nuclear film's strength and limitation lies in this combination artistry and issue advocacy.
>
> At this point, it should be clear that a nuclear film cannot stand in the classroom on its own pedagogical merits. How, then, is the instructor to best round out the presentation? As a beginning, the teacher must recognize that a film confronts students with an array of images that is beyond strict faculty control. Blinding flashes, swift missiles, radiated bodies—these and other elements of nuclear films leave impressions on students which can be quite unintended and, occasionally, quite revolutionary. When using the printed word, the job of the teacher is to breathe life into paragraphs and pages of sometimes obtuse commentary. With films such as these, a fundamental task is that of bringing some semblance of order—order to students who may forget that the film is more conceptually and politically potent than a mere fantasy, and order to those gaps in knowledge and understanding that prevent the student from challenging the biases and alleged historicity of the presentation. (Robert W. Zuber, "The Role of Film in Nuclear Education," *Social Education* [November–December 1983])

17. Herb Mack and Ann Cook, who is co-director of the Inquiry Demonstration Project, have successfully directed programs in schools as diverse as Bronx Science, Bronx Regional High School, and Erasmus High School in Brooklyn, New York. Mack and Cook do not conceive of their work as nuclear-age education, but the critical thinking encouraged by projects they have directed is, in fact, the kind of thinking that is central to nuclear-age education. Distinguishing her point of view from that of peace educators, Ann Cook commented to me, "Teachers should be neutral. They've done their job if they get kids to think about all sides of an issue. If a teacher advocates one point of view then any open discussion is a kind of fake. The cards are stacked. Teachers shouldn't really be teaching about peace. They

should be teaching about how to function in a democracy." But, Cook points out, students often guess exactly where a teacher stands politically. In such a case, it behooves the teacher to be more than usually careful to examine every point of view, rather than to attempt to conceal his or her own.

18. Tony Wagner, "Two Challenges for Chapters," *Forum* (Educators for Social Responsibility newsletter) 2, no. 2 (1983): 1.

19. The remarks of a teacher, Katherine Schultz, are pertinent:

> If students find projects with concrete results, they can see progress from their actions and they often feel more encouraged. I am not an advocate of encouraging children to write letters to the President and other elected representatives. While I think that this is a very important skill for adults, the results are often too obscure for a child and it is difficult to see that the letter has actually made a difference. If this project is initiated by students, then adults should work with them to write letters that reflect what the children think and feel. Often children write letters that reflect what adults would like them to say. In general, I think that it is most useful to listen to students' concerns and help them find ways to act when it seems appropriate.
>
> The year I began teaching, the girls in my fourth- and fifth-grade class decided that they wanted their gym classes to be co-ed. We brainstormed the ways that they could act on this strong desire. Their first step was to write an article which was published in the high school's newspaper. Their next steps were to talk to the appropriate people—their gym teacher, the Director of Athletics and the principal. They also talked to their friends in other classes to see if there was general agreement for this idea. Finally, they asked adults they knew, parents and teachers, to bring up the issue at a parents' meeting. They were successful and the school now has co-ed gym classes for fourth and fifth graders.
>
> Another student was perturbed by the fact that it was very difficult for her to cross a street next to the school. She decided that the difficulty was due to the number of cars that went "right on red" at that corner. She discovered that another student in her class had a father who worked for the city. This student gave her information on how to write a letter and to whom it should be written. Within weeks a "no turn on red" sign was installed on that corner. I like to imagine how proud and powerful this student must feel when she sees the sign on her way to school.
>
> A third example involves a whole class of mine. The class was disturbed over the news of starvation in Cambodia. They decided that they wanted to do something about this. After brainstorming, the class chose to sell pens to raise money. They studied about Cambodia and various relief organizations and decided to give the money to the American Friends Service Committee to be sent to Cambodia. I think that doing something made them feel less hopeless about the situation. However, if the children can have a more direct contact with the people that they are helping, for instance actually running a soup kitchen for a day, then they can actually see the results of their labor.
>
> What all of these examples have in common is that they were student-initiated. Before they decided to act, the students felt good about themselves. They had a sense that they would be listened to and that their actions counted. While the actions are not directly related to preventing nuclear war, they gave the children a sense that they were able to exert some control over their future and the lives of others. (Katherine Schultz, "Nuclear Education in the Elementary School," unpublished article. If interested in complete article, contact Katherine Schultz, 704 West Mt. Airy Avenue, Philadelphia, PA 19119.)

20. For an excellent discussion of these issues see Robert N. Bellah, Richard Madsen, William M. Sullivan, Ann Swidler, and Steven M. Tipton, *The Habits of the Heart* (Berkeley: University of California Press, 1985). With respect to pragmatism and the peace movement specifically, see Christopher Lasch's *The Minimal Self,* chapter 7, particularly pages 253–59.

21. Lasch, *Minimal Self,* 255.

22. In their debate about the MX, Brian's eighth grade settled in the end for a "piece of what they wanted"—that is, they were very pragmatic in their fight for their ideals. Although virtually the whole class was opposed to the MX missile when they first began to discuss the issue, they ended up voting for thirty-three missiles —on the condition that the president would accept their choice for INF negotiator in Geneva. The choice of a negotiator who would pursue a strategy in line with their ideals eventually seemed to them a more immediate problem than stopping the MX entirely.

23. See Seymour B. Sarason, *The Culture of the School and the Problem of Change* (Boston: Allyn and Bacon, 1971). The phrase "consititutional rights" in relation to student–teacher relationships and to the teacher's relationship to the "system" is drawn from chapter 11, "The Teacher: Constitutional Issues in the Classroom."

24. Ernest Boyer, *High School: A Report on Secondary Education in America* (New York: Harper & Row, 1983), 29. Boyer draws these figures from "Citizenship/Social Achievement Trends Over Time," a paper by Ina Mullis presented at the March 1978 Annual Meeting of the American Educational Research Association, Toronto, Canada (page 9) and from *National Assessment of Educational Progress, Education for Citizenship: A Bicentennial Survey* (Denver: Education Commission of the States, November 1976), 26–27.

25. Boyer, *High School,* 105.

26. Ibid.

27. Mortimer J. Adler, *The Paideia Proposal* (New York: Macmillan Co., 1982), 27.

28. Ibid., 77.

29. The most public airing of the issue of bias was associated with the curriculum *Choices: A Unit on Conflict and Nuclear War,* a joint project of the Union of Concerned Scientists and the Massachusetts Teachers Association, with the support of the National Education Association. When it appeared in 1983, it was condemned as biased by sources as diverse as the *Washington Post,* the conservative magazine *Human Events,* and indirectly by President Reagan himself, who applauded the American Federation of Teachers—always in the opposite political camp to the NEA—for its "bright contrast to those who have promoted curriculum guides that seem to be more aimed at frightening and brainwashing American schoolchildren than . . . stimulating balanced, intelligent debate" (quoted in *Newsweek,* July 18, 1983). In fact, the biggest problems with *Choices,* as with the majority of materials on nuclear weapons and the arms race prepared specifically for high school students, is its informational skimpiness and the dubious equation it implies between conflict at the interpersonal level and conflict between national powers equipped with modern weaponry. With respect to this latter deficiency one reviewer noted:

> Major portions of *Choices* are based on the assumption that conflicts between nations resemble those between individuals. Students are asked to solve imaginary teenage problems like a conflict over turns at PacMan, and they are asked to participate in classroom games which are designed to demonstrate the benefits of cooperation. An escalating schoolyard quarrel is used to explain the process of military escalation. Questions in the teacher's guide frequently attempt to elicit from students the generalizations that fighting is unproductive and cooperation is desirable. Much of this has an unfortunate aura of heavy-handed adult moralizing. More importantly, students may be

learning the wrong lesson. The monstrous forces wielded by the superpowers have nothing in common with the kinds of force students use in their own disputes. The devastating nature of nuclear weapons may in fact transform normal notions of when fighting is justifiable and may urge cooperation between parties who would ordinarily see no reason to resolve their differences. In failing to present these arguments, *Choices* may leave students feeling that opposition to nuclear weapons must be predicated on pacifism in daily life, or that the horrors of nuclear war in some sense represent a logical development from children's own squabbles. (Hemphill, "Curriculum Responses")

30. Fitzgerald, *America Revised,* 178.

31. Mack, "Resistances to Knowing," 264.

32. I agree that the nuclear issue should not be an explicit part of the curriculum at the elementary level, although teachers should be prepared to answer specific questions as they come up. However, making conflict resolution skills the content of nuclear-age education at the elementary school level (as the Milwaukee and many other programs do) is built on the premise of a similarity between interpersonal and international conflict, as suggested in note 29 in this section. In the long run, the most significant aspect about this approach may not be the conceptual flaws suggested above but the fact that an ideal essential to life in a dangerous, crowded, and interdependent world is made explicit to young children, thus contributing to change in the moral environment.